Lecture Notes in Economics and Mathematical Systems

MW01226684

For further volumes:
http://www.springer.com/series/300

Marcus Brandenburg

Quantitative Models for Value-Based Supply Chain Management

 Springer

Dipl. Math. Marcus Brandenburg
Chair of Supply Chain Management
University of Kassel
Kassel, Germany

ISSN 0075-8442
ISBN 978-3-642-31303-5   ISBN 978-3-642-31304-2 (eBook)
DOI 10.1007/978-3-642-31304-2
Springer Heidelberg New York Dordrecht London

Library of Congress Control Number: 2012950141

Springer is part of Springer Science+Business Media (www.springer.com)

Foreword

The increasing relevance of supply chains for a wide range of products shifts competitiveness from the single company to the supply chain level. While this seems an agreed upon fact, appropriate instruments allowing the in-depth analysis of different value drivers for supply chain management are rather scarce so far. Much of the previous analysis stays on a descriptive level, where the assessed effects are explained mainly by qualitative arguments.

This is the research gap that Marcus Brandenburg addresses in his thesis on "Quantitative Models for Value-Based Supply Chain Management". Therefore, these different methodological approaches are taken and combined with applications and empirical pieces of research. Taking a look at the overall thesis, the highlights are the following: (1) a wide coverage of relevant literature and a respective formal literature review, (2) the mathematical formulation of a so far conceptual framework for value based supply chain management and (3) the different applications of this model with links to benchmarking, supply chain planning and new product introduction. Therefore, the author applies a range of both formal quantitative and empirical research methods. The thesis is exceptionally, starting from literature coverage to theoretical foundations and empirical application.

The doctoral thesis of Marcus Brandenburg makes a highly relevant contribution to the further development of supply chain management and supply chain controlling literature. Hence, one can only wish for a good reception of the thesis into academic research and practical application.

Kassel, Germany   Stefan Seuring

Preface

Supply chain management and value-based management are two concepts which have gained a significant and still growing scientific and practical relevance during the last decades. Supply chain management is characterized by process orientation and inter-organizational collaboration while focusing on customers and their requirements. Hence, contention in business environments nowadays seems to be shifted from market rivalry of single firms towards competition between supply chains. Although it is taken for granted that an improved supply chain management results in financial benefits of a firm, efficiency and effectiveness of related processes are often influenced by and assessed based on non-financial factors.

Value-based management strives for managing all parts of a firm in such a way that the value of a company is increased. Taking into account the increasing importance of supply chain management and value-based management, the link between both concepts should be evident and thoroughly assessed. Contrastingly to this expectation, both disciplines seem to follow opposed perspectives with contradictory objectives. Considering the competition of capital markets and the expectations of company shareholders, value-based management places the value of a single firm into the focus of all considerations and hence seems to separate the inter-organizational aspects which supply chain management aims to integrate. Beyond this, value-based management combines aspects of profitability and capital lockup under consideration of time and hence perceives cash as the major influencing factor, while supply chain processes mainly deal with the flow of material and information.

The objective of this dissertation is a thorough analysis of this seemingly contradictory coherence of supply chain management and value-based management, comprehended as value-based supply chain management. While most approaches of related scientific research employ conceptual frameworks which are predominantly substantiated by qualitative arguments, the thesis at hand aims at suggesting quantitative models that are suitable to measure and compare impacts of supply chain management on company value. The proposed models take into account the configurational and operational dimensions of supply chain management and cover all phases of the product life cycle. These models consist of financial factors influencing profitability and capital lockup as well as of non-financial value drivers including the dynamics and uncertainties that occur in supply chains. Hence, this thesis elaborates on value-based supply chain management in breadth rather than providing an in-depth assessment of selected value drivers or an analysis that covers the whole length of an inter-organizational supply network. The chosen research design comprises theoretical and empirical methodologies in a balanced way, and thus, the thesis at hand is of relevance for academic researchers as well as for industrial practitioners. The specific structure of this monograph enables the reader to select chapters of particular interest for reading without losing the understanding of the arguments or the view for the central theme of this dissertation.

Kassel, Germany   Marcus Brandenburg

Acknowledgements

I am heartily thankful to my supervisor, Professor Dr. Stefan Seuring, University of Kassel, whose encouragement, guidance and support enabled me to develop a deeper understanding of scientific research on supply chain management and to accede the academic world. In this context, I would like to thank all participants of the doctoral seminaries, especially my fellow PhD students as well as Professor Dr. Martin Müller, University of Ulm, and his team, for the fruitful discussions and exchanges of experiences.

Beyond this, I would like to thank Professor Dr. Richard Vahrenkamp, University of Kassel, for the second review of this dissertation and particularly Dr. Robert Schilling, Catholic University of Eichstätt-Ingolstadt, for his cooperation on different conference papers and publications. For reprinting papers in this monograph, I am indebted to the courtesy of Erich Schmidt Verlag, Berlin, EUL Verlag, Lohmar, Shaker Verlag, Aachen, and Springer Verlag, Heidelberg.

Lastly, I offer my regards and blessings to all of those who supported me in any respect during the completion of the dissertation project, and I may express my deepest gratefulness humbly: "Trust in the LORD with all thine heart; and lean not unto thine own understanding" (Proverbs 3:5).

Kassel, Germany   Marcus Brandenburg

Contents

List of Figures

List of Tables

Acronyms

Acronyms

AD	Axiomatic descriptive
AHP	Analytic hierarchy process
AN	Axiomatic normative
APS	Advanced planning system
AS	Axiomatic simulation
C2C	Cash to cash
CAGR	Compound annual growth rate
CAPM	Capital asset pricing model
CFROI	Cash flow return on investment
COGS	Cost of goods sold
CPFR	Collaborative planning, forecasting and replenishment
CRP	Collaborative replenishment program
CU	Currency unit
CVA	Cash value added
DC	Distribution center
DCF	Discounted cash flow
DES	Discrete event simulation
DPO	Days payables outstanding
DSI	Days sales of inventory
DSO	Days sales outstanding
EAN	European article number
EBIT	Earnings before interest and taxes
ECR	Efficient consumer response
ED	Empirical descriptive
EDI	Electronic data interchange
EN	Empirical normative
ERP	Enterprise resource planning
EU	Europe

EVA	Economic value added
FCF	Free cash flow
FMCG	Fast moving consumer goods
FTL	Full truck load
IJLM	International Journal of Logistics Management
IJPDLM	International Journal of Physical Distribution and Logistics Management
IT	Information technology
KPI	Key performance indicator
LTL	Less than truck load
m	Million
MIP	Mixed integer programming
NPI	New product introduction
NPV	Net present value
OEM	Original equipment manufacturer
OOS	Out-of-stock
P&L	Profit and loss
PPE	Property, plant and equipment
POS	Point of sale
PLC	Product life cycle
R&D	Research and development
RFID	Radio frequency identification
RLT	Replenishment lead time
ROA	Return on assets
ROCE	Return on capital employed
ROI	Return on investment
ROIC	Return on invested capital
ROS	Return on sales
ROTA	Return on total assets
RQ	Research question
S&OP	Sales and operations planning
SC	Supply chain
SCOR	Supply chain operations reference
SCM	Supply chain management
SCMIJ	Supply Chain Management: An International Journal
SCNVA	Supply chain network value added
SKU	Stock keeping unit
TCU	'000 currency units
TSCD	Tactical supply chain design
UK	United Kingdom
UOM	Unit of measurement
US	United States
US GAAP	United States Generally Accepted Accounting Principles
VBM	Value-based management
vs.	versus
WACC	Weighted average cost of capital

Company Abbreviations

AVO	Avon Products Inc.
BDF	Beiersdorf AG
CPA	Colgate-Palmolive Company
ELA	The Estée Lauder Companies Inc.
HEN	Henkel KGaA
KAO	Kao Corporation
KMB	Kimberly-Clark Corporation
PRG	The Procter and Gamble Company
RCU	Reckitt Benckiser Group plc
UNI	The Unilever Group

Currencies

€	Euro
GB£	British Pound Sterling
JP¥	Japanese Yen
US$	US Dollar

Symbols

α	Factor
α_p	Disaggregation ratio for period p
α^C	Disaggregation ratio for SC cost
α^W	Disaggregation ratio for working capital
Δ	Difference, change of a parameter
$\lambda^C(C_p)$	Ratio of SC cost C_p and sales S_p in period p
$\lambda^W(W_p)$	Ratio of working capital W_p and sales S_p in period p
$\sigma(y_t)$	Standard deviation of forecast demand y during replenishment time t
C_p	SC cost of period p
c_p	Target SC cost of period p
cf_t	Net cash flow in period t
ci_t	Cash-in in period t
co_t	Cash-out in period t
$COGS_p$	Cost of goods sold in period p
D	Debt (derived from book value)
D_p	Depreciation expenses of period p
d_t	Demand in period t
E	Equity (defined as market capitalization)

E_p	Capital expenditure of period p
fc	Total production costs of finished goods incl. transport
FCF_p	Free cash flow of period p
fg_t	Finished goods produced and shipped in period t
I_p	Inventory of period p
i_t	On-hand inventory in period t
j_t	On-order inventory in period t
k_D	Cost of debt D
k_E	Cost of equity E
ls_t	Lost sales in period t
lt_{sd}	Lead time from origin s to destination d
ncc	Non-cash items of total finished goods production costs
p	(Fiscal) time period
P_p	Trade payables of period p
p_t	Packaging material received in period t
pc	Packaging costs incl. transport
q	Capital costs
r	Review period
R_p	Trade receivables of period p
S_p	Sales of period p
S_t	Target inventory level in period t
SS_t	Safety stock in period t
t	Time period
tp	Transfer price
T	Tax rate
T_p	Tax rate of period p
V	Net present value
va_p^C	Target value contribution of SC cost in period p
va_p^W	Target value contribution of working capital in period p
va^{Total}	Total target value contribution
VA^A	Total value created by fixed assets
VA_p^A	Value created by fixed assets in period p
VA^C	Total value created by SC cost
VA_p^C	Value created by SC cost in period p
VA^{COGS}	Total value created by COGS
VA_p^{COGS}	Value created by COGS in period p
VA^S	Total value created by sales
VA_p^S	Value created by sales in period p
VA^{SCM}	Total value created by supply chain management
VA_p^{SCM}	Value created by supply chain management in period p
VA^{Total}	Total value created by sales and working capital
VA^W	Total value created by working capital
VA_p^W	Value created by working capital in period p

w_p	Target working capital of period p
W_p	Working capital in period p
$WACC$	Weighted average cost of capital
$WACC_p$	Weighted average cost of capital in period p
x_t	Inventory order in period t
y_t	Forecast demand in period t
z	Normal distribution safety factor

Units of Measurement

%	Percentage
d	Days
pcs.	Pieces
pp	Percentage point

Chapter 1
Introduction

Abstract In this chapter, the research area of value-based supply chain management is introduced. Based on research gaps that are pointed out, the underlying research questions of this thesis are raised. Methodology and approaches of this thesis to answer these questions are outlined and the structure of the thesis is illustrated.

1.1 Introduction

For several decades, supply chain management (SCM) has developed to a source of competitive advantage for enterprises from all industries (Mentzer et al. 2001). Characterized by process orientation and customer focus, SCM is driven by collaboration on intra-organizational level between various functions of the same company as well as in inter-organizational networks comprising different companies of the same supply chain (SC) (Alvarado and Kotzab 2001; Attaran and Attaran 2007; Jüttner et al. 2010; Pero et al. 2010; Simatupang and Sridharan 2005). Nowadays it is undoubted that competition does not only occur between individual organizations, but additionally between competing supply chains (Christopher 2005). This circumstance has fostered the awareness for SC performance management, which is categorized into effectiveness and efficiency (Beamon 1999; Gunasekaran and Kobu 2007; Shepherd and Günter 2006; Walters 2006). SC effectiveness is mainly assessed by the extent to which the needs of (ultimate) customers are covered, while SC efficiency is most often measured by metrics that are related to SC processes and structures (Christopher and Towill 2002; Huan et al. 2004; Lockamy and McCormack 2004; Min et al. 2007).

In financial terms, SC efficiency is most often linked to cost reduction and profit increases, which offer considerable optimization potential (Huan et al. 2005; Meixell and Gargeya 2005). This perception is complemented by SC efficiency aspects of capital employed. Improved utilization of property, plants and equipment (PPE) for production and logistics indicates the adequacy of SC structures and

M. Brandenburg, *Quantitative Models for Value-Based Supply Chain Management*, Lecture Notes in Economics and Mathematical Systems 660, DOI 10.1007/978-3-642-31304-2__1, © Springer-Verlag Berlin Heidelberg 2013

increases the efficiency of fixed assets (Gunasekaran et al. 2004). Besides an appropriate utilization of such fixed assets, working capital is identified as another considerable lever for cash creation by SCM (Farris II and Hutchison 2002; Metze 2010; Randall and Farris II 2009b). In this context, the relevance of inventory management for SC performance has been explored and explained thoroughly (Silver et al. 1998). The rising awareness for the monetary working capital components trade payables and trade receivables has brought the management of financial flows in SC, comprehended as "financial chain management" or "supply chain finance", in focus (Pfohl and Gomm 2009; Randall and Farris II 2009a). Efficiency and effectiveness of an SC are furthermore influenced by non-financial factors, which range from strategic criteria to operational aspects including flexibility and responsiveness of an SC or delivery performance and service level (Christopher 2000; Sanchez and Perez 2005).

Thus one of the key questions in SCM is how effectiveness and efficiency of an SC can be ensured and improved (Walters 2006). This question is reflected in all tasks related to configuration or operation of an SC (Seuring 2009). The configuration of an SC aims at designing appropriate structures and relationships for SCM, such as network design or supplier selection, while the operation of an SC is focused on appropriate execution of SC processes and systems (Beamon 1998; Gunasekaran et al. 2004; Hübner 2007; Jayaram 2008; Melo et al. 2009; Truong and Azadivar 2005). The complexity of these tasks is considerably amplified by SC dynamics and uncertainties (Wilding 1998). Uncertainties, in most cases related to ambiguous or missing information on quantities, durations or financial figures, can occur on demand or supply side of an SC triggered by external or internal factors (Blackhurst et al. 2004; Datta and Christopher 2011; Saad and Gindy 1998). SC dynamics are often caused by process variations or demand oscillations, which are amplified by the interplay of different SC actors (Christopher and Lee 2004; Lee et al. 1997b). Therefore, efficiency and effectiveness of SCM are most often brought in context to inter-organizational networks.

In contrast to the inter-organizational network perspective of SCM, the concept of value-based management (VBM) puts forward a single enterprise and strives for increasing the value of a firm. One of the key questions in VBM is how to manage all parts of a company in such a way that its value is increased in a long-lasting way. In this coherence, the value of a firm is determined by its ability to create future cash flows (Damodaran 2011a). These cash flows are driven by profitability and capital efficiency as well as cost of capital (Damodaran 2011b). One answer to this question is attempted to be given by the idea of shareholder value, which is affected by cash flow from operations, discount rate and debt which in turn are influenced by management decisions of operating, investment and financing (Rappaport 1998). This approach to VBM is supported by a broad field of valuation models including discounted cash flow (DCF) valuation, liquidation and accounting valuation, relative valuation or contingent claim valuation that allow for quantifying the value of an asset (Damodaran 2005). These models can be applied to determine company value, which is furthermore assessed by suitable metrics including return on sales (ROS), return on capital employed (ROCE), return on investment (ROI) or economic value added (EVA) (Hawawini and Viallet 2002). To operationalize the VBM concept, such metrics are disaggregated by value driver hierarchies that illustrate influencing factors on operational level and how they are linked to company value (Copeland et al. 2005; Weber et al. 2004).

The combination of the inter-organizational concept of SCM and the intra-organizational VBM approach leads to the question how SCM performance contributes to company value. The related field of research can be comprehended as value-based SCM. The SC hypothesis states that an efficient and effective SCM results in commercial benefits for the whole SC as well as for each of its members and thus can be seen as a basic conjecture of value-based SCM (Jehle 2005; New 1996). This conjecture is nowadays widely accepted and substantiated by frameworks that outline the coherence between SC performance, customer satisfaction and financials (Otto 2002; Reiner and Schodl 2003). Since the turn of the millennium, various conceptual frameworks for value-based SCM are suggested which identify value drivers such as revenue growth, operating cost or capital employed and outline their coherence to SCM and company value (Christopher and Ryals 1999). Other frameworks elaborate on the coherence between logistics and company value or aim at linking SCM processes and investments to extended financial statements and figures on the inter-organizational network level (Lambert and Pohlen 2001; Otto and Obermaier 2009; Walters 1999). The frameworks are complemented by numerous value-based metrics to measure and steer SC-related value drivers (Keebler et al. 1999; Lambert and Burduroglu 2000; Lambert and Pohlen 2001). These conceptual frameworks and metrics are supported by empirical research which assess the correlation between SCM improvements or deficiencies and the financial performance of a company in secondary data analyses or which focus industrial case examples that outline implementation aspects of value-based SCM concepts (Hendricks and Singhal 2003, 2005b; Hendricks et al. 1995; Hofmann and Locker 2009; Losbichler and Rothböck 2006). Compared to these exhaustive conceptual frameworks for value-based SCM and the detailed empirical research on this field, scientific research on quantitative models for value-based SCM seems to fall short because related scientific publications predominantly elaborate on selective aspects of value-based SCM. Such examples comprise suggested approaches to assess value impacts of SC configurations, e.g. by applying the DCF method to network design decisions, or normative models to optimize value contributions of SC operation which deliberately exclude specific value drivers, such as fixed asset investments or monetary working capital components, from observation or limit the focus of analysis to one particular value driver, for instance working capital (Chopra and Meindl 2007; Hahn and Kuhn 2010, 2011; Kannegiesser et al. 2009). Limitations of such approaches can be seen in the degree to which the field of research on value-based SCM is reflected holistically, i.e. by covering value impacts of SC configuration and SC operation under consideration of all phases of the product life cycle (PLC) and by assessing financial profitability- and capital-related value drivers of SCM as well as non-financial SC performance criteria. Academic publications that thoroughly deal with quantitative models for value-based SCM in such a holistic way have to the best of the author's knowledge not been found.

The thesis at hand picks up this gap and contributes to scientific research on value-based SCM by elaborating on three questions. The first question is how SCM-related value impacts of profitability-related value drivers, sales growth and SC cost, and of asset-related value drivers, fixed and working capital, can be quantified and financially compared. Quantitative models to answer this question must be suitable to reflect complementary effects stemming from different value drivers, e.g. improvements in warehousing cost that result from inventory reductions, as well as to compare competing effects, such as extended supplier payment periods that lead to working capital improvements and cost increases due to lost cash discounts. The second question aims at identifying and substantiating relevant criteria and influencing factors for value creation. On the one hand, timing aspects and volatility of developments of SC-related value drivers have to be assessed regarding their influences on company value. On the other hand, non-financial SC-related value drivers – especially SC dynamics and uncertainties – and their relevance for value creation are of particular interest in this context. The third question is how financial performance related to company value can be linked to tactical and operational SCM activities. All phases of the PLC as well as SC configuration and SC operation should be considered to answer this question.

To elaborate on these research questions, a model-based quantitative research design is chosen for the thesis at hand (Bertrand and Fransoo 2002; Golicic et al. 2005; Shapiro 2007). The research of this dissertation is grounded on a conceptual framework for value-based SCM designed in a theorizing desk research (Halldorsson and Arlbjørn 2005). To provide a terminological foundation and to explore the current status of research on this field, a content analysis of related literature is performed (Mayring 2008; Seuring et al. 2005). Descriptive models are proposed to quantify value contributions stemming from SCM influences on four financial value drivers – sales, SC cost, working capital and fixed assets – identified by Christopher and Ryals (1999). Based on these models, the relevance of timing aspects and continuity of value driver developments, which Srivastava et al. (1998) explained by qualitative arguments, is systematically explored and mathematically substantiated. Beyond this, these descriptive models are developed further to a normative approach for value-based strategic SC planning. Discrete-event simulation (DES) models are designed to assess value impacts of tactical SC design decisions for new product introduction (NPI) under consideration of influences arising from the non-financial factors SC dynamics and uncertainties (Kleijnen 2005). The quantitative models are validated and the findings are substantiated by empirical research, which is performed by a secondary data analysis and by an industrial case example (Reiner 2005; Seuring 2005, 2008). The empirical research focuses the fast moving consumer goods (FMCG) industry, which is characterized by short PLCs, considerable SC dynamics and high uncertainties and thus is suitable for this research (Schilling et al. 2010).

The thesis at hand is structured as follows. Chapter 2 contains a thorough introduction of the concepts VBM, SCM and value-based SCM. Furthermore, a terminological clarification and a survey of related manuscripts are given in this chapter. The research methodology applied in this thesis and the coherence of its subsequent chapters are outlined in Chap. 3. This chapter comprises the conceptual framework for value-based SCM on which the quantitative models of this thesis are grounded. A content analysis of related literature on value-based SCM is given in Chap. 4 in order to systematically assess the current status of research and the applied terminology on this field. A quantitative model introduced in Chap. 5 allows for determining value impacts stemming from developments of SC cost and working capital. This model is empirically validated by a secondary data analysis of value impacts at ten globally operating FMCG manufacturers described in Chap. 6. This empirical analysis furthermore provides insights on the importance of timing and continuity of value driver developments for value creation. Besides, the relevance of working capital components and cost of capital for value creation are explored in greater detail. In Chap. 7, a quantitative approach for value-based strategic SC planning is described which is derived from the model introduced in Chap. 5. Chapter 8 deals with aspects of SC dynamics and uncertainties in tactical SC design. The interplay of these factors and company value is outlined in a conceptual model introduced in this chapter which is validated by a DES model and a case example from FMCG industry introduced by Schilling et al. (2010). Chapter 9 contains an extension of this DES model by a DCF-based valuation approach which allows for quantifying the value impacts stemming from tactical SC design decisions, SC dynamics and uncertainties. This approach is illustrated by the case example from FMCG industry, too (Schilling et al. 2010). Chapter 10 comprises an extension and mathematical validation of the model introduced in Chap. 5. This extension enables to quantify and compare SC-related value impacts of all four financial value drivers – sales growth, SC cost, working capital and fixed assets – introduced by Christopher and Ryals (1999) and is complemented by qualitative arguments that explain how these value drivers are linked to operational SCM activites. Beyond this, a mathematical substantiation of the value creation criteria identified by Srivastava et al. (1998) is provided in this chapter. The thesis concludes with a summary of findings, limitations and further research prospects discussed in Chap. 11.

The Chaps. 4–10 contain manuscripts that are published or submitted for publication in journals or edited books. The article structure of these manuscripts is inherited unchanged to the respective chapters in order to facilitate reading selected chapters of this thesis. Additionally, most of these manuscripts were presented at scientific conferences. Detailed information on publication status and these presentations are given at the beginning of each chapter and in Sect. 12.4 of this thesis.

Chapter 2
Terminology and Related Literature

Abstract This chapter provides the terminological basis for the research of the thesis at hand and a review of related literature. The first section, which deals with value-based management (VBM), outlines what is comprehended by the term "value", how it can be measured and what factors influence company value. This section ends with a discussion of empirical aspects of VBM. The second section comprises a comprehensive introduction of supply chain management (SCM). After terminological aspects and characteristics of SCM are discussed, special focus is put on types of flows through supply chains (SC). Furthermore constituents and components, relationships and benefits of SCM are explained and an SCM framework is outlined to position the research of this thesis. Under consideration of the empirical and case-related parts of this dissertation (Chaps. 6, 8 and 9), SC dynamics and uncertainties as well as SCM in the fast moving consumer goods (FMCG) industry are thoroughly discussed. The last section of this chapter is related to value-based SCM. Finanical impacts of SCM, driven by sales, cost and capital, are outlined. Beyond this, 20 selected manuscripts are reviewed to illustrate the broadness of this field of research, its current status and recent developments.

2.1 Value-Based Management

This section deals with key questions in scientific research on VBM. These concern the perception, definition and determination of value. Besides, influencing factors and drivers of company value are of particular interest for academic research and managerial practice. To reflect these regards, the shareholder value concept is introduced and delineated from stakeholder value and customer-perceived value. An outline and discussion of valuation models and value drivers provide the basis for the approaches to quantify value impacts of SCM which are presented in the thesis at hand. A survey on empirical aspects and managerial implications of VBM illustrates the practical relevance of this scientific area.

M. Brandenburg, *Quantitative Models for Value-Based Supply Chain Management*,
Lecture Notes in Economics and Mathematical Systems 660,
DOI 10.1007/978-3-642-31304-2__2, © Springer-Verlag Berlin Heidelberg 2013

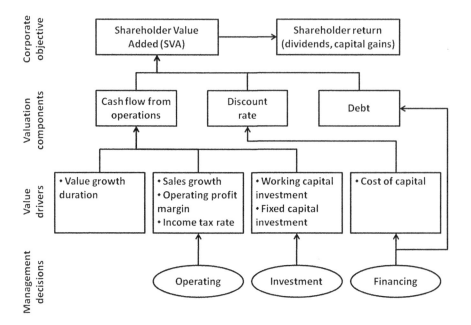

Fig. 2.1 Shareholder value network (Rappaport 1998, p. 56)

2.1.1 Value

The concept of value-based management (VBM) is linked to the term shareholder value introduced by Rappaport (1998): Shareholder value and debt are seen as complementary portions of the total economic value of a company or business unit. The maximization of shareholder value is perceived as primary objective of a company, and hence VBM stipulates that all parts of a company are managed in such a way that the equity value of this entity is increased, i.e. shareholder value is added. Being obliged to this objective by defined targets and effective compensation packages, management can apply decision making in financing, investing and operating in order to improve the operating profit, increase the capital turnover and reduce the effective tax rate. These value drivers in turn have an impact on the valuation components cash flow, discount rate and debt and ultimately influence the shareholder value of a company (see Fig. 2.1). Based on the comprehension of Modigliani and Miller (1958), the financial value of a firm is determined by the present value of its future cash flows.

A different perception of value has come up with the theory of stakeholders, which are defined as "any group or individual who can affect or is affected by the achievement of the organization's objectives" (Freeman 1984, p. 53). While (shareholder) value maximization obliges managers to strive for increasing the total market value of the firm, stakeholder theory aims at managerial decision-making under consideration of the interests of all stakeholders in a firm (Jensen 2001). The conflictive aspects of these two value perceptions, which are thoroughly discussed and compared in scientific literature (see e.g. papers in Wall and Schröder 2009), are illustrated by a statement from Smith (2003): "Stakeholder theory demands that interests of all stakeholders be considered even if it reduces company profitability" (Smith 2003, p. 86). Nevertheless, stakeholder management may complement shareholder value creation and thus contribute to increasing competitive advantage (Hillman and Keim 2001).

The conventional input-output-perspective of a corporation, which Donaldson and Preston (1995) compare to the stakeholder conception, focuses the value perceived by customers: investors, employees, and suppliers act as contributing inputs, which the firm transforms into outputs, from which in turn mainly customers benefit. This concept of customer-perceived value can be brought in relation to the management of supply chains, which creates tangible benefits for customers and whose members should monitor to which extent the customer realizes these benefits and mitigate factors that may impede their realizations (Brewer and Speh 2000).

2.1.2   Valuation

Various valuation approaches are suggested to determine and measure the extent and changes of company value. For an introduction, the categorization and explanations of valuation approaches given by Damodaran (2005) are outlined in this subsection and summarized in Table 2.1.

The first category of valuation approaches consists of DCF methods, which relate the value of an asset to the present value of its expected future cash flows. DCF approaches are differentiated further between discount rate adjustment models (equity DCF models, firm DCF models), excess return models and beyond this certainty equivalent models and adjusted present valuation models. Discount rate adjustment models either value the entire business (firm DCF models) by discounting free cash flows to the firm at weighted cost of capital or focus discounting expected cash flows to equity investors at a company risk rate (equity DCF models). Excess return models, such as economic value added (EVA) (Stewart 1991) or cash flow return on investment (CFROI) (Madden 1998), separate the expected cash flows between normal return cash flows, obtained by earnings that represent the risk-adjusted required returns, and excess return cash flows, which exceed the expectations formulated by risk-adjusted required return rates. Certainty equivalent models comprise utility models, risk and return models or cash flow haircuts (see Damodaran 2005). In such models, the uncertain expected cash flows are replaced by certainty equivalent cash flows obtained by applying risk adjustment processes, which are comparable to the methods by which discount rates are adjusted. Methods that separate the effects on value of debt financing from the asset value of a business are categorized as adjusted present value models. Examples for this category are suggested by Myers (1974), Luehrmann (1997) or Kaplan and Ruback (1995).

Table 2.1 Valuation approaches according to categorization by Damodaran (2005)

Valuation approach	Model	Basic idea	Examples
Discounted cash flow (DCF) approaches	Discount rate adjustment models	Future cash flows discounted by risk-adjusted rates	Firm DCF models, equity DCF models (see Damodaran 2005)
	Excess return models	Differentiate between normal and excess return cash flows by risk-adjusted required return	Economic value added (EVA) (Stewart 1991), Cash flow return on investment (CFROI) (Madden 1998)
	Certainty equivalent models	Replace uncertain expected cash flows by certainty equivalent cash flows	Utility models, risk and return models, cash flow haircuts (see Damodaran 2005)
	Adjusted present value models	Value of fully equity financed business adjusted for present value of expected tax, benefits of debt and bankruptcy cost	Models from Myers (1974), Luehrmann (1997) or Kaplan and Ruback (1995)
Liquidation and accounting valuation	Book value based valuation, liquidation valuation	Determine asset value based on accounting estimates or book value	Book value, book value plus earnings, liquidation value (see Damodaran 2005)
Relative valuation approaches	Standardized values and multiples	Estimate the value of an asset in relation to pricing of "comparable" assets	Ratios of price to earnings or price to revenue, Tobin's Q (see Damodaran 2005)
Contingent claim valuation	Option pricing models	Measure the value of assets with option characteristics	Black-Scholes-model (Black and Scholes 1973)

The second category of valuation approaches comprises liquidation and accounting valuation to determine the value of existing assets of a firm based on accounting estimates of value or book value. Liquidation valuation estimates the company value that would be obtained by liquidating the firm. This approach considers urgency influences and violates the going concern assumption of a firm and hence is likely to result in lower value estimates compared to DCF valuation. Accounting valuation approaches assume that book value of the assets of a firm is a good proxy for its market value. Therefore, these valuation approaches are considered applicable rather for companies with a comparably high share of fixed assets and a limited potential for further growth or excess returns.

Relative valuation approaches, which form the third valuation category, estimate the value of an asset by looking at the pricing of "comparable" assets. To value an asset, a comparable asset is determined which is priced by the market, the market price is scaled appropriately and adjusted for relevant differences between both assets. Commonly used multiples comprise ratios of price to earnings or price to revenue as well as Tobin's Q (see Damodaran 2005). Over pricing or under pricing effects stemming from market behavior can result in considerable deviations between relative valuation and approaches based on DCF.

The fourth category of valuation approaches includes contingent claim valuation, which employs option pricing models to measure the value of assets that share option characteristics. The basic idea behind this is grounded on the combination of equity investors' option to liquidate assets at simultaneously limited liability, which allows equity to have features of a call option (see Damodaran 2011a, p. 658, 659): In case the equity investors exercise their option to liquidate, they receive the liquidation value of the firm reduced by the face value of debt, while the limited liability cuts their losses to their investment in the firm. One often applied option pricing model is developed by Black and Scholes (1973).

2.1.3 Value Drivers and Influencing Factors

In the context of VBM, the question of drivers and influencing factors on company value is of particular interest for academic science and managerial practice. One approach to analyze cause and effect chains between company value and managerial decision making or operational business activities is represented by value driver trees, as illustrated in Fig. 2.2. Such trees are based on the idea that free cash flow (FCF) is split into income and expense figures which are disaggregated further into influencing factors (strategic and operational value drivers) until an applicable level of detail is reached that allows for integrating these value drivers into operational systems for management and controlling of business activities and performance (see Knorren and Weber 1997). Therefore, value driver trees link the strategic and operational level of a company (Knorren and Weber 1997): Value drivers enable the assessment of strategy options and sensitivity analysis of influencing factors in strategic planning, from which operational business activities of selected strategies are derived, executed and controlled. Hence the value drivers can be assigned to different levels of a value driver tree and are linked by cause-effect-relations which can be mathematically quantified or substantiated by qualitative arguments.

The postulate of VBM to manage all parts of a company with a focus on value increase leads to the conjecture that value drivers can be identified in various areas of managerial decision-making and different functions of a company. As one answer, Coenenberg and Salfeld (2003) illustrate thoroughly the relevance of company

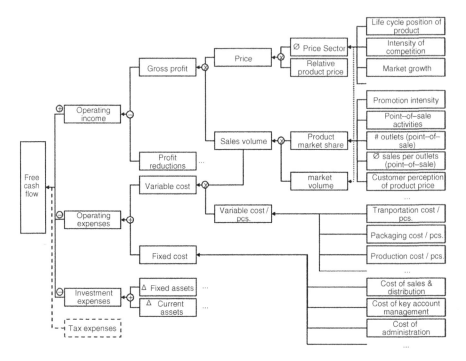

Fig. 2.2 Possible value driver hierarchy for an FMCG manufacturer (Based on Knorren and Weber 1997, p. 32)

growth, operational efficiency and effectiveness, capital structure and portfolio management for value creation. Academic research has provided further arguments to substantiate this conjecture. Scientific papers point out the influences on company value that stem from research and development (R&D) (Kelm et al. 1995) and from new product introduction (NPI) (Hendricks and Singhal 1997; Pauwels et al. 2004) as well as from SCM (Hendricks and Singhal 2003, 2005b) and from marketing (Srivastava et al. 1998) and last but not least from customer satisfaction (Anderson et al. 2004; Gruca and Rego 2005).

Based on 501 announcements about developments or introductions of new products, Kelm et al. (1995) evaluate the reaction of stock market prices on these announcements. The authors classify R&D projects as being in an innovation stage ending or a commercialization stage beginning when a new product is launched in the market. Technology variables, which describe the R&D intensity of an industry or company are distinguished from market variables such as industry concentration, sales growth or company size. Based on this categorization, their study shows that technology variables have a higher relevance in the innovation stage, while in the commercialization stage both technology and market variables are important. Further findings comprise the observations that capital markets react positively on small firms announcing R&D projects, on technology leading companies making announcements in the innovation stage or when firms in concentrated industry sectors announce NPIs.

Positive impacts of NPI on sales, profit and firm value are assessed by Pauwels et al. (2004) in an empirical study from the US automotive industry. Results obtained by a vector-autoregressive model indicate that, contrary to sales promotions, NPI increases the financial metrics in both short- and long-term. Hendricks and Singhal (1997) empirically evaluate impacts on market stock price of a firm stemming from delays in NPI. Based on 101 delay announcements from firms between 1984 and 1991 they observe that market value decreases on average by 5.2 %, and in 1991 the total loss of market value accounted for 119.3 m US$. Statistically significant influences on the degree of the impact arise from industry sector, company size or the degree of diversification of the firm.

In two other papers (Hendricks and Singhal 2003, 2005b), the authors assess the influences on market stock price of a company caused by announced SC disruptions. In 519 and 827 observations from industrial practice respectively, an abnormal short-term value decrease of 10.3 % and average abnormal long-term stock return reductions of nearly 40 % respectively are identified. It is observed that SC glitches cause stronger value deteriorations at smaller firms or at firms with higher growth expectations.

Srivastava et al. (1998) suggest a conceptual framework to assess impacts of market-based assets on shareholder value. The proposed framework comprises relational market-based assets, e.g. relations to customer, retailers and distributors, and intellectual market-based assets, i.e. the knowledge of a firm about emerging and potential market conditions and the entities in it. Similar to Barney (1991), the authors explain that market based assets are more likely to create value if they are convertible, i.e. adequate to exploit opportunities or mitigate threats, rare, e.g. possessed by no or only few competitors, imperfectly imitable or not perfectly substitutable. Qualitative arguments are provided for their potential influence on four strategic value drivers: (i) accelerated cash flows, (ii) increased level of cash flows, (iii) reduced risk associated with cash flows (obtained by lower volatility or vulnerability of future cash flows) that reduces the firm's cost of capital and (iv) the residual value of the business.

The positive association between customer satisfaction and shareholder value is substantiated by Anderson et al. (2004). By a proposed conceptual framework it is outlined how customer satisfaction affects the level, timing and risk of cash flows. These qualitative arguments are supported by an empirical evaluation of the correlation between overall customer satisfaction index and company value measured by Tobin's Q at 200 publicly traded firms between 1994 and 1997. The findings of Srivastava et al. (1998) and Anderson et al. (2004) are validated empirically by Gruca and Rego (2005). Based on a model that integrates the customer satisfaction level with cash flows and earnings of a company, a study of 840 firm-year observations from 1994 to 2003 shows that customer satisfaction can increase a company's cash flow and reduce its variability.

The managerial relevance of VBM and its occurences in various functions of a firm are reflected by its implementation and application in industrial practice. This aspect is illustrated in the following Sect. 2.1.4.

2.1.4 Empirical Aspects and Managerial Relevance

It is widely accepted in academic research that a comprehensive and integrated VBM system can be obtained by adding appropriate instruments for business planning and performance management to decision-making processes and incentive schemes (Hawawini and Viallet 2002). In accordance with Young and O'Byrne (2001) or Chenhall (2005), VBM can be comprehended as "a management accounting system linking value-maximization to strategic objectives, a coherent set of performance measures, and compensation through cause-and-effect chains" (Lueg and Schäffer 2010, p. 5). The subsequent questions, which are of interest for scientific research as well as for managerial practice, challenge if VBM implementations have a positive impact on company performance and what best practices for this implementation are identified in theory and observed in practice.

In a review on VBM, Lueg and Schäffer (2010) categorize 120 empirical studies regarding performance outcomes, capabilities, contingency factors and competencies and furthermore cluster the reviewed studies by the analytic breadth by which the VBM implementation is analyzed and the VBM orientation of the performance variables applied for these analyses. It is observed that a positive correlation between VBM implementation and company performance is indicated, and that stronger indications are provided by studies which combine a broad holistic investigation of VBM implementation with objective performance measures, such as stock returns. Besides, the authors address the need for further tests of the conjectured correlation between achieved level of the VBM implementation and objectively measured increase of company performance.

Two studies of Ryan and Trahan (1999, 2007) elaborate further on the VBM performance metrics applied in industrial practice and the impacts on company performance stemming from VBM implementations. Ryan and Trahan (1999) empirically assess the perception of VBM by financial managers from 184 publicly owned industrial firms and observed that EVA and DCF are the two VBM metrics that most managers are familiar with. Besides, CFROI and return on invested capital (ROIC) (see Copeland et al. 2005, for an introduction) were mentioned in this survey. DCF was identified as the predominantly applied metric. Areas of implementation focus on investment decisions, long-term planning and performance measurement, mainly on corporate and divisional level. It is furthermore detected that a link to compensation, in most cases by bonus systems, is realized throughout for executives and to a certain extent on professional level.

The use and efficiency of VBM systems is analyzed at 84 firms between 1984 and 1997 by Ryan and Trahan (2007). The main observation is that the implementation of VBM systems is positively associated with an increase of residual income. At a sample of 84 firms between 1984 and 1997, the ratio of industry- and performance-adjusted residual income and invested capital was increased by approximately 7 pp for 5 years after a VBM system was implemented. In this analysis, small firms showed larger improvements after VBM adoption than larger companies.

According to Weber et al. (2004), seamless implementation approaches for VBM systems must reflect the aspects of planning and target setting, compensation and incentive schemes, value reporting and investor relations as well as performance measurement and value driver trees. Weber et al. (2002b) differentiate between three maturity levels of VBM adoption. On a basic level, VBM is focused on external reporting and communication to capital markets. An advanced level can be achieved by linking the management compensation to value-based key figures, which are integrated with strategic and operational planning. The highest maturity level is characterized by a seamless adoption of VBM across all levels of management hierarchy and a balanced reflection of financial and non-financial performance metrics in a value driver tree. Weber et al. (2002a) assess to which extent four German corporations[1] achieve the highest maturity level and reveal deficiencies, especially in the transformation of shareholders expectations into strategic targets and in the degree to which long-term aspects of value creation are considered. The authors furthermore point out that standardized instruments are not adequate for value reporting, which should be performed in a monthly frequency and include both strategic and operational value drivers to provide information on the current, planned and forecasted business situation. Besides, penalty payments and upper limits for incentives are suggested.

The correlation between managerial behavior and compensation plans is elaborated by Wallace (1997) in a longitudinal analysis based on a sample of 40 firms. This study indicates a positive association between residual income performance measures and managerial decision-making for investing, financing and operating. It is observed that managers who are evaluated and compensated under consideration of the residual income of the firm tend to increase asset dispositions and to decrease investments, to use existing assets more intensely and to increase shareholder payments.

Numerous scientific publications comprise case examples for the implementation and application of VBM systems in various industries. Weber et al. (2004) provide examples from six globally operating German corporations[2] which illustrate the realization of value-based performance metrics, processes for planning and targeting, incentive schemes or value reporting in managerial practice. Claes (2006) elaborates on the VBM implementation in three multinational Dutch organizations[3] and the resulting effects on the management control system, behavior, decision making and performance. Papers in Schweickart and Töpfer (2006) discuss VBM

---

[1] Not particularly named market-listed holding companies.

[2] Bayer AG, Beiersdorf AG, Bosch Siemens Haushaltsgeräte GmbH, Deutsche Lufthansa AG, Deutsche Post AG, Deutsche Telekom AG.

[3] Akzo Nobel N. V., Heimans N. V., Schiphol Group N. V.

applications at nine German internationally or globally operating corporations[4] from strategic, process-oriented or customer-related perspectives. Three of these case examples indicate the link between VBM and operations management: A value creation program initiated at ThyssenKrupp AG comprises nearly 400 different projects, out of which 56% aim at increasing the operational efficiency and additional 6% focus on improving the productivity of fixed assets and working capital (Berlien et al. 2006). The importance of working capital is furthermore pointed out by Brandt and Zencke (2006), who exemplify that the optimization of working capital is considered a priority topic at SAP AG. Meyer (2006) describes the relevance of fixed asset reduction for value creation at Heidelberger Druckmaschinen AG. Beyond these examples, the managerial awareness for SCM in the context of value creation is illustrated by Cappello et al. (2006) with the example of the chemical industry or by Brandenburg and Menke (2008) with the example of six FMCG manufacturers.[5]

2.2 Supply Chain Management

The heterogeneity of terms for SCM used in academic research and industrial practice fosters the need of an adequate terminological basis and an appropriate framework for SCM. Both are given in this section to provide an appropriate basis for the thesis at hand and to position it to extant literature. An outline of dynamics and uncertainties of supply chains prepares the focusing of these aspects in the case examples presented in Chaps. 8 and 9. A discussion of scientific research on SCM in the FMCG industry reflects the emphasis of the thesis at hand for this field of research.

2.2.1 Terminology and Characteristics of Supply Chain Management

An SC can be comprehended as a structure that comprises "entities (organizations or individuals) directly involved in the upstream and downstream flows of products, services, finances, and/or information from a source to a customer" and that exists independent whether it is managed or not (Mentzer et al. 2001, p. 4 et seq.). The awareness for SCM has continuously increased during the last decades. In the 1950s and 1960s, the primary strategy was grounded on mass production to

---

[4]Altana AG, BMW Group, DaimlerChrysler AG, Deutsche Bank AG, Heidelberger Druckmaschinen AG, Metro AG, SAP AG, Stinnes AG, ThyssenKrupp AG.
[5]Beiersdorf AG, Colgate-Palmolive Company, Henkel KGaA, The Procter & Gamble Company, Reckitt-Benckiser Group plc, The Unilever Group.

minimize unit cost, while in the 1970s topics like materials' requirements planning enlarged the focus of SCM by materials' management (Tan 2001). In the 1980s, just-in-time concepts were developed as the importance of non-financial objectives such as quality, flexibility and reliability grew, while strategic suppliers and logistics functions have been included in the value chain since the 1990s (Tan 2001). Fostered by pioneering progress in the information technology (IT) (Croom et al. 2000; Günther 2005) and continuously enhancing globalization (Caniato et al. 2010; Christopher et al. 2006; Humphrey 2003), the perspective on SCM has evolved from a narrow focus to an encompassing view on this topic (Stock and Boyer 2009). The development of SCM was amplified by its relevance to a large variety of industry sectors including computer assembly and automotive as well as consumer goods and retail (Burgess et al. 2006).

Academic research on SCM is characterized by its multi-disciplinary perception of this topic. In a narrow sense, SCM is perceived as somehow advanced concept of purchasing and supply or logistics and transportation, which was extended by aspects of strategic management and organizational behavior (Croom et al. 2000). Furthermore, institutional sociology and contingency theory or economic development has contributed to the development of SCM (Croom et al. 2000). Numerous academic publications and research directions reflect the scientific variety and relevance of SCM. Stock and Boyer (2009) explicate that more than 7,000 refereed journal articles on SCM have been published between 1994 and 2008. In a content analysis of 22 literature reviews on SCM, Seuring and Gold (2012) identified seven sub-fields of SCM ranging from SC risk and performance to SC integration and sustainable SCM. Despite the long-ranging and continuously growing popularity of this field, the topic is characterized by a lack of terminology and clarity of perception of SCM, which varies from definitions based on operational terms, perceptions as management philosophy and views as a management process (Mentzer et al. 2001). More than half of the 100 scientific publications on SCM reviewed by Burgess et al. (2006) were not grounded on any definition for the term SCM, in further 21 % of the articles one of the various existing definitions was applied and in the remaining papers, new definitions were introduced as a terminological basis. To examine the terminological heterogeneity and provide a basis to develop further SCM theory, Stock and Boyer (2009) have examined 173 different definitions of SCM suggested in more than 1,000 academic publications from 30 journals and numerous scientific books and reports. The authors identified three main themes considered defining characteristics of SCM, which are

- activities including physical, logical and financial flows in networks of internal and external relationships,
- constituents and components comprising all operations, systems, business functions and organizations involved in the management of a particular SC, and
- benefits consisting of efficiency, effectiveness and value creation.

These three main themes are adopted for the thesis at hand. Thus they will be outlined in the following Sects. 2.2.2–2.2.4 and brought into context of an SCM framework in Sect. 2.2.5.

2.2.2   Physical, Logical and Financial Flows in Supply Chains

Physical flows comprise all activities to transform or distribute materials and goods within an SC. These flows are seen as integral part of SCM, which is substantiated amongst others by the coherence of SCM and logistics, comprehended as that part of the SC process that plans, implements and controls flow and storage of materials, inventory and goods from the point of origin to the point of consumption (Burgess et al. 2006; Cooper et al. 1997; Lambert and Cooper 2000).

Logical flows comprise transactions to share information, e.g. on inventory and capacity availability, quantity and timing of demands or point of sale (POS) data, within a function or across different organizations (Vanpoucke et al. 2009; Yang 2000). These transactions are supported by IT (Vahrenkamp 2005, Chap. 4) for enterprise resource planning (ERP) (Akkermans et al. 2003; Haug et al. 2010) and advanced planning systems (APS) (Günther and Meyr 2009; Günther and van Beek 2003; Stadtler 2005), electronic commerce (Vahrenkamp 2005, Chaps. 7 and 13) enabling electronic data interchange (EDI) (Cachon and Fisher 1997; Tan et al. 2010) or bar coding (O'Leary 2000) and radio frequency identification (RFID) technology (Palsson and Johansson 2009) as well as web-based applications for global SCM (Handfield and Nichols 2002; Tan et al. 2000, Chap. 8). By accelerating the information exchange and smoothing the physical flow, such IT implementations help reduce cost (Cachon and Fisher 2000) and improve quality, deliver reliability, lead times and flexibility (Schnetzler and Schönsleben 2007).

Financial flows represent the interface between finance and operations and result from activities of these two areas (Hofmann and Elbert 2004). SCM focuses on optimally designing and integrating them with flows of goods and information (Franke et al. 2005; Stemmler and Seuring 2003). This integration is comprehended as "SC finance" or "financial chain management" and aims at reducing cost, optimizing the financial structure and improving the cash flow situation within an SC (Metze 2010; Pfohl and Gomm 2009; Stemmler 2002). Tasks of SC finance include the collaborative financing of assets and working capital or optimization of financial processes between SC partners (Gomm 2010; Metze 2010). To optimize financing on an inter-organizational level, SC finance strives to integrate financial processes and increase value of customers, suppliers and service providers (Pfohl and Gomm 2009).

2.2.3   Relationships, Constituents and Components of Supply Chains

Relationships along which these physical, logical and financial flows stream can be categorized as internal or functional interfaces within an organization, dyadic links to immediate suppliers or customers, chain-related connections between first and second-tier suppliers and customers along the SC and network-related conjunctions between all members of the SC (Harland 1996; Lambert et al. 1998).

Constituents and components of SCM are defined differently in academic publications. Constituent parts of an SC can include single entities such as material suppliers, production facilities, distribution services and customers (Gunasekaran and Kobu 2007), various functions ranging from purchasing, production and logistics to finance, marketing and sales (Cooper et al. 1997) or heterogeneous processes including product development, order fulfillment and customer service management (Croxton et al. 2001). From an organizational perspective, Lambert and Cooper (2000) define members of an SC as "all those autonomous companies or strategic business units who carry out value-adding activities (operational and/or managerial) in the business processes designed to produce a specific output for a particular customer or market" (Lambert and Cooper 2000, p. 70). Facing this surfeit of appropriate perceptions, Stock and Boyer (2009) suggest that constituents and components of SCM comprise all operations, systems, business functions and organizations involved in the management of a particular supply chain.

2.2.4 Benefits of Supply Chain Management

SCM strives to achieve efficiency and effectiveness and ultimately to contribute to the financial value of a company (Christopher and Ryals 1999; Walters 2006). In this context, the efficiency of an SC is expressed by the performance of its processes (Croxton et al. 2001; Walters 2006). Walters (2008) differentiates between quantitative performance criteria striving for strategic and operational financial performance or customer response and qualitative performance criteria aiming at conformance, sustainability and environmental and social responsibility. The performance of an SC can be measured by appropriate SC metrics (Gunasekaran and Kobu 2007; Shepherd and Günter 2006) categorized into quality, speed, cost, flexibility and delivery dependability (White 1996). The effectiveness of an SC can be comprehended as customer satisfaction (Heikkilä 2002) which measures to which extent a company meets the requirements of its customers (Reiner and Schodl 2003). The value of a company is determined by its ability to create cash flows which are mainly influenced by its financials sales, profit margin and capital (as discussed in Sect. 2.1.1). A framework suggested by Reiner and Schodl (2003) as displayed in Fig. 2.3 helps to explain the interplay between these three benefits of SCM.

Efficiency and performance of SC processes can directly influence the customer satisfaction: Discussing cause effect relationships of efficient consumer response (ECR), Zimmermann and Seuring (2009) outline that improvements of the forecasting and replenishment processes increase the ability to deliver which in turn affects customer satisfaction. Taking into account the direct positive impact of customer satisfaction on company value (as discussed in Sect. 2.1.3), it becomes clear that SC efficiency also has an indirect influence on company value.

Fig. 2.3 SCM benefits
(Based on Reiner and Schodl
2003, p. 310)

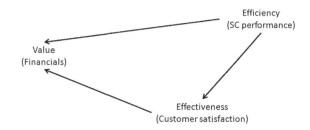

The efficiency of SC processes furthermore has a direct impact on the financial value of a firm. The profit margin of a company can be increased by improving the cost efficiency of its SC processes (Walters 2006). Improving the SC process efficiency results in lower inventory, prolonged supplier payment periods or shortened customer payment periods and thus reduces the working capital requirements of a company (Randall and Farris II 2009a). A more efficient utilization of production capacities and hence a higher return on assets (ROA) can be obtained by improved manufacturing processes (Fullerton and Wempe 2009; Gunasekaran et al. 2004). The impacts of SCM on sales, cost and capital will be discussed in greater detail in the following Sect. 2.3.

2.2.5   Supply Chain Management Framework

The complexity of SCM is driven on the one hand by product-related factors including expanding variety and shorter product life cycles (PLC) and on the other hand by structural aspects of an SC comprising increasing outsourcing and globalization of businesses (Lee 2002). The product-relationship-matrix (see Fig. 2.4) is a conceptual framework which combines SC dimensions with PLC dimensions (Schmenner and Swink 1998; Seuring 2009). The SC dimensions are differentiated between on the one hand configuration fields covering activities of network design and adaptation to reach the performance frontiers of an SC and on the other hand operational design focusing on organizing the physical, logical and financial flows in the SC in an even and swift manner (Seuring 2009). The PLC is separated into a pre-phase including product introduction and sales growth, a market phase covering the maturity of a product, and a post-phase which consists of decline and phase-out of a product.

The management of an SC can be seen from a strategic, tactical or operational perspective (Stock and Boyer 2009). Based on a definition of these levels given by Hübner (2007), this differentiation can be adopted to the product-relationship-matrix. Strategic aspects aim at ensuring long-term success of a company and focus on decision making on the product portfolio and the overall network configuration in a time horizon of 3–10 years. Tactical aspects consider the implementation of the strategic objectives under consideration of launch and discontinuation of

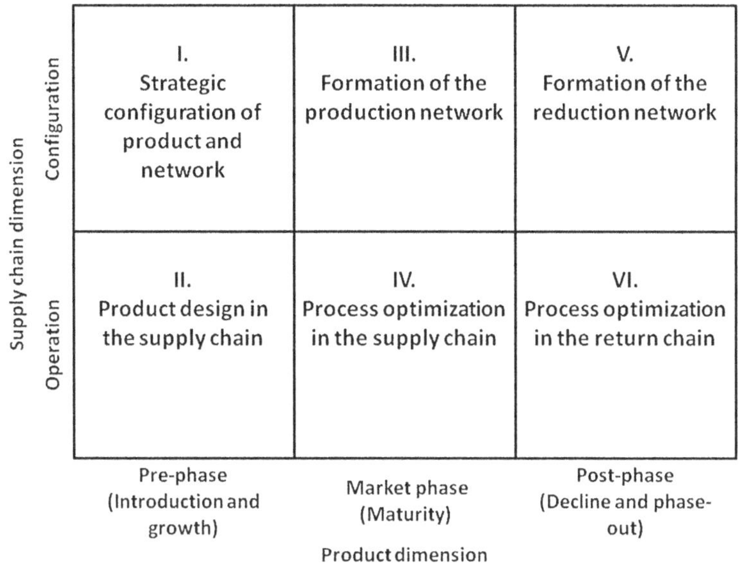

	I. Strategic configuration of product and network	III. Formation of the production network	V. Formation of the reduction network
Configuration			
Operation	II. Product design in the supply chain	IV. Process optimization in the supply chain	VI. Process optimization in the return chain

(row label left side: Supply chain dimension)

Pre-phase (Introduction and growth)	Market phase (Maturity)	Post-phase (Decline and phase-out)

Product dimension

Fig. 2.4 Product-relationship-matrix (Seuring 2009, p. 225)

specific products or categories as well as capacity adjustments and product transfers within the existing network over 1–3 years. Operational aspects strive for efficiently executing decisions taken on strategic and tactical level to ensure continuous product supply and optimal asset utilization within 1 year.

SC design can be comprehended as process of planning an SC that facilitates an effective and efficient SCM on tactical and operational level (Freiwald 2005). Hence it can be considered as strategic configuration of an SC and thus assigned to field I. of the product-relationship-matrix. Configuration decisions can be categorized into structural decisions reflecting location, capacity and transportation channels and co-ordination decisions including supplier selection, partnerships or inventory ownership (Reiner and Schodl 2003; Truong and Azadivar 2005). SC design problems comprise variables for location-allocation, inventory, production technology and capacity (Melo et al. 2009) as well as for production and shipment quantities, supplier selection options and transportation modes (Meixell and Gargeya 2005). SC design aims at determining the best configuration to achieve a high performance level (Truong and Azadivar 2005) which is in most cases measured by cost and profit metrics (Meixell and Gargeya 2005; Melo et al. 2009). Challenges in SC design can arise from geographical distances affecting transportation cost and lead times, infrastructural deficiencies, cultural differences in relationships to SC partners from other regions (Caniato et al. 2010) as well as inadequately skilled workforce and increased financial, economical or political risks (Meixell and Gargeya 2005). Multitudinous scientific publications deal with SC design problems. Based on a literature review, Kumar et al. (2010) categorize quantitative models for SC design by analytic hierarchy process (AHP), linear and non-linear programming or models using time compression and just-in-time methods. Quantitative models and methods designed by Freiwald (2005) can be applied to optimize SC designs with a focus on supplier selection and robustness of decisions taken. Hübner (2007) suggests a mathematical model for optimized production network design and applied this method in a case study of a special chemical company. Neuner (2009) proposes a conceptual framework for the configuration of manufacturing networks under consideration of uncertainty which is tested in four case studies from different industries.[6] The potential of value-oriented simulation models for improved SC configuration planning is explained by Labitzke et al. (2009), who apply DES models that include cost accounting models in an industrial case of a German steel manufacturer. In another case example from the steel industry,[7] Labitzke et al. (2011) adapt such a combined approach to the redesign of logistics processes.

Besides strategic approaches for widespread structural redesign of the entire SC network, NPI can raise the need for comparably slighter adaptations of the SC structure (Graves and Willems 2005) which hence can be considered tactical (Schilling et al. 2010). Such NPI-driven tactical SC designs comprise structural decisions on production capacity or allocation (Schilling et al. 2010) and coordination decisions, e.g. on selection and early integration of suppliers (Jayaram 2008; Wynstra and ten Pierick 2000). Depending on the degree of required SC adaptations, NPI activities can be assigned to the fields II., III. and IV. of the product-relationship-matrix (Seuring 2009). Driven by increases in time-based competition and customer requirements for innovative products, the rates of NPI continuously grow (Caridi et al. 2009; Fisher et al. 1997). This trend is accompanied by an increasing scientific relevance of the topic, reflected by academic literature which can be categorized into NPI-oriented publications focusing on anticipating constraints arising from the SC design and SCM-related scripts that mainly deal with aspects of planning and managing SC activities (Pero and Sianesi 2009; Pero et al. 2010). Caridi et al. (2009) state that the degree of product novelty, distinguished between innovation and adaptation, determines the extent to which the introduction of this product results in an SC redesign requirement. In empirical assessment of 20 innovation cases from different industries,[8] the authors identify a positive correlation between product innovativeness and SC complexity caused by process innovativeness. Pero et al. (2010) elaborate on the impacts of product characteristics on SC complexity and conclude that an improved match between SC design and product characteristics modularity, innovativeness and variety positively affects the SC performance. Based on five case studies from different industries,[9] the authors reveal the impacts on SC performance stemming from the adjustment of NPI and SCM activities and explain

---

[6] Apparel industry, chemical industry, packaging industry, technology industry.

[7] Salzgitter Flachstahl GmbH.

[8] These industries comprise automotive, bioengineering systems, furniture, household appliances, mechanical components, photo, power systems and tooling machines.

[9] Apparel industry, engine industry, weapon industry.

that during the design phase of a product, its SC-related characteristics and hence a considerable share of the expected SC cost are determined (Pero et al. 2010). Ayag (2005) points out that 60–80 % of these cost are committed in the early stages of product development and commercialization. Under consideration of the mutual correlation between SC performance and product performance, Pero and Sianesi (2009) propose a framework to align product development activities, which affect SCM by "created variety", and SCM processes that influence the SC performance by "transported variety". The authors emphasize the importance of this alignment by explaining the limited possibilities to alter the design of a product after it is launched in the marketplace (Pero and Sianesi 2009). The continuously decreasing length of PLCs (Caridi et al. 2009; Fisher et al. 1997) fosters this need to integrate both processes, especially because once introduced in the marketplace, products with comparably short life cycles might not leave enough time to adjust or improve the SC (Higuchi and Troutt 2004). Fisher et al. (1997) describe extreme cases in which the supply lead time of a product might even exceed the duration of its selling period. As a consequence of the interaction between NPI and SCM, SC decisions have to be taken before the development of a product has ended and its market reception can be adequately forecasted (van Hoek and Chapman 2006). Butler (2003) and Butler et al. (2006) have thoroughly analyzed influences on SC design decisions stemming from uncertainties of demand, cost or market conditions and dynamics arising from changes that occur during the PLC. The impacts of uncertainties and dynamics on SCM will be discussed in greater detail in the following Sect. 2.2.6.

Process optimization in the supply chain (field IV. of the product-relationship-matrix) aims at ensuring a swift and even flow of existing products (and related information and financial resources) through established networks (Schmenner and Swink 1998). SC performance measurement and management is adopted to control and improve the efficiency of such operational processes (Gunasekaran and Kobu 2007; Gunasekaran et al. 2004; Weimer and Seuring 2009), which can furthermore be linked to aggregated financial figures comprising profitability, cost or capital (see Fig. 2.2 on page 12). Another commonly applied method to assess, compare and enhance the SC process efficiency is benchmarking (Bhutta and Huq 1999; Fong et al. 1998; Gilmour 1999; Wong and Wong 2008). The coordination of operational SC processes and activities is supported by SC planning (see e.g. papers in Günther and Meyr 2009). SC planning on tactical level covers a mid-term horizon of several months or quarters (Shapiro 2007) and strives for optimizing the fixed assets' utilization, avoiding delayed product deliveries and reducing inventory and cost (see e.g. Berning et al. 2002; Brandenburg and Tölle 2009) to ensure both capital efficiency and profitability simultaneously.

The explanation of the product-relationship-matrix ends with a brief characterization of reduction networks (field V. of the product-relationship-matrix) and return chains (field VI. of the product-relationship-matrix), which are related to return flows of material for proper disposal (open loop) or remanufacturing (closed loop) (Krikke et al. 2002). Closed-loop SCM is comprehended as "the design, control, and operation of a system to maximize value creation over the entire life cycle of a product with dynamic recovery of value from different types and volumes of returns over time" (Guide Jr. and van Wassenhove 2009, p. 10). Krikke et al. (2004), and also Morana and Seuring (2007) categorize such product returns by end-of-life returns, end-of-use returns, commercial returns and re-usable items. Unlike the material flow in forward supply chains, return products flow back from many points of consumption to few points of origin, recovery or disposal (Fleischmann et al. 1997). These return flows are managed by reverse logistics, which can include retailers, manufacturers and service entities across several functional areas and can have considerable economic, environmental, managerial, regulatory, and strategic implications (Dowlatshahi 2005). The benefits of closed-loop SCM are affected by uncertainties of quality, quantity and timing of return products (Guide Jr. et al. 2003). Morana and Seuring (2011) distinguish three relationship levels of return chains and reduction networks: The society level deals with societal or stakeholder demands and related political decisions. The chain level describes the overall product life-phases and related return processes. On the actor level, the single actor's transaction costs for product returns are assessed. The research streams on closed-loop SCM are categorized by Atasu et al. (2008) into the areas of industrial engineering/operations research, design, strategic competition and behavioral problems. Scientific literature on reverse logistics can be categorized into integration between reverse and forward networks and fully concentrated on recovery activities (Melo et al. 2009). In a review, Fleischmann et al. (1997) classify quantitative approaches on reverse logistics in models for distribution logistics, inventory control models and production planning models.

2.2.6 Dynamics and Uncertainties in Supply Chains

Strong influences on the complexity and performance of an SC arise from uncertainties and dynamics which are hence of particular interest for academic research (Blackhurst et al. 2004; Wilding 1998). Dynamics are caused by variations of physical and logical flows within an SC as well as by demand oscillations over time. Uncertainties define any practically unavoidable deviation from the purely theoretical ideal of full knowledge of a system and thus distinguishes stochastic from deterministic supply chains (Datta and Christopher 2011).

Customer demands, information exchange and applied order or replenishment rules determine the rates at which products flow within an SC (Daganzo 2003). Supply chains in which reorder policies are exclusively based on the status of a supplier and the order history of its direct customer are characterized by variability in order sizes and inventory levels that increases upstream (Daganzo 2003). This phenomenon, known as the "bullwhip effect" (Lee et al. 1997a) and first observed by Forrester (1961), can be amplified by different factors. Fischer (1997) observed that an overuse of price promotions at the Campbell Soup Company negatively influenced the efficiency of the physical flows within the SC of this company. Lee et al. (1997b) identified demand signal processing, order batching and shortage gaming as further amplifiers of this phenomenon. Based on a system dynamics model comprising four echelons of the SC of a Mexican food company, Villegas and Smith (2006) exemplified that order quantity oscillations resulting in the bullwhip effect can be induced by safety stock policies. By applying the "beer distribution game" it is shown that the behavior of SC members creates or augments the bullwhip effect (Sterman 1989). This finding is validated by Nienhaus et al. (2006) by an online simulation of this game with more than 400 participants. Based on analytical models, Lee et al. (2000) show that sharing sales information can help manufacturers to reduce both inventory and cost.

Demand oscillations over time causing internal dynamics can arise in NPI situations, when a considerable amount of the total expected demand of a product must be available shortly after it is introduced in the marketplace. The resulting effect of "pipeline filling" (Schilling et al. 2010) occurs when major product quantities are produced and distributed before the product is actually launched (van Hoek and Chapman 2006). Fischer (1997) illustrates this phenomenon with the example of Campbell Soup Company, which deploys enough inventory of newly introduced products to cover the most optimistic demands for the first months after product launch. Another example for the impacts of dynamic PLCs is given by Lee (2002) who describes that computer manufacturers are challenged by suppliers that do not meet the ramp up speed required in the product introduction phase or that overproduce at the end of the PLC.

The issue of dynamics in an SC is closely related to SC uncertainties, which can create or foster the bullwhip effect (Lee 2002). Uncertainties in an SC can be caused by external or internal factors (Datta and Christopher 2011) on demand or supply side (Lee 2002; Saad and Gindy 1998). Its dimensions comprise quantities, such as demand volume or supply capacities, time, e.g. durations or due dates, financials including cost, price or exchange rates, information which can be ambiguous or missing, as well as managerial or technical aspects, e.g. business priorities or quality of goods and products (Blackhurst et al. 2004; Chopra and Meindl 2007). The influences of uncertainties on SC performance are assessed by Petrovic (2001), who applies a simulation model in a multi-echelon SC to validate the negative impacts of uncertainties in an SC on its cost and delivery performance. Forecasting errors, caused by demand uncertainties, result in markdowns and stockouts and hence create additional cost, which in some industries even exceed the total cost of manufacturing (Fisher et al. 1994). Safety stocks represent one attempt to mitigate negative effects of demand and supply uncertainties on customer service (Silver et al. 1998). Optimized safety stock levels in production networks can be determined by a stochastic optimization model developed by Jung et al. (2004), which is tested in a case example of a US polyethylene producer. Other approaches to decrease demand uncertainties comprise information sharing and centrally coordinated material flows, as Datta and Christopher (2011) demonstrated by applying an agent-based simulation model in an industrial case from a paper tissue manufacturer. Blackhurst et al. (2004) distinguish between different quantitative methods including interval analysis, fuzzy methods and statistical approaches, to represent uncertainties in an SC. The authors outline the deficits, especially loss of relevant information, computational complexity and difficulties in data analysis or manipulation, of these models and propose a network-based methodology which is empirically validated in a case study of a metal fabrication shop.

There is a seamless transition from the concept of uncertainties to the idea of risk, which in context to SCM is defined as variation of potential events assessed by their occurrence probability and subjective value with a negative impact on the business processes of at least one SC member (Kersten et al. 2006). With reference to academic publications (e.g. papers in Kersten and Blecker 2006; Vahrenkamp and Siepermann 2007), the broad scientific field of supply chain risk management, comprehended as all adequate methods to mitigate supply chain risks (Kersten et al. 2006), will not be discussed further in this thesis.

Both dynamics and uncertainties can influence the configuration of an SC. Gabriel (2003) states that the combination of demand dynamics, stable or volatile, and product structure, physical-assembled or chemical-biological, determines the adequate configuration of an SC. In this approach, SC configurations are categorized in lean designs for automotive industry, agile designs for electronics industry, connected designs for the chemical and pharmaceutical industry and rapid SC designs for consumer goods industry. This categorization is validated by four case studies from companies[10] of the respective industries. Lee (2002) bases the appropriate SC configuration on the degree of uncertainties of supply processes and product demands. Regarding the demand uncertainties, functional products with low uncertainties are distinguished from innovative products with high uncertainties. With regards to the supply uncertainties, stable processes with low uncertainties and evolving processes with high uncertainties are differentiated. The proposed SC configurations comprising efficient, responsive, risk-hedging and agile designs are illustrated by numerous case examples from different industries.[11]

2.2.7 Supply Chain Management in the Fast Moving Consumer Goods Industry

SCM in FMCG is of particular interest for academic research. Clustering SC configurations by demand volatility and product structure, Gabriel (2003) assigns the FMCG sector to rapid SC which distribute products with incremental innovations to mature markets with price- and quality-conscious consumers and mainly require a high reactivity and efficiency throughout all sourcing, production and distribution processes. Lee (2002) differentiates SC configurations by demand and supply uncertainties. Depending on the consumer goods category, an SC from FMCG industry can be ascribed to different fields of this framework: SC for grocery and basic apparel, functional products requiring stable processes with low

---

[10]BASF AG, Ford Werke AG, Hewlett-Packard CSDE, Sara Lee Household & Body Care.

[11]Apparel industry, automotive industry, computer industry, electronics industry, food industry, semiconductor industry, steel industry.

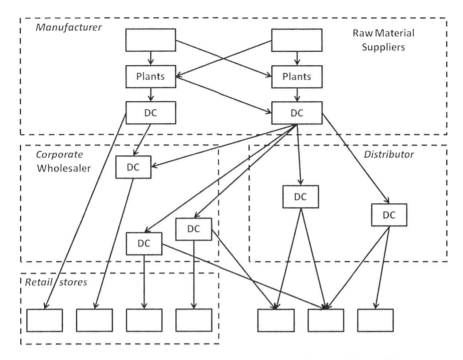

Fig. 2.5 Supply chain of a manufacturer of consumer products (Shapiro 2007, p. 489)

demand and supply uncertainties, are attributed as efficient, i.e. referred to focusing on economies of scale and adopting optimization concepts. SC for some food products requiring evolving processes show high supply uncertainties and hence are peculiarized as risk-hedging. In such an SC, resources are pooled and shared to cover uncertainties on the supply side. Fashion apparel and computer electronics categorized as innovative products with stable processes require a responsive SC, in which mass customization and order accuracy are most relevant success factors.

FMCG like cosmetics and toiletries, electronic gadgets or batteries, household goods or paper products are merchandises which at high turnover and comparably low cost can considerably contribute to profitability (Pourakbar et al. 2009). Managerial decisions about changes in the FMCG assortment have to be taken under consideration of tradeoffs between beneficial incremental sales achieved by an improved coverage of consumer preferences and disadvantageous additional cost caused by an increase in the complexity of the product portfolio (Danne and Häusler 2010). This assortment complexity is determined by various factors like packaging size, prints and labels, the composition of ingredients and flavors and number of new products (Bilgen and Günther 2010). An SC for consumer products, as illustrated in Fig. 2.5, consists of manufacturers, wholesalers, distributors and retailers comprising a considerable number of factories, outlets, transshipment points and department stores and thus exhibits a high structural complexity (Gudehus and Kotzab 2009; Shapiro 2007). These complexities of SCM in the

FMCG sector are fostered by two main trends on the demand side of the SC (Miebach Consulting 2004): Hybrid behavior and declining brand loyalty of consumers confront the SC members with demands of an increasing number of products that continuously shortens PLCs (Teller and Kotzab 2003). Beyond this, producers face increasing requirements regarding delivery performance and cost efficiency amplified by enlarged concentration and price competition in the retail sector (ELA 2004; McKinnon and Forster 2000).

SCM in FMCG industry has undergone a change from traditional "egoistic" relationships between customers and suppliers towards cooperation and partnering between retailers, vendors and logistics service providers in order to improve the flows of goods and information between the channel members (Teller and Kotzab 2003). Handfield and Nichols (2002) exemplify such collaborative relationships by FMCG manufacturers which established dedicated customer teams to facilitate appropriate information sharing and handle logistics, finance, accounting and supply issues with its major retail accounts.[12]

The physical flows through FMCG networks are determined by the assignment of consumer products to the various plants in the network, which are often operated in make-and-pack mode comprising one single production stage to manufacture the final products that are subsequently packed for shipment (Bilgen and Günther 2008, 2010). Palletized finished products are distributed from production plants to retail outlets either directly or via regional logistics centers and warehouses (Gudehus and Kotzab 2009). Distribution logistics can be executed either in full truck load (FTL) mode, in which the manufacturer hires a full truck to ship finished goods to various destinations, or in less than truck load (LTL) mode, in which a carrier bundles loads from various pick-up locations (Bilgen and Günther 2010). To maximize full trailer movements, inventory turns and the delivery quality, the logistical distribution of consumer products is often supported by cross-docking processes, which facilitate shipments without putting the respective product into storage before it is sent to retail outlets or department stores (Handfield and Nichols 2002). Since the adaptation of the continuous replenishment program (CRP), this physical flow has evolved from pushing product from inventory holding areas driven by supply to pulling products onto grocery shelves driven by consumer demands (Lummus and Vokurka 1999).

In order to link logical flows of POS data to these physical flows of consumer goods and thus enable adequate reactions to consumer needs, the ECR concept which is characterized by various tools and techniques including EDI, cross-docking and SC integration has been designed in the beginning of the 1990s (Bahrami 2002; Bhutta et al. 2002; Frankel et al. 2002). In a case survey of 45 Austrian companies, Teller and Kotzab (2003) identified the adoption of European article numbers (EAN), EDI and category management as success factors for ECR cooperations. On the supply side of an SC this concept is complemented by the intersectoral collaborative planning, forecasting and replenishment (CPFR) initiative (Handfield

---

[12]The Procter & Gamble Company and Wal-Mart Stores, Inc., mentioned in particular.

and Nichols 2002, p. 321 et seq.). Especially in branches with many seasonal products and promotional items, long replenishment lead times (RLT) and frequent NPIs resulting in short PLCs, CPFR supports the integration of physical and logical flows between suppliers, manufacturers and retailers and fosters increases of sales and profitability at reduced inventory levels and RLT (Seifert 2002). These benefits of CPFR are demonstrated by dyadic case examples from the FMCG industry[13] in which retailers and manufacturers significantly reduced the inventory and RLT while simultaneous improvements of fill rates and product availability resulted in considerable sales increases (Frankel et al. 2002; Handfield and Nichols 2002; Seifert 2002, p. 326 et seq.).

These case examples illustrate the high relevance of customer satisfaction in FMCG industry. Both manufacturers and retailers are obliged to ensure product availability to the consumer, who likely buys a substitute article from a different brand or in another store if the desired product is not available on the shelf of a grocery store (Christopher 2005; Corsten and Gruen 2003; Meyr and Stadtler 2008). Additionally, FMCG manufacturers and retailers strive for efficiency improvements regarding delivery flexibility, inventory levels and cost for production, transportation and warehousing (Bilgen and Günther 2010; ELA 2004; Miebach Consulting 2004). The coherence between operational value drivers linked to these objectives and the cash flow of an FMCG manufacturer is exemplarily illustrated in Fig. 2.2 on page 12.

Dynamics and uncertainties are decisive factors for SCM in the FMCG sector, as can already be seen by its positioning in the frameworks proposed by Lee (2002) and Gabriel (2003) or some of the case examples mentioned in Sect. 2.2.6. Both phenomena are highly interrelated on the demand side to the buying behavior of consumers and on the supply side to shortened PLCs often caused by incremental product innovations brought to markets by manufacturers. The relevance of product availability in FMCG industry amplifies the importance of the retailers' and manufacturers' ability to accurately forecast consumer demands (Adebanjo and Mann 2000). This circumstance is exemplified in an industrial case example[14] by Cachon and Fisher (1997). Strong amplifications of variations in consumer demands resulting in the bullwhip effect are observed by Lee et al. (1997a) in case examples from the FMCG industry.[15] These phenomena are described and analyzed in greater detail by Handfield and Nichols (2002, p. 295 et seq.) and Chopra and Meindl (2007, p. 497 et seq.). The short-term uncertainties and volatility of consumer demands affecting the operational business is complemented by the dynamics of demand quantities during short PLCs and the uncertainties of the mid- and long-term market potential of consumer goods and product ranges. To ensure on-shelf availability of newly developed consumer goods, manufacturers fill all stocking points of the distribution channel with large quantities of these new products before they are

---

[13] K-Mart Corp. and Kimberly-Clark Co., Nabisco and Wegmans Food Markets, Inc., Wal-Mart Stores, Inc. and Warner-Lambert Co.

[14] Campbell Soup Company.

[15] 3M Company and The Procter & Gamble Company and furthermore Hewlett-Packard Company.

actually launched in the marketplace (Schilling et al. 2010). Shortage gaming
retailers tend to place "phantom orders" in order to ensure sufficient product supply
during the beginning of the commercialization phase (Higuchi and Troutt 2004).
These behaviors result in boosted demand quantities during the product introduction
phase followed by a sharp decline after this phase, but both developments to an
unforeseeable extent. Hence FMCG manufacturers are more and more challenged
by redesigning the SC for new products or new product categories before their
market reception is known and before an adequate basis for accurate demand
forecasts is available (van Hoek and Chapman 2006). Higuchi and Troutt (2004)
illustrate the resulting misalignments in the SC configuration by a case example
of an electronics toy manufacturer[16] that was confronted with tremendous out of
stock situations and boosting customer demands shortly after product launch. The
company tried to react on this by adjusting its SC setup and in the end of the
short life cycle of its product was confronted with significant excess capacities
and surplus stocks. These case examples illustrate that overall, short-, mid- and
long-term demand uncertainties and dynamics in FMCG industry affect inventory
levels, the utilization of available capacities, the identification of additional fixed
asset requirements and adequate partnerships in the SC (Adebanjo and Mann 2000;
Schilling et al. 2010).

   Based on the product-relationship-matrix introduced in Sect. 2.2.5, the discussion
on scientific research on SCM in the FMCG industry is completed. SC design
(field I. of the product-relationship-matrix) is focused by Camm et al. (1997) in
a case study on the restructuring of the North American production and distribution
network at a major FMCG manufacturer.[17] In order to streamline the operational
processes, to eliminate value destroying activities and to consolidate the production
plant network, a quantitative optimization model was designed and linked to
scenario design based on human decision making. The restructuring was preceded
by an assortment harmonization of raw materials, packaging components and
finished products and by a significant reduction of PLCs from 5 years to 18–24
months on average. The consolidation of every fifth production location resulted in
considerable cost reductions.

   The case study from Higuchi and Troutt (2004) mentioned above deals with
aspects of new product introduction (field II. of the product-relationship-matrix).
Based on a scenario-based dynamic simulation model comprising three echelons of
this case, it is concluded that the introduction of new products should be preceded
by thorough quantitative analyses including assessments of various design options
and different scenarios for customer and consumer behavior. The authors state
that the determination of product and SC specifications is more important than
later adjustments, which might be timely limited by the short PLC. Based on the
example of a globally operating FMCG manufacturer,[18] van Hoek and Chapman

---

[16]Bandai Co., Ltd.

[17]The Procter & Gamble Company.

[18]Reckitt Benckiser Group plc.

(2006) elaborate on the alignment between SCM and NPI regarding forecasting and capacity planning in order to avoid disadvantageous out-of-stock (OOS) situations and significant cost for later adjustments.

A stochastic model to optimize reconfigurations of and operations in the production and distribution network (fields III. and IV. of the product-relationship-matrix) is proposed by Tahmassebi (1998). The suggested model is suitable to reduce inventory levels and cost at improved service level under consideration of demand, process and supply uncertainties. It is shown that this model can be applied to the FMCG sector as well as to the chemical process industry.

The model-based optimization of operational processes (field IV. of the product-relationship-matrix) is furthermore focused by Bilgen and Günther (2008, 2010). The authors propose scheduling approaches based on mixed integer programming (MIP) for block planning of a consumer goods production plant, which are tested in case examples from the beverage industry. In a quantitative simulation-based analysis of the dyadic relationship between an FMCG manufacturer and a retailer, Dekker et al. (2009) evaluate different options for intermodal transportation regarding cost, lead time and delivery performance. Potential advantages of intermodal transportation and floating stocks are illustrated at the example of a manufacturing plant that supplies four regional distribution centers. Sandholm et al. (2006) apply mathematical optimization models to improve decision making in strategic sourcing of raw materials, packaging components and transportation services at The Procter & Gamble Company. Improvements of operational SC processes and reductions of the assortment complexity at Gillette Co. are illustrated by Duffy (2004). In this case example, significant improvements in delivery performance, cost efficiency and inventory levels were achieved.

A quantitative model developed by Wojanowski et al. (2007) helps to optimize the design of the return chain (field V. of the product-relationship-matrix) for deposit-refunds in the retail sector. The analytical framework incorporates the design of the collection facility network and pricing decisions for finished goods.

In a review of case studies on reverse logistics (field VI. of the product-relationship-matrix), de Brito et al. (2002) find that more than half of the reviewed case studies focused on metal products, machinery or technical equipment. The authors state that reverse logistics are in most cases applied for products with a high residual value. It can be concluded that return chains in FMCG industry mainly focus the return of deposit or transport packaging, which accounted for up to 50 % of the total domestic garbage before increasing environmental consciousness of consumers and stricter legal obligations forced manufacturers and retailers to adopt functional, economic and ecologic packagings (Vahrenkamp 2005, Chap. 14). Bloemhof-Ruwaard et al. (2002) elaborate on cost and environmental aspects of packaging recycling in a case example of a dairy company.[19] Aspects of bottle recycling in the optimization of filling and distribution processes are furthermore dealt with by Förster et al. (2006) in a case example of a beverage company.

---

[19]Campina Melkunie B. V.

2.3 Value-Based Supply Chain Management

In this section, the mergence of VBM and SCM to the concept of value-based SCM is described. An outline of the coherence between SC performance and profitability- and capital-related financial value drivers provides the basis for the conceptual elements of the quantitative models proposed in this thesis. In a review of 20 selected manuscripts that complements the content analysis presented in Chap. 4, conceptual frameworks for value-based SCM are introduced which are extended to quantitative models in the subsequent Chaps. 5–10. Furthermore this review illustrates the broadness of academic research on value-based SCM and represents the current status and recent developments of related scientific research.

2.3.1 Financial Impacts of Supply Chain Performance

Due to the interplay between efficiency and effectiveness of SCM and the resulting financial impacts described in Sect. 2.2.4, SCM decisions affect the financial shape of a company and thus the value of its shares (Shapiro 2007). Hence, it can be concluded that company value is considerably influenced by SC performance, which can be measured and managed by appropriate metrics (Gunasekaran and Kobu 2007; Gunasekaran et al. 2004). Such metrics can be distinguished between quantitative measures which can be directly described numerically and qualitative measures that do not facilitate a single direct numerical measurement (Beamon 1998). The former category includes indicators such as fill rate, product tardiness or lead time, examples for the latter category are customer satisfaction, flexibility or integration (Beamon 1998). Losbichler and Rothböck (2006) state that SCM affects financial performance levers growth, profitability and capital, to which Beamon (1998) assigns four quantitative SC performance metrics: sales, cost, working capital and fixed assets. In the following, these four financial metrics are defined to ensure terminological clarity. Besides, difficulties of the interplays between these metrics are outlined and a brief discussion on related literature is given.

The sales of a company are defined by its revenue, i.e. all transactions apart from the issuance of new shares that increase the owners' equity, reduced by trade discounts and allowances (Hawawini and Viallet 2002). They can be distinguished between intercompany sales, e.g. resulting from shipments between different segments or affiliates of the same corporation, and external sales stemming from deliveries to external customers which do not belong to the selling corporation (Shapiro 2007). From an SC perspective, sales are mainly determined by the sales price and the quantity of sold products and strongly influenced by customer satisfaction (Kannegiesser et al. 2009; Vickery et al. 2003). The major challenge in this context is that the exact correlation between customer service created by SCM and sales obtained by the company cannot be quantified or calculated, although this conjectured causality is supported by qualitative arguments stating that superior service to customers can increase their loyalty to a specific supplier and hence result in higher sales (Christopher 2005). Other approaches to substantiate sales impacts of SCM spotlight OOS situations, which are mainly caused by insufficient planning, ordering or replenishment processes (Marquai et al. 2010). Although the unavailability of consumer products in the retail industry most often results in replacement purchases of final customers, the question to what level and at which effort the product availability should ideally be improved remains open (Marquai et al. 2010). Such lost sales exhibit a functional relevance for SCM, cost accounting and marketing and besides do not only affect the final tier of an SC, but furthermore all upstream members (Perona 2002). Product availability can be measured by OOS rates, which can either be reported as an average over all categories or be determined by counting the number of times a consumer unsuccessfully searches a specific item on shelf (Corsten and Gruen 2003). The former metric is limited by its inability to adequately indicate lost sales, while the latter measure can only be quantified by estimates based on historical sales data (Corsten and Gruen 2003).

SC cost can be categorized by direct cost for acquiring material and labor, activity-based cost that account for administration activities of the organizational framework and transaction cost related to inter-organizational interactions between SC members (Seuring 2001). A major part of SC cost is reflected by cost of goods sold (COGS) which include direct and overhead cost associated with physical production of products for sale (Poston and Grabinski 2001). Slagmulder (2002) expounds that SC cost management is an inter-organizational approach to take advantage of synergies between SC members and hence would extend the cost assignment from products towards customers and suppliers. Limitations of SC cost management already arise on company level from difficulties of traditional management accounting to clearly define, measure and appropriately assign relevant cost categories (Beamon 1999). A good example for this problem are logistics cost which can differ significantly even between companies from the same sector and represent a considerable amount of total cost, but however are not uniquely defined or properly assigned to related cost categories (Gudehus and Kotzab 2009). In most scientific papers, financial benefits of SCM are related to cost (Meixell and Gargeya 2005; Melo et al. 2009; Villegas and Smith 2006), and research on SC cost management comprises concepts, instruments and models (see e.g. papers in Seuring and Goldbach 2001). Goldbach (2002) supports the comprehension that SC cost management extends cost management within a firm to the entire SC and clusters this area by a functional dimension focusing managing cost optimization activities and an institutional dimension referring to managerial responsibilities for cost-related decisions. In this publication, instrumental aspects are reflected in context to activity-based costing which attributes overhead cost appropriately to total product cost and to target costing which adjusts allowable cost determined based on assumed market price and margin expectation by standard cost of a product (Goldbach 2002). In an empirical analysis of 126 medium- and large-sized Swiss firms, Wagner (2008) identifies 18 different cost management practices in SCM, which are functionally related to purchasing, supplier relationship management or integrated logistics and which comprise different approaches for target costing, total cost of ownership, activity-based costing and supplier lifetime value. Numerous scientific publications illustrate the relevance of SC cost management for managerial practice. Gudehus and Kotzab (2009) state that logistics cost account for 5–15 % of the turnover of manufacturing firms and 10–25 % of the turnover of trade companies. In an enquiry of 3,767 Austrian corporations, Kotzab and Teller (2002) discover that on average logistics represents a cost volume of more than 15 % of total cost and up to 9 % of total sales. Inventory carrying cost can account for approx. 25 % of COGS (Fischer 1997).

In scientific research and industrial practice, working capital is most often defined as sum of inventory and trade receivables reduced by trade payables (Brealey et al. 2008). In some definitions, working capital is extended by other components such as cash, prepaid expenses or accrued expenses (Hawawini and Viallet 2002; Ross et al. 2002). Working capital is an important SC-related value driver, especially because it usually has a life-span of less than 1 year and strongly influences the liquidity position and thus the economic value of a company (Schilling 1996). Working capital combines intra- and inter-organizational physical and financial flows and thus can be seen from an SCM perspective and complementary from a financial view (Farris II and Hutchison 2003). From the SCM perspective, working capital links material activities with suppliers, manufacturing and operations processes to sales activities with customers (Farris II and Hutchison 2002). From the point of time at which cash expenditures for acquisition of raw materials are made through the time interval of production and inventory storage within a company to the collection period during which funds for sold products are received from customers, working capital circulates synchronously to the operating cycle of a company (Schilling 1996). This SCM-related perception of working capital is complemented by a financial comprehension that focuses on cash flow. The length of the circulation period of working capital, named cash to cash (C2C) cycle, measures the time period between cash outflow and cash inflow and expresses the working capital performance of a company (Farris II and Hutchison 2002). The C2C cycle can be decomposed into days sales outstanding (DSO), days sales of inventory (DSI) and days payables outstanding (DPO), three metrics that quantify the performance of each working capital component (Lambert and Pohlen 2001):

$$DSO = \frac{\text{Trade receivables}}{\text{Sales}} \cdot 365 . \qquad (2.1)$$

$$DSI = \frac{\text{Inventory}}{COGS} \cdot 365 . \qquad (2.2)$$

$$DPO = \frac{\text{Trade payables}}{COGS} \cdot 365 . \qquad (2.3)$$

$$C2C = DSO + DSI - DPO . \qquad (2.4)$$

These coherent concepts are depicted in Fig. 2.6. The cash turnover, defined as the reciprocal value of C2C, indicates the minimum liquidity requirement of a company (Schilling 1996).

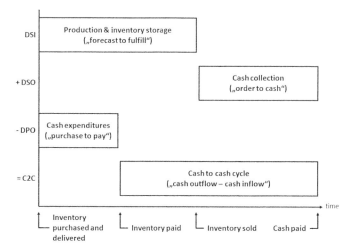

Fig. 2.6 The C2C cycle and its components

Farris II and Hutchison (2002) explain that the working capital performance of a company can be improved by extending the payment period to suppliers, by shortening the production cycle within a company or by reducing the collection period of sales to customers. The authors distinguish cooperative optimization methods comprising electronic payment or cash discounts from concurring approaches, e.g. the adjustment of payment frequencies at suppliers' expenses or the adaptation of just-in-time strategies. Randall and Farris II (2009a) discuss three aspects of collaborative working capital management. The determination of payback/leverage points of change, which indicate one time and recurring improvements, for each working capital component helps to compare trading partners within an SC. Shifting inventory within the SC upwards to the suppliers helps to reduce the overall inventory carrying cost of the SC. Financial levers of SC transactions can be shifted among SC members to the company with the lowest cost of capital. The authors illustrate these aspects by numerical examples and conclude that companies can increase their profitability by adopting an inter-organizational and collaborative perspective on working capital management.

Hofmann and Kotzab (2006) point out that working capital reductions create one-time benefits that increase free cash flows and thereby shareholder value. In their paper, it is furthermore explained that working capital metrics are relevant from perspectives of accounting, to measure liquidity and organizational efficiency, and of SCM, to bridge flows into and out of a firm by common accounting principles. The authors emphasize the need to consider inter-organizational aspects of working capital optimization and propose a conceptual model for collaborative working capital management. In this framework, financial flows within an SC network are distinguished from flows towards external interfaces resulting in two interrelated optimization tasks, the network-internal optimization of working capital and the outward looking optimization of cash flows. The authors explain the similarity of these optimization problems which both comprise payment periods at external intersections as well as internal inventory periods and conclude that improving working capital at the expense of SC members is counterproductive regarding value creation within the SC network. This finding is supported by a case example from the FMCG industry.[20] The idea of inter-organizational collaborative working capital management is elaborated further by Hofmann and Kotzab (2010), who describe that powerful focal companies tend to force their weaker SC partners to finance their working capital requirements. The authors distinguish between three research categories in this area. First working capital research that typically focuses the single company perspective, for which key figures for working capital can be derived from published financial statements of publicly traded firms. Second, management accounting that increasingly focuses inter-firm relationships and inter-organizational cost management but neglects working capital and cash flow figures. Third, academic research on SCM that analyzes the influences of collaborative information exchange without consideration of financial impacts or management accounting support. In their paper, Hofmann and Kotzab (2010) furthermore explain that value "is added when the overall net cash flow of the business exceeds the cost of all the capital employed to produce the operational performance" (Hofmann and Kotzab 2010, p. 314). Additionally it is observed that deteriorations of working capital performance can stem from operational deficiencies of the processes "order to cash", which aims at sales and receivables management on demand side, "forecast to fulfill", which includes production, warehousing, forecasting and order management, and "purchase to pay" comprising sourcing and expenditures management (Hofmann and Kotzab 2010). Based on this observation, which is supported by industry examples,[21] the authors suggest an integrated approach for collaborative C2C cycle management.

In many cases, empirical research on working capital management is based on benchmarking. Randall and Farris II (2009b) illustrate the potential of benchmarking the C2C cycle based on publicly available United States Generally Accepted Accounting Principles (US GAAP) financial data by three case studies from different industry sectors,[22] in which one selected company is compared against a sample group of more than 100 competitors. This approach outlines that difficulties in capturing useful data can be resolved by applying US GAAP figures for benchmarking, although financial data are reported in aggregated form and such an approach furthermore limits the sample group to publicly traded firms. The authors conclude that benchmarking the working capital performance helps to identify optimization potentials and that such a study can be extended by including customers and suppliers of the considered firms. A structural and geographical focus is taken by Padachi (2006) in an empirical evaluation of the working capital performance between 1998 and 2003 at 58 small Mauritanian manufacturing firms.

---

[20]The Unilever Group and its tea suppliers in Kenya, Indonesia and Sri Lanka.

[21]Dell Inc., The Procter & Gamble Company.

[22]Business service industry, electronics service industry, semiconductor industry

Based on secondary data from financial statements, a positive correlation between return on total assets (ROTA) and working capital performance as well as negative correlations between operating profit margin, capital turnover ratio and ROTA are observed.

Other empirical studies evaluate the impacts of inventory management on the financial performance of firms. Capkun et al. (2009) elaborate on the coherence of the inventory performance and the financial performance in a statistical analysis of US-based manufacturing firms between 1980 and 2005. Across a broad array of manufacturing industries, a strong correlation between both performance criteria is indicated. The results of this analysis furthermore show that compared to raw materials and work in progress, finished goods inventory show the strongest link to financial performance. Obermaier and Donhauser (2009) investigate long-term inventory developments between 1993 and 2005 on firm and industry level in 100 German companies. Although industry specific trends are observed with considerable reductions in the textile and apparel industry or the chemical process industry and significant increases in the food sector are detected, evidence for the impact of inventory levels on firm performance is not found.

Fixed assets have a life time of more than 1 year and can be differentiated between tangible assets including PPE and intangible assets comprising patents, trademarks, copyrights and goodwill (Hawawini and Viallet 2002). Capital expenditures describe the amount of cash which is invested to acquire tangible assets while depreciation expenses determine the calculatory cost of the period and systematic value-reduction process of a tangible asset (Hawawini and Viallet 2002). Fixed assets in SC network mainly comprise PPE, in particular facilities that typically are allocated to production sites, storage facilities, major warehouses or smaller distribution centers and that perform functions of procurement of materials, transformations of these materials into intermediate and finished products, and distribution of these products to customers (Tsiakis et al. 2001). The management of PPE in SC networks requires strategic, tactical and operational decision making on location, e.g. to determine number, size and physical location of plants, warehouses or distribution centers, and physical flows through these locations, mainly to determine quantities and timing of transformation, storage and transportation of material (Tsiakis et al. 2001). Strategic decisions to allocate and dimension the production and logistics capacities strive for suitable economic results and desired customer satisfaction levels (Guillen et al. 2005).

One of these strategic options is capacity expansion, which can be realized by enlarging existing facilities, constructing new facilities, acquiring plants from competitors, improving efficiency or hiring new staff, restarting previously closed plants or using new technology (Hendricks et al. 1995). Capacity expansion decisions represent one of the most critical managerial decisions that influence competitiveness and profitability, because they must be made under consideration of multiple criteria such as technological aspects, demand developments, competitor behavior and cost and besides because wrongly dimensioned capacities can result in expensive excess capacities, losses of market share or competitors entering the markets (Hendricks et al. 1995). In an empirical investigation of the influences of

233 capacity expansions announcements on the market value of a firm, Hendricks et al. (1995) observe significant value impacts which increase in growth rate and are negatively related to demand variability.

Partial or widespread restructuring or redesign of the SC network represents another strategic option for managing fixed assets, which in many cases are accompanied by re-engineering of SC processes or organizational realignments (Camm et al. 1997; Handfield and Nichols 2002). Camm et al. (1997) describe a major consolidation of the North American SC network of a global FMCG manufacturer,[23] which affected more than 60 production plants, 15 distribution centers, hundreds of suppliers and more than 1,000 customers. A reduction of the number of plants by almost 20 % resulted in considerable cost savings of over 200 m US$ annually. Horstmann (2003) deals with the restructuring of the European production network at a cosmetics manufacturer.[24] This realignment was achieved by four steps comprising network consolidation, process optimization, organizational integration and continuous improvement programs and resulted in considerable improvements of utilization, efficiency and flexibility of production capacities and thus reduced both product cost and capital employed. Wouda et al. (2003) elaborate on the consolidation and specialization of production plants at a dairy company in Hungary.[25] In a network of 400 supplying farmers, 9 production plants and 17 distribution centers, the number of plants, their locations and the allocation of products to the plants was optimized.

On tactical and operational level, an optimal utilization of available equipment to fulfill given or predicted demands is aimed at by SC planning (see e.g. papers in Günther and van Beek 2003). The resulting planning tasks strive for multiple objectives that combine criteria of profitability, including cost and sales-related service level, and capital, comprising inventory levels and utilization rate of production facilities (see e.g. Berning et al. 2002; Brandenburg and Tölle 2009).

2.3.2   Status of Related Academic Research

Shapiro (2007) points out that SCM decision making must be integrated to financial decisions about asset investments, profit growth and sales increase, as these factors affect shareholder value, which in turn indicates the financial health of a company. This integration of VBM with SCM can be comprehended as "value-based SCM", which requires a holistic and balanced approach to all financial aspects and hence exceeds focused SC-related perspectives on selected financial levers such as improvements of SC cost efficiency or inventory reductions. Although SCM and VBM both have been in focus of scientific research and managerial practice for

[23]The Procter & Gamble Company.
[24]Schwarzkopf and Henkel Production Europe GmbH & Co. KG.
[25]Nutricia Dairy & Drinks Group.

several decades (see e.g. Copeland et al. 2005; Mentzer et al. 2001), value-based SCM has gained awareness of academic research since the end of the 1990s, i.e. for hardly more than 10 years (see e.g. the distribution of related papers over time illustrated in Fig. 4.1 on page 70). A structured content analysis of related literature on value-based SCM is given in Chap. 4, which elaborates on terminological and conceptual aspects as well as on current status and future directions of academic research in this field. Complementary, 20 selected publications, which are suitable to illustrate the broadness of related approaches to the scientific field with respect to value comprehension, SCM perception and research approach, are reviewed in this Sect. 2.3.1 to provide a comparative and explanatory discussion of conceptual frameworks, quantitative models and empirical studies on value-based SCM. On this basis, the research questions of the thesis at hand are derived (as formulated in Sect. 3.1) and furthermore a positioning of the thesis to scientific literature on this research area is given in Sect. 11.2. In the literature reviewed in this Sect. 2.3 three aspects are exposed. Firstly, the comprehension of SCM and VBM on which the respective publication is based is elaborated. Secondly, the articles are categorized by the applied research methodology. Thirdly, findings and contributions of each manuscript are summarized.

Conceptual frameworks represent the majority of value-based SCM approaches proposed by the reviewed scientific papers. Christopher and Ryals (1999) propose a conceptual framework that comprises four SC-related value drivers, namely (i) revenue growth, (ii) operating cost reduction, (iii) working capital efficiency and (iv) fixed asset efficiency. This framework is based on the strategic perspective of SCM which is comprehended as the coordination of all logistics activities encompassing the management of physical and logical flows in a network of organizations linked by processes producing products and services that add value to the final consumer. Perceiving financial value created for shareholders, most often measured by EVA, as returns that exceed the investors total cost including risk premiums, the authors apply the definition of VBM as a concept to maximize long-term value creation with a managerial focus on the four above mentioned key value drivers. In their paper, Christopher and Ryals (1999) point out the relevance of timing and volatility of cash flows realized by compressing the total end-to-end SC. In particular, reductions of replenishment lead times at suppliers' side, eliminations of non-value-adding times and activities within internal processes as well as increases in demand transparency on the customers' side are discussed in this context. The authors relate this approach to Srivastava et al. (1998) who explain the relevance of accelerated and increased cash flows, reduced risk and residual values for value creation. Furthermore, several industrial case examples[26] are mentioned to illustrate the value creation potential of product availability, supplier integration, postponement strategies or integrated product design.

---

[26]BHS Ltd., Cisco Systems Inc., Compaq Computer Corporation, Hewlett-Packard Company, Nissan Motor Co. Ltd., Nokia Corporation, Smart division of Daimler AG, The Procter & Gamble Company.

The conceptual framework suggested by Lambert and Pohlen (2001) links SC strategy and corporate performance to operational efficiency. In this approach, an SC is perceived as an inter-organizational multi-level network comprising a focal company with various tiers of customers and suppliers that are linked by eight SC-related processes introduced by Lambert et al. (1998). The basic idea of this framework intends to gradually evaluate and align the profitability of all customer and supplier interfaces in this network beginning with a focal company. This approach aims at maximizing the shareholder value, measured by EVA, for the total SC and for each of its members. This value maximization is achieved by seven steps including the design and assessment of customer and supplier profit and loss (P&L) statements, the realignment of SC processes and the establishment of performance metrics to measure and compare the value contribution in each link. In order to cascade performance metrics from SC and company level down to operational activities, the non-financial measures are aligned with EVA via the P&L statements. In an explanatory numerical analysis of a fictitious company, the authors illustrate the relevance of the SC position and the actual performance level for value-creating inventory optimization.

Six different concepts to measure value impacts stemming from logistics are discussed by Lambert and Burduroglu (2000). The assessed concepts range from customer satisfaction as being the least quantitative to shareholder value identified as the most comprehensive financial measure. It is explained that customer satisfaction, achieved by fulfilling obligations of product, price, promotion and place, can result in higher service level and thus affects the financial performance, but has to be related to associated cost and revenues. Customer value-added as a more quantitative metric relates the perceived value of a company's offer, defined as the ratio of perceived customer benefit and perceived customer sacrifice, to the perceived value of the competitors' offers. Based on this metric it is outlined that product and service improvements can lead to higher sales, profit margins or market shares and ultimately increase shareholder value. Total cost analysis is discussed as a third measure which, opposed to the former two concepts, does not leave the determination of the economic benefits to the customers. The basic idea of this measure is to consider the total cost of ownership by considering all logistics activities instead of focusing cost reductions. Total cost analysis requires the conversion of non-financial metrics such as fill rate or lead times into financial metrics. Revenue aspects, which are neglected by total cost analysis, are reflected in profitability related value metrics. Profitability analysis, which deducts variable and fixed cost from revenues and thus supports the evaluation strategic options regarding their revenue and cost implications, assesses the impact of logistics on the profitability of a business or a segment. This concept can be extended to strategic profit models, which additionally take into account the cost related to fixed assets and hence demonstrate impacts of asset and margin management on shareholder's investments. Strategic profit models must consider logistics performance which can increase sales price and volume, accelerate new product introductions, reduce cost of production and distribution processes or improve sourcing conditions. Furthermore it is necessary to measure logistics impacts on cost and inventory levels, customer satisfaction and fixed assets.

• Accounts receivables
• Inventory levels

• Order cycle management times
• Use third party companies to increase profitability from low volume customers
• Increase revenue/profit/cash flow from service responsive customers

Strategic cash flow management

Productivity management

Shareholder value planning

Profitability management

• Capacity requirements/utilization
• Systems: EDI, QR

Financial and investment management

• Increase capital equipment applications to enhance capital utilisation and customer service and customer response

Fig. 2.7 The elements of shareholder value planning (Walters 1999, p. 251)

A major shortfall of strategic profit models is their neglect of cash flow aspects. In contrast to traditional financial measures, shareholder value concepts focus on cash flow and consider the time value of money and the risk of investments. The authors base their explanation on the value drivers explained by Rappaport (1998) and provide qualitative arguments to validate the finding of Christopher and Ryals (1999) that logistics affect shareholder value by influencing revenue, operating cost, working capital and fixed assets.

Based on the assumption that logistics create shareholder value by impacts on cash, invested capital or cost of capital, Walters (1999) designs a conceptual model to link EVA with options for logistics decision making. The proposed framework brings strategic and operational management criteria and value drivers in context to shareholder value. This framework is substantiated by stating that strategic value drivers have a direct impact on shareholder value while operational value drivers, especially sales growth rate, operating profit margin and income tax rate, are influenced by operating decisions during strategy implementation. Furthermore investment decisions affect the structure of fixed and working capital. Based on these conclusions, shareholder value planning is related to the management of productivity, strategic cash flow, profitability and investments, and logistics activities are assigned to each of these managerial areas (see Fig. 2.7). The case example of a fictitious manufacturing company for industrial durable goods illustrates how logistics decision making can positively influence EVA. In this article, the implications of shareholder value planning for logistics decision making are explored and difficulties in implementing VBM on operational level are outlined. The author concludes that logistics management must aim at two major tasks, the identification of drivers for customer satisfaction and the impact of customer service cost on shareholder value.

A framework designed by Otto and Obermaier (2009) is suitable to structure and reveal the impacts of SC network investments on firm value. The authors state that the complexity of inter-organizational SC networks comprising physical, logical and financial flows as well as social and institutional relationships prevents from quantifying SC value on network level. Instead the authors focus firm value as primary managerial objective measured by DCF or residual income and differentiate five components in the suggested framework to assess value impacts. The first component considers the dimensions of networking given by the flows and relationships within the network. Mechanisms of networking causing variations of arcs, frequency and objects form the second component. Effects of networking, i.e. processes, behavior and resources, represent the third component. The non-financial quantification of networking, categorized as fourth component, reflects aspects of efficiency and effectiveness as well as power, innovation or uncertainties. The fifth component, dealing with the financial quantification of networking, incorporates sales, cost, taxes, capital and cost of capital. The framework integrates financial and SC aspects, but is limited by shortened applicability to managerial practice or restricted possibility of empirical testing.

A conceptual framework for value-based SC performance management is designed and empirically tested by Hofmann and Locker (2009). This concept matches operational SC performance indicators to company value, measured by EVA and its components sales, cost and capital, via value drivers that are assessed and weighted by magnitudes, sensitivities and changes of financial and non-financial figures. The authors comprehend an SC as a network of different firms that are linked by planning, sourcing, manufacturing and delivery processes as well as physical and logical flows and that strive for efficiency and effectiveness to benefit from performance and customer achievements. The concept is tested in a case example from the packaging industry.[27] Limitations of this approach arise from the circumstance that only selected performance aspects are evaluated and incorporated in the EVA calculation. In particular, long-term sales effects of SC flexibility and customer satisfaction are not integrated in the approach. Furthermore, interactions between assessed indicators and applied metrics are neglected.

A further conceptual model for value-based SC performance management is outlined by Losbichler and Rothböck (2006). This concept is grounded on the perception that SCM, in accordance with Cooper et al. (1997), comprehended as the end-to-end integration of value-adding business processes, affects growth, profitability and capital of a company and thus its financial performance measured by EVA. The assessment of these effects comprises five steps. Firstly value gaps are identified, e.g. by applying benchmarking, which secondly are mapped to SC processes and strategy. In a third step, appropriate SCM tools to bridge these gaps are identified and ranked. Appropriate projects to realize the identified optimization

---

[27]SIG Combiblock

potential are defined in the fourth step, which is followed by the assessment of resulting business cases. In the empirical part of this paper, the working capital development between 1995 and 2004 is compared between 6,295 European (see Sect. 2.3.1 for a brief summary of this benchmarking). The authors conclude that the integration of SCM and shareholder value facilitates the identification of value gaps and the inception of SC initiatives that contribute to company value. In this integration, all drivers of financial performance must be considered.

In German academic literature, value-based SCM is strongly related to SC management accounting,[28] which is distinguished by three major directions (Seuring 2006; Stölzle 2002). Rationality-oriented approaches to SC management accounting focus on aspects of competitiveness and performance in SCM, coordination-oriented methods aim at SC integration and information-oriented concepts are designed to prevent and resolve information distortions in SCM (Seuring 2006; Stölzle 2002). Neher (2003) discusses general principles on which a value-oriented SC management accounting can be grounded. The author assigns three tasks – the creation of value potentials, the optimized utilization of available values and the adjustment of value within an SC – to value-based SCM and derives three tasks for value-based SC management accounting. The first task is to determine an appropriate terminology for value-based SCM, i.e. to appropriately define what in this context is comprehended by the term "value". The second task consists of the collection, assessment and steering of value contributions and is associated with the coordination- and information-oriented direction of SC management accounting. The third task, the creation of adequate value adjustments within the SC that are compatible with incentive schemes, relates to the rationality-oriented direction of SC management accounting. In this paper, Neher (2003) categorizes the term "value" into financial capital and intangible capital, which can be differentiated further into external human, customer and partner capital and internal image, structure and organization capital. The author states that although the expression "shareholder value" dominates VBM in academic science and managerial practice, the value terminology in SC context is heterogeneous and unresolved. SC value can be comprehended as maximization of individual company value under consideration of targets defined on network level. Furthermore, customer perceived value, which includes delivery performance and cost, or supplier perceived value, which comprises direct and indirect functions of customer relation, are suggested concepts for value-based SCM that consists of monetary and non-monetary value drivers such as quality, time or flexibility. The author concludes that holistic approaches to value-based SCM and SC management accounting are missing so far, and especially the integration of system and network perspective shows conceptual deficits.

Lasch et al. (2006) state that VBM is grounded on a financial perspective on corporate management, and hence the financial correlation between value drivers and company value has to be considered. A conceptual model is designed to outline the impacts of logistics performance on company targets: Efficiency and

---

[28]In German named "SC Controlling" (Seuring 2006)

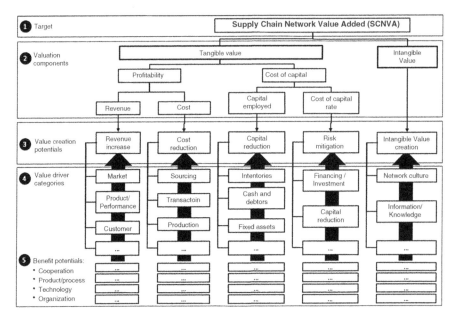

Fig. 2.8 Model to link supply chain network value added with operational level (Based on Möller 2003, p. 72)

effectiveness of logistics contribute to the profitability of a company, competitive advantages arising from logistics performance ensure the economic future of a firm, and customer benefits of logistics performance increase customer satisfaction. In this paper, four value drivers – sales growth, profit margin, investments and cost of capital – are related to the basic strategies of cost leadership and differentiation. The authors explain that due to intense competition FMCG manufacturers have to consider both strategic dimensions in order to achieve competitive advantages from SCM improvements.

Based on the SC hypothesis that SCM improves the profitability of a firm, Möller (2003) designs a conceptual framework for value-based SCM and adds management support to the above mentioned directions of SC management accounting. The author comprehends SCM as the planning, steering and control of physical, logical, financial and service-related flows through intra- and inter-organizational networks, which are characterized by focal or polycentric allocation of power, in order to improve efficiency and effectiveness. The author furthermore outlines that the value discussion has evolved from a market-based view on five forces of competitive advantage (see e.g. Porter 1998) in the 1970s and a resource-based view comprising physical, financial and intangible resources in the 1980s to a value-based view quantified by shareholder value, DCF, CFROI or EVA since the 1990s. In this paper it is stated that operational and strategic planning dimensions have to be integrated, e.g. as outlined by Knorren and Weber (1997) (see Fig. 2.5 on page 27), in order to achieve value-related targets on company or network level. Möller (2003) proposes a conceptual model (see Fig. 2.8 on page 44) consisting of five levels to achieve this integration. The SC network value added (SCNVA) on top level is disaggregated on the second level into tangible and intangible valuation components. The third level consists of five value creation potentials, namely revenue increase, cost reduction, capital reduction, risk mitigation and intangible value creation. The fourth level comprises value driver categories for each value creation potential, and the fifth level includes operational benefit potentials such as cooperation, product and process, technology or organization. The author points out the necessity to quantitatively link SC value creation with the operational level in a calculation model, in order to facilitate a goal-oriented control of the SC network, a clear formulation of strategies, a transparent representation of benefits and a comprehensible value determination. It is explained that especially the quantification of intangible value creation is seen as problematic, while the creation of tangible value can be determined by profitability and cost of capital.

Quantitative models for value-based SCM are most often applied in SC planning in order to create value impacts in sales & operations planning (S&OP). Kannegiesser et al. (2009) combine value- and volume-based S&OP on tactical level in a normative model to optimize the profitability over a time horizon of 6–12 months. The approach integrates demand-oriented revenue management concepts with supply-oriented logistics management concepts under consideration of contract and spot demands and volatility of prices and quantities in a two stage model. The first step comprises a sales model to determine sales quantities for maximum profitability subject to production and procurement capabilities, sales price and supply cost. The second step consists of a supply model to determine production and procurement quantities under consideration of available capacities and existing demands. The model is tested in a case example from chemical process industry.

A quantitative normative model for S&OP over a mid-term horizon of 6–18 months designed by Hahn and Kuhn (2010) is suitable to optimize physical and financial flows in procurement, production, distribution and sales. Opposed to purely conceptual frameworks, which disaggregate the top level performance measured by EVA to operational level, this model helps to determine production and transportation quantities, payments and collection periods and product-related marketing activities on company level. Besides operating profit margin, working capital is identified as a major mid- and short-term SC-related value driver. Due to the length of the considered planning horizon, the time value of money as well as fixed assets investments are omitted in the model. The model is validated based on an industrial case of an FMCG manufacturer. This approach is one of the first to integrate the concepts of EVA and shareholder value with quantitative normative modeling from operations research.

In another paper (Hahn and Kuhn 2011), the authors extend the approach of Hahn and Kuhn (2010) to a quantitative normative model for value-based S&OP under consideration of risk aspects. A two-stage stochastic programming model enables robust optimization of the impacts of profitability and working capital on EVA. Although fixed assets (dis-)investments are neglected in this model, it can be considered a holistic framework for value-based SC performance and risk management.

In most cases, empirical research on value impacts of SCM is performed by applying secondary data analysis or by case studies. Motivated by the circumstance that clear evidence for the link between SCM, profitability and shareholder value is missing, Hendricks and Singhal (2003) elaborate on the impacts of SC disruptions on the market value of a firm. The authors analyze the correlation between 519 SC glitches announced between 1989 and 2000 in financial newspapers by publicly traded firms from approximately 50 different industries and short-term changes of the market value of the respective firms. The assessed glitches, which comprise planning and forecasting errors, operational constraints and breakdowns, affect SC cost, delivery performance, inventory levels or capacity utilization. Several days around the dates of SC glitch announcements, a decrease of shareholder value by 10.3 % caused by SC deficiencies is observed. It is furthermore detected that the stock price of smaller or fast growing companies is affected more strongly. A correlation between the capital structure on the extent of market value impacts is not observed.

In another paper (Hendricks and Singhal 2005b), the authors evaluate 827 disruptions announced in the same period and their long-term impacts on market value of the respective firms. Over a horizon of 3 years (1 year before and 2 years after the glitch), the authors identify average abnormal stock returns of 40 % at firms with disruptions and furthermore observe significant negative impacts on equity risk, asset risk and financial leverage of the concerned companies. It is concluded that firms do not easily recover from disruption effects.

The analysis of short-term impacts of announced SC glitches on the market value of a company is extended to 838 disruptions between 1989 and 2001 in a third paper from Hendricks and Singhal (2008). The observations confirm the extent of negative impacts of SC deficiencies on market value, which Hendricks and Singhal (2003) observed prior to this analysis. Hendricks and Singhal (2008) additionally explore influences of company size, industry sector and disruption cause. It is concluded that the stock price of smaller or faster growing firms is more vulnerable to SC deficiencies. Strongest reactions are observed in the wholesale and retail sectors and in computers and electronics industry. Stock prices of firms from the automotive or aircraft industry and of agricultural or construction companies seem to be more resistant towards negative influences of SC glitches. Part shortages, customer order changes, or problems in production or ramp-up are mentioned most often as causes for SC glitches. SC interruptions caused by customer responsibility show the strongest impacts on company value, while natural disasters apparently cause slighter effects.

A more focused analysis of stock price impacts of deficient SCM is provided by Hendricks and Singhal (2009). Based on a sample of 276 announcements of excess inventory made between 1990 and 2002, the authors assess the short-term impacts on the market value of the respective firm 1 day before and 2 days after the proclamation. The authors observe negative stock market reactions at three quarters of the sample firms with a median of approximately 6.8 %. The magnitude of the observed effects amplifies downwards the SC and correlates positively to debt-equity ratio of a firm and negatively to company size.

Driven by lacking empirical quantification of the link between SC performance and financial performance, Johnson and Templar (2011) analyze this coherence at 117 publicly traded UK manufacturing firms. For these companies, the metrics of cash generation ratio, i.e. the ratio between net cash inflow and sales, and asset efficiency, i.e. the ratio of sales versus assets and liabilities, are compared between 1995 and 2004. It is explained that SC-related levers of company value comprise profitability, which is affected by sales and cost, liquidity, which is mainly influenced by working capital, and productivity, which is related to fixed assets. The authors conclude that SCM can positively influence company value and hence main tasks of SC managers should focus on the increase of cash generated from operations and on the optimization of total assets employed in the SC.

Reiner and Hofmann (2006) combine dependency analysis and data envelopment analysis to assess the performance of SC processes and the impacts on financial performance of a firm. In an empirical benchmarking study based on process definitions and performance metrics of the supply chain operations reference (SCOR) model, the SC performance of 65 European and North American companies was assessed. The authors observe strong dependencies between operational performance and financial success of a company. In particular, a negative correlation between the working capital performance and the profitability of a firm is detected. The authors conclude that efficient SCM contributes to the financial performance of a firm.

Case study research on value-based SCM is applied by Sridharan et al. (2005). The authors elaborate on disruptions that occur during the implementation of SCM software and the impacts on stock price. In this paper, IT is comprehended as element that enables an effective SCM which comprises all activities, functions and facilities involved in the inter-organizational flow and transformation of goods and services. Three case studies of manufacturing firms[29] illustrate benefits of successful web-based supplier integration, negative impacts of delayed implementations of heterogeneous IT systems[30] on stock price and deficient implementations of SCM software[31] causing deteriorated inventory management resulting in sales and margin losses.

This review of selected manuscripts indicates different aspects of scientific research on value-based SCM. The majority of the reviewed papers deals with conceptual models that integrate the profitability-related drivers sales and cost with the asset-related drivers fixed and working capital. Other factors such as cost of capital, taxes or risk are reflected in some papers only. Similarly, the time value of money, intangible value and SC deficiencies are taken into account in only few manuscripts. In most cases, the value perception is focused on company level, predominantly based on the shareholder value concept and measured by DCF models or market value of a firm indicated by stock price, while network aspects of SCM are considered seldom. Quantitative approaches represent the smallest part

---

[29]Dell Inc., Hershey Foods Corp., Nike Inc.

[30]Systems from Manugistics Group Inc., SAP AG, Siebel Systems.

[31]i2 Technologies.

Table 2.2 Value-based SCM in selected research papers

Paper	Value comprehension		Research method
	Value term/metric	Value driver	
Christopher and Ryals (1999)	Shareholder value, EVA	Sales, cost, working capital, fixed assets	Conceptual model
Walters (1999)	Shareholder value, EVA	Logistics-related activities	Conceptual model
Lambert and Burduroglu (2000)	Shareholder value as most comprehensive	Profitability- and capital-efficiency, time value of money, risk	Comparison of six qualitative concepts
Lambert and Pohlen (2001)	Shareholder value, EVA	Customer and supplier profitability	Conceptual model, illustrative numerical example
Hendricks and Singhal (2003, 2005a, 2008, 2009)	Market value of a firm	Short- and long-term value impacts of SC disruptions and of excess inventory	Empirical secondary data analysis
Möller (2003)	SC network value added	Intangible and tangible value (profitability, cost of capital)	Conceptual model
Neher (2003)	Need of clarification of terminology addressed	Financial and intangible capital	Conceptual model
Sridharan et al. (2005)	Stock price	Implementation of IT for SCM	Three industrial case studies
Lasch et al. (2006)	Company value	Effectiveness, efficiency, competitive advantage, customer orientation	Conceptual model
Losbichler and Rothböck (2006)	Shareholder value, EVA	SC performance	Conceptual model
Reiner and Hofmann (2006)	Financial success of a company	SC performance metrics	Empirical secondary data analysis
Hofmann and Locker (2009)	Shareholder value, EVA	Sales, cost, capital, operational drivers	Conceptual model, case example
Kannegiesser et al. (2009)	Profitability	Sales price and quantity, production and procurement cost and quantity	Quantitative normative model for sales & operations planning (S&OP)
Otto and Obermaier (2009)	Company value, DCF	SC network investments	Conceptual model
Hahn and Kuhn (2010)	Shareholder value, EVA	Operating profit margin, working capital	Quantitative normative model for S&OP

(continued)

Table 2.2 continued

| Paper | Value comprehension | | Research method |
	Value term/metric	Value driver	
Hahn and Kuhn (2011)	Shareholder value, EVA	Operating profit margin, working capital, risk	Quantitative normative model for S&OP and risk management
Johnson and Templar (2011)	Cash generation ratio	Profitability, liquidity, productivity	Empirical secondary data analysis

of reviewed papers and comprise normative planning models that include sales, cost and inventory but exclude value aspects of fixed assets from observation. Most of the reviewed empirical papers describe ex-post secondary data analyses of financial figures to assess the correlation between SC disruptions and market value of a firm. Furthermore, case study research illustrates negative value impacts of deficient IT implementations. These observations are condensed in Table 2.2 and substantiated by a systematic content analysis of related literature in Chap. 4.

Chapter 3
Methodological Aspects

Abstract This sections comprises a formulation of the research questions of this dissertation and outlines the chosen research approach and how it is reflected by the structure of the thesis. Additionally, the coherence of its chapters is described. Furthermore, conceptual elements are defined and a conceptual framework for value-based SCM is designed as a basis for the quantitative models proposed in the thesis at hand.

3.1 Research Question and Delineation

This thesis contributes to scientific research on value-based SCM by proposing quantitative models to assess impacts of SCM on company value. The proposed models strive for a holistic comprehension of value creation in which capital- and profitability-related influences are combined, as proposed by Christopher and Ryals (1999), and by which influencing criteria, e.g. the factors identified by Srivastava et al. (1998), are determined. The research design is appropriate to reflect financial and non-financial facets of SC performance outlined in Sect. 2.2.4 and to study all aspects of the product-relationship-matrix introduced in Sect. 2.2.5. On the product dimension, all phases of the PLC will be covered in this research. On the relationship dimension, aspects of SC configuration are covered as well as SC operation. In this context, the proposed models reflect the whole spectrum ranging from strategic SCM to operational SCM activities. In particular, this dissertation aims at elaborating three research questions (RQ) on value-based SCM:

- RQ1: How are value contributions of SCM quantified in such a way that profitability-related changes of sales or SC cost and capital-related changes of fixed assets or working capital are financially comparable?
- RQ2: Which criteria and influencing factors are relevant for value creation?
- RQ3: How are financial performance figures to measure company value brought into context with tactical and operational SCM activities?

M. Brandenburg, *Quantitative Models for Value-Based Supply Chain Management*,   51
Lecture Notes in Economics and Mathematical Systems 660,
DOI 10.1007/978-3-642-31304-2__3, © Springer-Verlag Berlin Heidelberg 2013

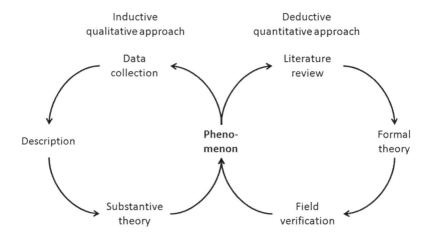

Fig. 3.1 Quantitative and qualitative research processes (Golicic et al. 2005, p. 20)

The research objective of this thesis is delineated by a clear focus on company value. A thorough elaboration on value impacts stemming from interactions between different SC members is not in focus of this thesis, although influences of the network structure are considered in Chaps. 8 and 9. Furthermore, a conception of an inter-organizational value terminology or a calculation scheme to mathematically determine value created by selected operational SC activities is not attempted.

3.2   Research Methodology

3.2.1   Qualitative and Quantitative Research Designs

Scientific research in management can be differentiated between qualitative and quantitative designs as described by Golicic et al. (2005): Qualitative approaches start with collecting data on a considered phenomenon in a natural setting followed by a description of this phenomenon from the perspective of the informants based on which in a third step substantive theory is built inductively. Quantitative research is grounded on a conceptual framework comprising specific variables and their expected relationships, which is derived from related literature being reviewed in a first step. Based on this conceptual framework, formal theory suitable to generate predictive statements is developed deductively in a second step. The third step of quantitative research consists of the verification of this formal theory which is usually done by testing the significance and strength of the proposed relationships based on real-world data. Both research designs are illustrated in Fig. 3.1.

3.2.2 Model-Based Quantitative Research

Model-based quantitative research is grounded on objective models that explain the behavior of real-life operational processes or capture decision-making problems managers face in real-life (Bertrand and Fransoo 2002). Such an approach is chosen for the thesis at hand. Meredith (1993) defines a model as "simplified representation or abstraction of reality" and differentiates between ionic, analogue or symbolic models (Meredith 1993, p. 5).[1] With regards to their basic character, models can be categorized as conceptual, defined as "set of concepts, with or without propositions, used to represent or describe (but not explain) an event, object, or process" (Meredith 1993, p. 5), or quantitative, which "are based on a set of variables that vary over a specific domain while quantitative and causal relationships have been defined between these variables" (Bertrand and Fransoo 2002, p. 242). Mathematical models that are suitable to "predict the outcome of an action, and theoretically evaluate various dynamic properties of complex problems, without incurring expensive and timely field studies" (Mikkola 2005, p. 495) represent a special type of quantitative models which is predominantly applied in this thesis. These models are categorized as deterministic, i.e. non-probabilistic models that assume all parameters are known and fixed, or stochastic, i.e. probabilistic models which are applied in optimal control theory or dynamic programming (Min and Zhou 2002).

Quantitative models can either have a normative or a descriptive purpose (Bertrand and Fransoo 2002; Shapiro 2007): Normative models focus on improving current situations by developed policies, strategies and actions or defined "norms that a company should strive, but maybe not be able, to achieve" (Shapiro 2007, p. 11). These models are synonymously called prescriptive models, because they prescribe decisions for a given decision-making problem, or optimization models due to the circumstance that they integrate input data in the analysis of a given problem and seek optimized solutions according to a manager's preferences (Bertrand and Fransoo 2002; Shapiro 2007). Descriptive models adequately help to describe and understand functional or process-related causal relationships that may exist in reality (Bertrand and Fransoo 2002; Shapiro 2007). Simulation models, which represent a major category of descriptive quantitative models, provide insights into cause and effects of SC performance (Kleijnen 2005) and hence are often applied for SC modeling (Chang and Makatsoris 2001). Simulation models can be differentiated further between spreadsheet calculation, system dynamics, business games and discrete-event simulation (DES) (Kleijnen and Smits 2003). Spreadsheet calculations are deterministic and static calculation models, which

---

[1] Meredith (1993) defines ionic models as rescaled physical replicas of a system, e.g. a photograph, analogue models as more abstract models that show similar behavior like the original system, such as color maps or architectural blue prints, and symbolic models as such models that allow for the greatest manipulation for analysis, e.g. mathematical equations or Monte Carlo simulations.

probably represent the most often applied method in managerial practice (Conway and Ragsdale 1997; Schilling et al. 2010). System dynamics were applied first by Forrester (1961) who perceived companies as systems with different types of flows and stocks which are managerially controlled by changing rate variables (Kleijnen and Smits 2003). Business games, e.g. the "Beer Distribution Game" developed at the Massachusetts Institute of Technology, are suitable to simulate economic or technical processes (Kleijnen and Smits 2003; Nienhaus et al. 2006). DES models represent individual events that occur in the system, describe the logic that prevails at occurrence of an event and process the events in a chronological order at simulated time (Reiner 2005). DES models are suitable to reflect stochastic influences and hence are often applied in academic research on SCM (Chwif et al. 2002).

3.2.3   Axiomatic and Empirical Quantitative Research

A model-based quantitative research design can follow an axiomatic or empirical approach. Bertrand and Fransoo (2002) explain that axiomatic quantitative research is "primarily driven by the (idealized) model itself" and strives "to obtain solutions within the defined model and to make sure that these solutions provide insights into the structure as defined within the model" and furthermore to "produce knowledge about the behavior of certain variables in the model" (Bertrand and Fransoo 2002, p. 249 et seq.). The authors categorize axiomatic quantitative research into axiomatic descriptive (AD) models that are scientifically derived from conceptual frameworks and skip the model solving phase, axiomatic simulation (AS) models that are applied in cases the problem complexity prevents from formal mathematical analysis, and axiomatic normative (AN) models which are suitable to solve complex decision problems. Following the authors' perception, the axiomatic quantitative research design consists of three phases: In a first phase, a condensed description of the considered operational process or decision-making problem is given by a conceptual model derived from accepted scientific standards. In a second phase, a quantitative model with formal, mathematical terms is specified based on the conceptual model. The third phase comprises the execution of mathematical or numerical analysis. In case of axiomatic quantitative simulation, i.e. computer simulation, the research design slightly differs: The justification of the research method and hypotheses to be tested is followed by setting up the experimental design and concluded by statistical analysis and interpretation of the obtained results.

Empirical quantitative research on the other hand aims at ensuring "that there is a model fit between observations and actions in reality and the model made for that reality" in order "to test the validity of quantitative theoretical models" (Bertrand and Fransoo 2002, p. 250 et seq.). The authors differentiate empirical descriptive (ED) models to model and validate a conceptual framework from empirical normative (EN) models that additionally range to model solving and implementation and describe the empirical quantitative research process as follows: At first, the basic assumptions regarding the operational process underlying the theoretical model and the process or problem type have to be identified. Further preparatory steps include the definition of criteria for deciding whether or not a real-life process belongs to the class of modeled processes as well as the development of basic assumptions and hypotheses regarding the behavior of these processes and objective ways to measure and observe these processes. The execution steps of the research process include data collection, measurement application and result documentation. The research process ends with interpretations of data by statistical analysis and of the obtained results related to the theoretical model.

In the thesis at hand, the quantitative research design is realized as follows: In a theorizing desk research (Halldorsson and Arlbjørn 2005), the conceptual framework on which the research of this is grounded, is derived from concepts that are accepted in management science and thoroughly discussed in related academic literature. To elaborate on the terminology applied, focus taken and future directions proposed in academic research on value-based SCM, the related literature is systematically reviewed by content analysis (Mayring 2008) as suggested by Seuring et al. (2005) and often applied in the scientific field of supply chain management (Seuring and Gold 2012). The formal theory is build by SC modeling, which in general combines concepts from various disciplines and, in particular in this dissertation, includes SCM, operations research, management accounting, corporate finance and valuation (Shapiro 2007). To verify the formal theory, the SC models are validated empirically based on explanatory real-life cases from the FMCG industry (Seuring 2005, 2008) or systematically by providing mathematical proof (Bertrand and Fransoo 2002) of their consistency with existing and scientifically accepted quantitative models.

The structure of the thesis and the coherence of its chapters are discussed in greater detail in the next Sect. 3.3.

3.2.4 Empirical Focus of the Research Design

The empirical research of this thesis is focused on the FMCG industry, and in particular on manufacturers of cosmetics and toiletries. SCM in this industry sector is of considerable relevance for academic research, as outlined in Sect. 2.3.1, and possesses a high structural complexity (Shapiro 2007). Although the quantitative models proposed in this thesis strive for being universally valid and applicable independent from industrial specifics, focusing on a particular industry sector increases the structural comparability, especially for the benchmarking study presented in Chap. 6. Furthermore, comparable short PLCs in FMCG industry allow for considering the whole PLC when assessing value impacts of SC design decisions in NPI situations in Chaps. 8 and 9. Besides, these empirical case examples exhibit both complexity drivers, uncertainties and dynamics, to a notable extent.

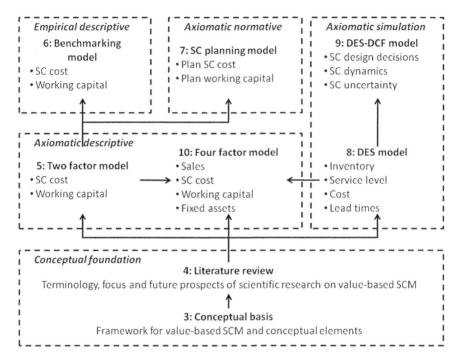

Fig. 3.2 Research design comprising a conceptual basis and four parts of quantitative modeling

3.3 Structure of the Thesis

The research design, based on which the three research questions of this thesis are elaborated, comprises a conceptual foundation and four categories of quantitative models (see Fig. 3.2). Section 3.4 of this Chap. 3 as well as Chap. 4 represent the conceptual foundation on which the quantitative models are grounded. The category of AD models consists of the models developed in Chaps. 5 and 10. The models introduced in Chaps. 8 and 9 form the category of AS models. The models proposed in Chaps. 6 and 7 are assigned to the categories of ED models and AN models, respectively.

In the next Sect. 3.4 of this Chap. 3, a conceptual framework for value-based SCM is introduced. This framework is developed in a theorizing desk research (Halldorsson and Arlbjørn 2005) based on well-known and scientifically accepted models and concepts of management science. The framework acts as the conceptual basis, on which the quantitative models proposed in Chaps. 5–10 are grounded.

A systematic review of literature on value-based SCM is given in Chap. 4, which provides the basis to position the proposed dissertation to current research. The objectives of Chap. 4 are furthermore to shed light on the current status (e.g. emphases, gaps, methodology) of academic research on value-based SCM, to analyse the terminology on which this research is based and to identify future perspectives for further research in this area. To ensure that this review is performed systematically, the method of content analysis (Mayring 2008) is applied. In this Chap. 4, four research questions are elaborated:

- Which aspects of SCM are in focus of academic research on value-based SCM?
- Which designs are preferably applied for academic research on value-based SCM?
- Which value definitions represent the terminological foundation for academic research on value-based SCM?
- Which future directions are suggested for academic research on value-based SCM?

Chapter 5 addresses RQ1 by proposing an AD model to calculate the value impacts stemming from changes of SC cost and working capital. This model is developed in a theorizing desk research (Halldorsson and Arlbjørn 2005) and conceptually grounded on the value-based SCM framework introduced in Sect. 3.4 and the DCF method outlined in Sect. 2.1. An industrial case example that illustrates how timing and continuity of the developments of SC cost and working capital influence value creation reflects RQ2 and forms one part of the numerical analysis of this model. This Chap. 5 provides answers to the following research questions:

- How can value contributions from SC value drivers be quantified efficiently?
- How can the financial comparability of EBIT-related changes of SC cost and asset-related changes of working capital be ensured?

The AD model proposed in Chap. 5 is empirically validated and numerically analyzed further in a benchmarking study (Wong and Wong 2008) presented in Chap. 6. In a secondary data analysis, ten companies from FMCG industry are compared regarding the developments and value impacts of SC cost and working capital. The main hypotheses of this ED model, which addresses RQ2, are that improvements of the SC-related value drivers SC cost and working capital positively correlate with the value impacts measured by the AD model proposed in Chap. 5 and that timing and continuity of these developments are decisive criteria for value creation. The analysis and interpretation of obtained results comprises a regression analysis of value driver developments and value impacts, a case specific evaluation of the relevance of timing and continuity of these developments, and an empirical sensitivity analysis of WACC influences on value creation. Furthermore, the importance of working capital components is assessed. In particular, two research questions are dealt with in this Chap. 6:

- Can empirical evidence be found that overall developments of SCM-related value drivers, in particular cost and working capital, have an impact on company value?
- What decisive criteria for value creation from these drivers can be identified empirically?

An AN model for value-based strategic SC planning is described in Chap. 7. This approach is developed in a theorizing desk research (Halldorsson and Arlbjørn 2005) based on the AD model presented in Chap. 5 and provides answers to

RQ3: The planning approach facilitates the disaggregation of long-term targets for company value to annual targets for SC cost and working capital and enables the integration of value-based strategic SC planning with financial planning and tactical SC planning. The numerical analysis is based on an illustrative example of a fictitious company. This approach can be considered an AN model, because it helps to improve strategic financial planning processes, which are currently limited by the underlying assumption that assets and profits develop proportionate to sales (Ross et al. 2002). The research question of this Chap. 7 is:

- What is an appropriate design for a value-based strategic SC planning concept for a long-term horizon of several years to determine targets for SC cost and working capital?

Additional answers to RQ2 are given in Chap. 8, which deals with influences of SC-related value drivers that arise from tactical SC design decisions as well as SC dynamics and uncertainties in NPI. Under consideration of RQ1 and RQ3, the influence of SC dynamics and uncertainties on the financial value drivers sales, cost and capital is illustrated by developing further the conceptual framework for value-based SCM from Sect. 3.4 in a theorizing desk research (Halldorsson and Arlbjørn 2005). In accordance with Reiner (2005), an AS model based on empirical data is applied to test the hypothesis that SC design decisions, SC dynamics and SC uncertainties influence inventory levels, lead times, service level and cost. The experimental design is to apply a DES model (Kleijnen 2005) in a case example of a decision-making problem of tactical SC design (TSCD) for NPI in FMCG industry (Schilling et al. 2010). To assess the influences on inventory levels, lead times, service level and cost, the results obtained by DES are statistically analyzed and thoroughly discussed. This Chap. 8 deals with two research questions:

- How do the SC complexity drivers dynamics and uncertainties link to SC-related drivers of company value?
- How and to what extent do these complexity drivers affect tactical supply chain design (TSCD) in new product introduction (NPI)?

Chapter 9 provides additional answers to RQ1 and empirical substantiation of the extended conceptual framework for value-based SCM from Chap. 8. To test the hypothesis that tactical SC design decisions, dynamics and uncertainties have direct influences on company value, an ED model is designed which integrates DES (Kleijnen 2005) and a valuation approach based on DCF (Damodaran 2005). Based on empirical data (Reiner 2005) this ED model is applied to the case example of a cosmetics manufacturer (Schilling et al. 2010). For the numerical analysis, various scenarios characterized by different levels of dynamics and uncertainties are developed and combined with different SC design options. The simulation results obtained for each scenario are statistically evaluated and interpreted. The research question of this Chap. 9 is:

- How can the impacts of TSCD options, dynamics and uncertainties in NPI situations be assessed and quantified in a value-based way?

In Chap. 10, the findings of Chaps. 5 and 8 are developed further. To provide further answers to RQ1, the AD model introduced in Chap. 5 is extended to an AD model comprising all four SC-related value drivers identified by Christopher and Ryals (1999): sales, cost, working capital, fixed assets. This extension is developed in a theorizing desk research (Halldorsson and Arlbjørn 2005) conceptually grounded on the value-based SCM framework introduced in Sect. 3.4 and the DCF method (Damodaran 2005). To validate the model systematically, mathematical proof is provided that the designed AD model can be derived from the DCF model by algebraic transformations. As an answer to RQ2, important criteria for value impacts stemming from characteristic developments of these SC-related value drivers are explored in a numerical analysis and substantiated by mathematical evidences, in particular the relevance of accelerated, enhanced and volatile value impacts is pointed out. Under consideration of RQ3, it is outlined by qualitative arguments how the conceptual framework for value-based SCM introduced in Sect. 3.4 can be extended to link financial performance metrics on strategic level to the operational level of SCM. This Chap. 10 provides answers to the following three research questions:

- How to calculate value contributions of SCM in such a way that the financial comparability of profitability-related changes of sales and cost with capital-related changes of fixed assets and working capital is ensured?
- What important criteria for value creation can be identified and substantiated?
- How can operational SCM activities and processes be linked to company value?

3.4 Conceptual Elements and Frameworks

The conceptual basis on which the model based quantitative research of this thesis is grounded, comprises a terminological introduction of the conceptual elements, i.e. the variables used for modeling, and a framework for value-based SCM which outlines how these elements are linked by (expected) causal relationships. The conceptual elements comprise "value", "sales", "SC cost", "working capital", "fixed assets", "SC design decisions", "SC dynamics" and "SC uncertainties", the conceptual framework is based on a model of a firm (Shapiro 2007), its financial process (Damodaran 2011a) and the company-internal SCM (Harland 1996; Stock and Boyer 2009) and furthermore a company value model (Damodaran 2011a; Rappaport 1998) and the four SC-related value drivers (Christopher and Ryals 1999).

3.4.1 Conceptual Elements

For the comprehension of VBM on which thesis is grounded, a financial perception of the term value is chosen that is based on the idea of shareholder value

(Rappaport 1998). Applying this financial comprehension, the market value of a firm is defined by the sum of the value of debt and the value of equity expressed by the ability of a company to generate future cash flows (Ross et al. 2002). Out of the four valuation approaches introduced in Sect. 2.1.2, the DCF approach is chosen as an appropriate basis for the quantitative models presented in this thesis. For this purpose, the DCF approach is either based on FCF to the firm, which is obtained by adjusting EBIT for taxes, capital expenditures, depreciation and changes in working capital, or quantified by cash flow from operations, i.e. the difference between operating cash inflows and cash outflows (Damodaran 2011a; Rappaport 1998). This approach is accepted and widely applied in academic research and can be considered in line with numerous frameworks for value-based SCM that are grounded on EVA (as illustrated in Sects. 2.1.2 and 2.3.1) due to the equivalence of the DCF model and the EVA concept (Hartman 2000). Reasons not to select one of the other three valuation approaches as a basis for the models presented in this thesis are derived from Sect. 2.1.2. Liquidation and accounting valuation are considered inappropriate, because these approaches are suitable for companies with a specific fixed assets' structure or growth potential or because they do not reflect the going concern assumption. Relative valuation models bear a risk of deviating valuation results caused by over or under pricing effects. Contingent claim valuation is based on equity investors' options to liquidate a business, which might be considered inappropriate regarding the going concern assumption of the assessed companies. The idea of valuation on inter-organizational or SC network level, as arrogated by e.g. Möller (2003) or Neher (2003) (see Sect. 2.3.1), is not in focus of the thesis at hand. Furthermore the value comprehension in this manuscript must be delineated to the ideas of stakeholder value or customer-perceived value discussed in Sect. 2.1.1.

For the models presented in this manuscript, sales will be comprehended as the value of products sold, each at a certain quantity and price, disregarding influences of trade discounts or allowances. This comprehension will be differentiated between external sales to other companies or, for the analysis in Chap. 9, as company-internal sales between a manufacturing affiliate and a sales affiliate of a firm. For the models presented in Chaps. 5 and 10, the SC-related extent of sales changes, obtained by e.g. improved SC effectiveness, is assumed to be known.

The comprehension of SC cost applied in this thesis comprises all costs related to SC activities including direct cost, activity-based cost and transactional cost (Seuring 2001). For the secondary data analyses and case examples presented in Chaps. 5, 6, 9 and 10, the SC cost are limited to COGS.

In this thesis, working capital is defined as the sum of inventories and trade receivables reduced by trade payables (Brealey et al. 2008; Ross et al. 2002).

Fixed assets are comprehended as tangible and SC-related PPE of a company. This PPE influences cash flow directly by capital expenditures and depreciation (Brealey et al. 2008; Ross et al. 2002). Furthermore, these fixed assets can have an indirect influence on cash flow, e.g. by sales increases, cost reductions or working capital improvements that are facilitated by investments in new PPE. Such effects can be quantified in the models presented in Chaps. 5 and 10 by determining the value impacts of changes of the respective SC-related value driver.

SC design decision-making in this thesis is focused on TSCD in NPI situations, in particular on the allocation of new products to existing production plants in different geographical regions of an inter-organizational SC network. According to Shapiro (2007), such a task to appropriately define the connections between a consumer goods' manufacturer and its markets for a new product or product category adheres a considerable complexity. In the evaluated empirical case examples (see Chaps. 8 and 9), greenfield scenarios for SC design were not considered.

The evaluation of value impacts stemming from SC dynamics and uncertainties is included in the TSCD scenarios of NPI situations (see Chaps. 8 and 9). Dynamics are differentiated between major demand volatility caused by pipeline filling and minor demand volatility resulting from different launch timings in the affected countries and regions. Demand oscillations arising from seasonality or changing consumer behavior are excluded from observation. The assessment of value influences from uncertainties in SC is focused to uncertainties on the demand-side. These comprise the mid- and long-term uncertainties of the overall market reception of a new product and the short-term uncertainties in forecasting product demands in the near future.

3.4.2   Framework for Value-Based Supply Chain Management

For the design of a conceptual framework for value-based SCM, a company is defined in accordance with the terminology suggested by Shapiro (2007): A firm can be perceived as an economic entity which comprises an organizational structure that consists of owners, managers and employees, a production process that generates goods and services, and a financial process that provides financing for projects and distribution of revenues to its stakeholders. This definition explains the organizational structure on a level of detail which is sufficient for the research purpose of this thesis. For the other two components of this definition, a more detailed terminological characterization is needed and hence given in the following.

The production process of a firm can be comprehended as the company-internal SCM, which is perceived as the integration of business functions involved in the physical, logical and financial flows from the inbound to the outbound end of the business (Harland 1996). In accordance with Stock and Boyer (2009), the terminology for SCM is characterized by three aspects (see Sect. 2.2.1):

- Activities: A supply chain is a network of entities which are linked by internal and external relationships comprising bi-directional physical, logical and financial flows.
- Constituents and components: A supply chain is composed of all operations, systems, business functions and organizations which collaborate and cooperate in this particular network from the original producer to the final customer.

- Benefits: SCM comprises the design, planning, controlling and execution of all operations in the network in order to increase the efficiency (i.e. profitability) of a SC, ensure the effectiveness (i.e. ensure customer satisfaction) and add value.

The financial process can be modeled under consideration of three financial principles (Damodaran 2011a): A firm follows an investment principle to determine where to invest resources, a financing principle to govern the mix of funding to fund these investments and a dividend principle to decide how much earnings to reinvest or to return to the owners of the firm. Effects of the financial principles are represented by three basic accounting statements of a company (Damodaran 2011a,b):

- A balance sheet consisting of assets and liabilities. Asset positions can be differentiated by fixed assets, current assets, financial investments and intangible assets. Liabilities comprise current liabilities, debt, other liabilities and equity.
- A P&L statement comprising revenues which are reduced by operating expenses, financial expenses and taxes and adjusted further by extraordinary losses (or profits), income changes associated with accounting principles and preferred dividends. These calculations result in earnings before interest and taxes (EBIT), which measures the profitability achieved in an accounting period (usually fiscal year or quarter).
- A cash flow statement which specifies the amount of cash a company has generated or spent from operating, investment and financing processes.

The total economic value of an entity such as a company or business unit, entitled as shareholder value, is the sum of the values of its debt and its equity (Rappaport 1998). The shareholder value network modeled by Rappaport (1998) illustrates the causalities of value creation (see Fig. 2.1): Shareholder value added is influenced by cash flow from operations, discount rate and debt. Discount rate in turn is affected by cost of capital, while cash flow from operations is driven by sales growth, profit margin and tax rate as well as by working capital and fixed assets and furthermore by value growth duration. Cost of capital is related to financing decisions, working capital and fixed assets are influenced by investment decisions, sales growth, profit margin and tax rate are stimulated by operating management decisions. According to Rappaport (1998), this links to the three financial principles of a firm as follows:

- Investment decisions influence the quality of the firm's projects resulting in future growth.
- Dividend decisions influence the amount reinvested back into business.
- Financing decisions affect the firm value through discount rate and potentially through expected cash flows.

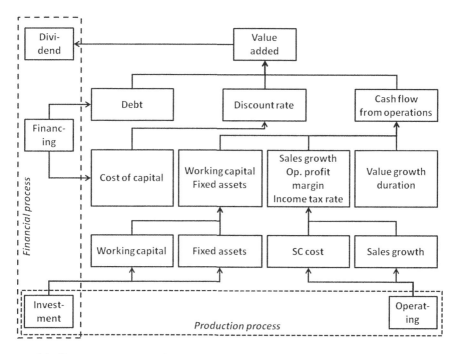

Fig. 3.3 Conceptual framework for value-based SCM

The conceptual design of a framework for value-based SCM (see Fig. 3.3) is completed by combining these models under consideration of Christopher and Ryals (1999) who state that SCM, in the shareholder value network (see Fig. 2.1 on page 8) comprehended as production process, influences company value by four financial drivers: sales, cost, working capital and fixed assets.

Chapter 4
Content Analysis of Literature on Value-Based Supply Chain Management

Abstract The question of value-based supply chain management has been of considerable interest for academics and practitioners alike over the last 10 years. Research in this area is characterised by heterogeneity in terminology and in applied methodologies. This chapter sheds light on the current status, applied terminology and future directions of research on value-based SCM. A systematical content-analysis has been applied to 65 relevant peer-reviewed manuscripts published by 2010 in 3 journals.[1]

4.1 Introduction

Supply chain management (SCM), which can be comprehended as the "integration of business processes from end users through original suppliers that provides products, services and information that add value for customers" (Cooper et al. 1997, p. 2), has gained significant relevance in academic research (Sachan and Datta 2008). It is widely accepted that SCM can be seen as a competitive advantage across all industries (Mentzer et al. 2001), especially because the profitability of a company can be increased by improving effectiveness and efficiency of a supply chain (SC) function (Gunasekaran and Kobu 2007; Lambert and Pohlen 2001). Furthermore, SCM has an impact on sales growth and capital performance and hence can positively influence the cash flow situation of a firm and finally the company value (Christopher and Ryals 1999). On the other hand, SC disruptions or performance gaps can negatively influence the market value of a firm (Hendricks and Singhal

---

[1]This chapter has been previously published as a paper (Brandenburg M (2011) A systematic review of literature on value-based supply chain management. In: Kersten W, Blecker T, Jahn C (eds) International supply chain management and collaboration practices. EUL Verlag, Lohmar, pp 283–296) and is reprinted in this dissertation by courtesy of © JOSEF EUL VERLAG GmbH, Lohmar. The content of this chapter has been presented at the Hamburg International Conference on Logistics HICL 2011 held in Hamburg, Germany, September 8–9, 2011.

M. Brandenburg, *Quantitative Models for Value-Based Supply Chain Management*,   65
Lecture Notes in Economics and Mathematical Systems 660,
DOI 10.1007/978-3-642-31304-2__4, © Springer-Verlag Berlin Heidelberg 2013

2003, 2005b). In the inter-organizational context, SCM aims at adding value for the final customer of a product or service (Cooper et al. 1997). These observations illustrate value impacts of SCM on functional, company or network level. This coherence between SCM and value based management (VBM), defined as a "management accounting system linking value-maximization to strategic objectives, a coherent set of performance measures, and compensation through cause-and-effect-chains" (Chenhall 2005; Lueg and Schäffer 2010; Young and O'Byrne 2001, p. 5), can be named value-based SCM.

The field of research on value-based SCM is characterized by heterogeneity in terminology and applied methodologies. This diversity can already be observed by a short survey on a small number of selected publications (Christopher and Ryals 1999; Hendricks and Singhal 2003; Hofmann and Locker 2009; Lambert and Burduroglu 2000; Lambert and Pohlen 2001; Sridharan et al. 2005). In these publications, the approaches to value-based SCM vary from functional or company specific perspectives to network considerations. Furthermore, the core concepts and value drivers addressed in these papers comprise different aspects of analysis, e.g. single functions, operational SC processes or SC strategy. The applied research methodologies range from theoretical designs with few references to empirical examples to extensive evaluation of several hundreds of cases. The objectives of this chapter are to shed light on the current status (e.g. emphases, gaps, methodology) of academic research on value-based SCM, to analyse the terminology on which this research is based and to identify future perspectives for further research in this area. This objective is elaborated by a thorough review of literature on value-based SCM. To ensure that this review is performed systematically, the method of content analysis (Mayring 2008) is applied.

The remainder of this chapter is structured as follows: Sect. 4.2 comprises an introduction of the conceptual elements SCM and VBM, followed by a description of the applied research methodology given in Sect. 4.3. The findings of the literature review are illustrated and thoroughly discussed in Sect. 4.4. The chapter concludes with findings, limitations and future research perspectives in Sect. 4.5.

4.2   Conceptual Basis

In this section, the terminology for SCM and VBM will be introduced as a conceptual basis for the content analysis of the reviewed literature. Defining characteristics of SCM will be introduced as a basis for analytic categories. The existence of different perceptions of value will be illustrated, which allows for categorizing the term "value" by "efficiency", "shareholder value" and "stakeholder value".

4.2.1   Supply Chain Management

Despite the fact that SCM has gained significant popularity in academic science and industrial practice, research on SCM has not resulted in a consensus terminology

(Mentzer et al. 2001). Stock and Boyer (2009) examined 173 definitions of the term "supply chain management" taken from scientific literature and digested three major themes of SCM, which are considered defining characteristics for this chapter:

1. SCM activities comprise flows of physical material, finances, services and information in networks of internal and external relationships.
2. Benefits of SCM can be categorised into value creation, efficiency increase and customer satisfaction.
3. Component parts of the network include suppliers, production facilities, distribution services and customers as well as functional areas and processes.

4.2.2 Value and Value-Based Management

In companies from various industries, a firm's profitability, driven by sales growth and cost decrease, is seen as one of the most important criteria for the business performance and value creation (Ramezani et al. 2002). It is widely assumed that sales growth is achieved mainly by marketing activities while SCM functions influence the profitability mainly by cost reductions (Godsell et al. 2010). As a consequence efficiency and effectiveness of SCM functions were identified as profit contributors and sources for value creation (Gunasekaran and Kobu 2007; Lambert and Pohlen 2001). An increasing awareness of the relevance of cash flow for value creation has moved the (working) capital efficiency in focus (Randall and Farris II 2009a).

Rappaport (1998) brought the idea of VBM in context to the term shareholder value, which stipulates all parts of a company to be managed in such a way that the equity value is sustainably increased. A survey and discussion of valuation concepts is provided by Damodaran (2005) differentiating between four approaches to valuation: (1) Discounted cash flow (DCF) valuation which "relates the value of an asset to the present value of expected future cash flows on that asset" (Damodaran 2005, p. 2). (2) Liquidation and accounting valuation which is based on accounting estimates of value or book value of an asset. (3) Relative valuation which determines the estimated value of an asset by "looking at the pricing of 'comparable' assets" (Damodaran 2005, p. 2). (4) Contingent claim valuation which measures asset values by option pricing models. The first category comprises firm DCF models which measure the value of a firm by free cash flows discounted by weighted average cost of capital and which are broadly accepted in academic research (Brealey et al. 2008), as well as excess return models such as economic value added (EVA) which measure the surplus value created by an investment (Stewart 1991; Young and O'Byrne 2001). The equivalence of both concepts has been proven by Hartman (2000). A thorough review of academic literature on VBM is given by Lueg and Schäffer (2010).

In SCM it is taken for granted that competition does not only occur between companies but furthermore between supply chains consisting of different companies (Christopher 2005). Hence, the creation of customer satisfaction (Fawcett et al. 2008) resulting in additional value for the final customer is comprehended as key objective and success criterion of SCM (Mentzer et al. 2001). A broader perspective on value is taken in the area of sustainability which leads companies and supply chains from striving for economic success to extending the view to a triple bottom line, including financial, ecological and social objectives (Seuring and Müller 2008). In this context, the view is shifted from value for shareholders or company to stakeholder value, which obliges managers to make decisions under consideration of the interests of all the stakeholders (financial claimholders, employees, customers, communities, government officials) in a firm including all individuals or groups who can substantially affect or be affected by the welfare of the firm (Jensen 2001). By testing the relationship between stakeholder management and shareholder value, Hillman and Keim (2001) found arguments which support the assumption that stakeholder management can lead to shareholder wealth creation.

4.3 Methodological Aspects

4.3.1 Research Question

The objective of this chapter is to analyze the current status and future directions of academic research on value-based SCM and the terminology on which this research is based. In this context it will be determined to which extent academic research on value-based SCM reflects cross-functional or inter-organizational aspects. In particular, this chapter deals with four questions:

1. Which aspects of SCM are in focus of academic research on value-based SCM?
2. Which designs are preferably applied for academic research on value-based SCM?
3. Which value definitions represent the terminological foundation for academic research on value-based SCM?
4. Which future directions are suggested for academic research on value-based SCM?

4.3.2 Research Methodology

These research questions are elaborated on in this chapter by a thorough review of literature on value-based SCM. To ensure that this review is performed systematically, the method of content analysis (Mayring 2008) is applied.

4.3.2.1 Material Collection

The material was collected from relevant peer-reviewed papers published up to 2010 in three journals, namely Supply Chain Management: An International Journal

(SCMIJ), International Journal of Physical Distribution and Logistics Management (IJPDLM) and International Journal of Logistics Management (IJLM). A structured search was performed in these journals based on the keywords "shareholder value" in title, abstract, keywords or full text. This keyword search resulted in an initial sample of 61 papers, from which 21 papers were deselected because they are not closely linked to value-based SCM and hence failed the paper validation test. Further 25 papers, which were found by literature search, based on one of the keywords "company value", "discounted cash flow", "economic value added" or "value-based", were added to the sample which in the end comprises 65 papers.[2]

4.3.2.2 Analytic Categories

The descriptive analysis shows formal aspects of the material, e.g. the distribution of publications across the time period and across the three journals, and furthermore helps to identify applied research methodologies. Based on descriptive categories ("case study", "conceptual", "literature review", "model", "survey") defined by Seuring et al. (2005), the papers are categorized by applied research methodologies.

The majority of the analytic categories was deductively derived from review elements defined by Halldorsson and Arlbjørn (2005). These criteria allow for structuring the material by the primary actor of analysis ("carrier", "manufacturer", "retailer", "warehousing", "wholesaler") and by the level of analysis ("function", "firm", "dyad", "chain", "network") as well as by the research purpose ("describe", "diagnose", "explain", "explore", "intervene", "normative", "understand"), by the considered time frame ("longitudinal", "snap shot") and by the functional area ("e-business / IT", "inventory management", "logistics", "purchasing", "quality management", "SCM", "SC risk management, "sustainable SCM", "others") focused in the reviewed manuscripts. Categories to cluster the value terminology ("efficiency", "shareholder value", "stakeholder value") applied in the papers were defined inductively in the course of the review.

4.4 Findings

4.4.1 Descriptive Analysis

The majority of the reviewed manuscripts were found in IJPDLM (37 relevant papers, 57 % of the paper sample). Additional 16 relevant papers (25 %) were taken from SCMIJ, the remaining 12 relevant papers (18 %) were published in IJLM.

---

[2]A complete list of the paper sample and the categorization of each reviewed manuscript is given in Sect. 12.1 of this thesis.

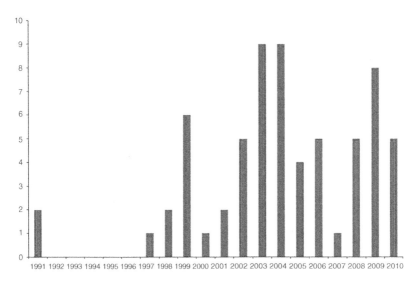

Fig. 4.1 Distribution of the papers on the time horizon

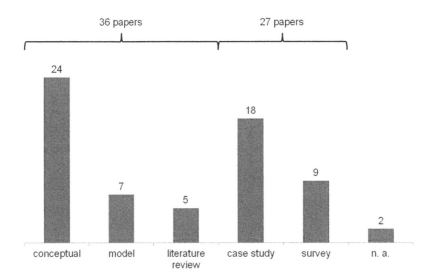

Fig. 4.2 Applied research methodologies

The distribution of papers on the time horizon (see Fig. 4.1) illustrates that the area of value-based SCM began to gain scientific attention at the end of the 1990s. Peaks occurred in 2003 and 2004 (9 papers per year) and 2009 (8 papers).

The assignment of papers to the applied research methodologies (see Fig. 4.2) illustrates that 36 papers are based on theory-driven methods (conceptual papers, quantitative models, literature reviews) while empirical approaches (surveys, case study research) are applied in 27 papers. Two papers were not categorized: Anderson and Katz (1998) who describe a consulting approach and Fawcett et al. (2008) who employ a triangulation method combining a literature review and a mail survey with 51 in-depth case analyses. An interesting finding is that most papers (4 out of 5) comprising literature reviews were published in 2008 or later.

4.4.2 Category Analysis

The majority of manuscripts (46 papers, 71 %) have an explanatory (21), explorative (17) or descriptive (8) purpose and hence mainly feature observations. The remaining 19 papers (29 %), categorized as normative (10), intervening (5) or diagnostic (4), represent a group of papers with more active involvement to the field of study. Most of the reviewed articles (45 papers, 69 %) do not mention the considered time frame, longitudinal studies were found in 6 papers (9 %).

The paper sample is nearly equally split, on the one hand manuscripts taking an intra-organizational perspective on firm level (29 papers, 45 %) or functional level (5 papers, 8 %), and on the other hand papers that follow inter-organizational approaches to value-based SCM: 7 papers (11 %) on dyads, 12 papers (18 %) on chains, 8 papers (12 %) on networks. Four papers (6 %) were not assigned to a specific level of analysis.

In most cases, research on value-based SCM seems to be done without taking into account a specific actor of analysis. Nearly two third of the manuscripts (41 papers) do not focus on a specific company category. Amongst these papers, all research designs and purposes can be found. On the contrary, all conceptual papers belong to this group. This might indicate that conceptual research on value-based SCM strives for universality of concepts. Most of the remaining papers consider manufacturing companies (16 papers, 24 %), the others deal with retailers or carriers (each: 4 papers, 6 %). Wholesalers or warehousing companies were not particularly focused on by these research papers.

Assessing the paper sample by the functional area indicates that holistic approaches to value-based SCM gain high awareness in science. Twenty-two papers (34 %) consider SCM in general without limiting the perspective to a specific function or area. Logistics (11 papers, 17 %) and purchasing (8 papers, 12 %) are functions which are considered comparably often in research on value-based SCM. Manuscripts dealing with inventory management or sustainability aspects (each: 5 papers, 8 %) illustrate the relevance of cash aspects and non-monetary considerations for value creation in SCM. The functional areas SC risk management and e-business/IT respectively are each covered by 3 papers (5 %). Four papers (Carr et al. 2004; Turner et al. 2004; Walters 2004a,b) deal with research topics that include but are not limited to SCM aspects. Surprisingly, no paper was found which focused on manufacturing in the field of study, and only one manuscript dealt with financial SCM (Randall and Farris II 2009a). The remaining 3 papers (5 %) of the sample shed light on value-based SCM approaches to operations management, quality management or SC planning.

4.4.3 Value Terminology and Research Perspective

Manuscripts that reduce the value perception to efficiency aspects were found comparably seldom (7 papers, 11 %). Apart from one exception (Emiliani and Stec 2005), none of these papers was published after 2003. This indicates that at a time when the scientific relevance of value-based SCM increased, the value terminology on which research in this area is based has been taken from a functional efficiency perspective to a more holistic view on value creation. Most reviewed manuscripts (37 papers, 57 %) base the research on "shareholder value" or "company value", but two thirds of these papers do not specify in greater detail what exactly should be understood by these value terms. Amongst specific definitions for value, DCF-based value definitions are predominantly applied (10 papers, 16 %). In 3 papers, different value terminologies are chosen to which SCM is related. Deitz et al. (2009) evaluate the impacts of SC technology on market value of a firm in a retail environment. Norrman and Jansson (2004) suggest the concept of business interruption value, defined as a product of gross margin and the time a business needs to recover from a disruption, as a value-based metric for SC risk management. A network perspective on the value terminology is taken by Randall and Farris II (2009a) by bringing financial metrics for working capital performance and cost of capital into a network context in order to reduce the financial cost for each member of an SC.

Value perceptions that go beyond the pure focus on financial performance of a single firm can be comprehended as stakeholder value. This approach is followed by 18 papers (28 %) of the reviewed sample. Thirteen of these papers (20 %) are related to customer value, which indicates that customer-orientation as a defining characteristic for SCM is well reflected in research on value-based SCM. Two papers (Emiliani and Stec 2002b; van Hoek 1999) seize social and ecological aspects of value creation respectively. Two other papers (Richey Jr. 2009; Turner et al. 2004) base their research on stakeholder value without giving a more specific definition of that term. Kennett et al. (1998) demonstrate value impacts stemming from product quality.

Future research perspectives addressed in the reviewed papers might indicate existing gaps in research on value-based SCM. Unfortunately 25 papers (39 %) did not include any suggestion for further research. Additional 16 papers (25 %) limited the perspectives to validating findings given in the respective paper or to slightly extending the research focus, e.g. by adding constraints to a proposed model. In the remaining 24 papers (37 %), different directions for future research are proposed.

Based on their evaluation of 173 definitions for SCM, Stock and Boyer (2009) propose discussing outcomes of SCM, defining appropriate metrics to measure these outcomes and elaborating best ways to obtain coordination between partners in an SC. Additional research in the field of decision making is stipulated by Randall and Farris II (2009a). In their paper, the authors considered network effects on company value and inspire further research to provide normative structures and SC financial tools for inter-organizational decision-making processes. Furthermore, the authors propose to develop optimization algorithms to maximize network profits. Blankley

(2008) assesses the financial impacts of SC technology investments and directs future research towards the evaluation of financial impacts of IT implementation and the influences arising from a firm's position in the SC or from network effects. Jüttner et al. (2010), who developed a strategic framework to integrate marketing and SC strategies, suggest investigating inter-organizational impacts on value creation and consequences of a combined market and SC orientation on corporate strategy. A detailed examination of factors behind aggregate performance metrics is proposed by Töyli et al. (2008) who have assessed 424 firms regarding the interplay between logistics and financial performance. Broadening the perspective of value creation to ecological and social aspects is suggested by Carter and Rogers (2008), who address the need to develop scales to measure the triple bottom line of sustainability.

4.5 Conclusion

In this chapter, current status and future perspectives of research on value-based SCM are elaborated in a review of 65 relevant papers published in three peer-reviewed journals. This field of study has gained scientific attention in the first decade of this millennium and considers intra-organizational aspects as well as inter-organizational facets. In the reviewed manuscripts, which in most cases have an observing research purpose, empirical research and theoretical approaches account for an equal share of methodologies applied. Research on value-based SCM is not limited to a specific actor of analysis, and the functional emphasis is put on SCM in general, logistics or purchasing. The value terminology on which research is based emphasizes "shareholder value" mainly complemented by "customer value", but in most cases without giving detailed specifications or definitions what exactly is meant by these terms. Future research directions are given for a broad field ranging from a more detailed elaboration of value-driving factors, appropriate structures and metrics to support decision making on company or network level to a broader comprehension of the term "value" which could include ecological or social facets. The research presented in this chapter is limited by the extent of the paper sample and the evaluated area. This vivifies validating the findings of this chapter, e.g. by assessing an increased paper sample which could be obtained by considering additional journals or more key words in the paper search, or to extend its evaluation spectrum, e.g. to discuss different conceptual frameworks and quantitative models proposed for value-based SCM.

Chapter 5
Quantifying Value Impacts of Supply Chain Cost and Working Capital

Abstract Supply chain management (SCM) is identified and accepted as a competitive advantage. Nevertheless holistic approaches for value-based SCM to leverage this advantage in a value adding way are missing so far. Efficient approaches to quantify and compare value contributions from supply chain (SC) value drivers are needed. This chapter contributes to this need by proposing a model to efficiently quantify and compare value contributions from SC cost and working capital, that affect the profitability and asset performance. Properties and characteristics of the model, which is based on the discounted cash flow concept, are illustrated by an industrial example of a single company. In this example, the relevance of timing and continuity of developments of SC cost and working capital for value creation is pointed out.[1]

5.1 Introduction

Supply chain management (SCM) has become a competitive advantage for companies from various industries (Christopher 2005; Mentzer et al. 2001), and competitive advantage is even considered a defining characteristic of SCM (Handfield and Nichols 1999). Supply chain (SC) performance improvements (Shepherd and Günter 2006) are initiated to increase this advantage. Improvements focusing on financial SC value drivers most often show conflicting effects on cost and capital respectively: methods to improve working capital components (inventory, trade payables, trade receivables) for instance often result in cost increases (e.g. negative

---

[1]This chapter has been previously published as a paper (Brandenburg M, Seuring S (2010b) A model for quantifying impacts of supply chain cost and working capital on the company value. Lecture notes in business information processing, vol 46. pp 107–117) and is reprinted in this dissertation by courtesy of © Springer Verlag, Berlin Heidelberg 2010. The content of this chapter has been presented at the 8th International Heinz Nixdorf Symposium IHNS 2010 held in Paderborn, Germany, April 21–22, 2010.

M. Brandenburg, *Quantitative Models for Value-Based Supply Chain Management*, 75
Lecture Notes in Economics and Mathematical Systems 660,
DOI 10.1007/978-3-642-31304-2__5, © Springer-Verlag Berlin Heidelberg 2013

effects on cash discount or production cost) and hence reduce the profitability, measured by e.g. earnings before interest and taxes (EBIT). One key question is how value contributions from SC value drivers can be quantified efficiently and how financial comparability of EBIT relevant changes of SC cost and asset relevant changes of working capital can be ensured.

To answer this question, a model based on a discounted cash flow (DCF) approach is suggested to quantify value contributions generated by reductions of these two SC value drivers by one aggregated figure. The conceptual elements are described in Sect. 5.2. Section 5.3 introduces the quantitative model, which is illustrated and discussed based on an industrial case example given in Sect. 5.4. The chapter concludes with summarized findings and future prospects for research in Sect. 5.5.

5.2   Conceptual Elements

5.2.1   Value-Based Supply Chain Management

The idea of value-based management (VBM) is strongly linked to the term shareholder value, which stipulates all parts of a company to be managed in such a way that the equity value is sustainably increased (Rappaport 1998). Different valuation approaches, such as economic value added (EVA) (Stewart 1991), cash flow return on investment (CFROI) (Madden 1998), cash value added (CVA) (Ottosson and Weissenrieder 1996), earned economic income (Grinyer 1985), have been developed and increased the popularity of VBM in academic science and managerial practice (Copeland et al. 2005; Damodaran 2005; de Wet 2005; Malmi and Ikäheimo 2003). One well known valuation approach is the DCF model, which is broadly accepted in academic research (Hawawini and Viallet 2002; Ross et al. 2002; Weber et al. 2004) and often applied in industrial practice (Geginat et al. 2006).

Existing literature emphasizes that the question of value-based SCM has been of considerable interest for academic research for the last 10 years. A thorough literature review would exceed the extent of this chapter. Hence, a survey on selective literature indicating the heterogeneity of approaches and concepts for value-based SCM is depicted in Table 5.1. Value-based SCM concepts vary from functional or company specific perspectives to network considerations. Core concepts and identified drivers for value-based SCM, which is most often linked to shareholder value and EVA, range from single functions, operational SC activities and processes to SC strategy. Empirical aspects are reflected differently – some rather theoretical papers give few references to industrial examples, some papers comprise case studies from one or few companies, some papers extensively evaluate several hundreds of observations.

Although it is taken for granted that SCM influences the cash flow and hence the shareholder value of a company (Christopher and Ryals 1999; Hendricks and

Table 5.1 Value-based SCM in selected research papers

Paper	SCM approach	VBM approach	Concept. value driver	Empirical aspects
Christopher and Ryals (1999)	Network of linked companies with internal processes and interfaces to suppliers and customers	Shareholder value, mainly EVA	SCM affects four drivers of shareholder value (revenue, cost, fixed capital, working capital)	Twelve observations from industrial or consulting practice
Lambert and Burduroglu (2000)	Functional (logistics)	Different approaches, shareholder value as most comprehensive	Logistics influence on revenue, cost, fixed capital, working capital	None
Lambert and Pohlen (2001)	Integration of eight key processes across companies to add value for customers and stakeholders	Shareholder value, EVA	Map 8 key processes to shareholder value	None
Hendricks and Singhal (2003)	Company-internal supply chain	Market value of a firm (stock price)	Examine impacts of production or shipment delays on stock price; SC strategy is linked to cash flow, earnings and assets	519 observations from industrial practice
Sridharan et al. (2005)	Functional (IT for SCM)	Market value of a firm (stock price)	Examine effects from implementation of IT for SCM on the market value of a firm	Three company case studies
Hofmann and Locker (2009)	Inter-organizational management of flows of goods and information to ensure performance and customer achievements	Shareholder value, EVA	SCM processes linked to EVA categories via key performance indicators (KPI)	Case study from packaging industry

Singhal 2003), value-based SCM approaches based on DCF models are found rather seldom. Furthermore little evidence exists that effective SCM is linked to shareholder value creation (Hendricks and Singhal 2003). Besides, future prospects in research address the need of cost effective ways to measure shareholder value impacts (Lambert and Burduroglu 2000) and the improvements regarding data used for evaluation (Hofmann and Locker 2009).

This chapter contributes to these gaps and future prospects in academic research on value-based SCM. An approach is proposed which links SC cost and working capital to company value. A quantitative model based on DCF allows for measuring shareholder value impacts of those two SC value drivers in a simple and efficient way by using published data. The approach is illustrated by a company example from the fast moving consumer goods (FMCG) industry.

5.2.2 Supply Chain Cost

Research in SC cost management ranges from concepts, instruments and models (see e.g. papers in Seuring and Goldbach 2001) to the link to other conceptual approaches, e.g. value based pricing (Christopher and Gattorna 2005) or logistics cost management (Suang and Wang 2009). SC cost comprise cost of goods sold (COGS), which reflect the direct cost and overhead associated with the physical production of products for sale (Poston and Grabinski 2001), and logistics cost for transportation, distribution logistics, inventory carrying and administration (Cohen and Roussel 2005):

$$SC\ cost = COGS + Logistics\ cost\ . \tag{5.1}$$

Furthermore, SC risks have a considerable influence on SC cost and SC performance (Lee 2008; Ritchie and Brindley 2007; Winkler and Kaluza 2006).

5.2.3 Working Capital

SC strategy and logistics management are linked to requirements of working capital (Christopher 2005), which has a strong influence on the liquidity position and the economic value of a company (Schilling 1996). In some definitions working capital comprises other components such as cash, prepaid expenses, accrued expenses (see e.g. Hawawini and Viallet 2002; Ross et al. 2002). For simplicity reasons, these components are neglected in the working capital definition applied in this chapter. Working capital is defined as the sum of inventories and trade receivables reduced by trade payables (Brealey et al. 2008, p. 145):

$$Working\ capital = Inventory + Trade\ receivables - Trade\ payables\ . \tag{5.2}$$

5.3   The Quantitative Model

The DCF method, which is introduced thoroughly by e.g. Hawawini and Viallet (2002) or Ross et al. (2002), is the basis for the proposed quantitative model. DCF determines the company value V, which is generated during time periods $p = 1, \ldots, P$, by the sum of the discounted free cash flows FCF_p:

$$V = \sum_{p=1}^{p} \frac{FCF_p}{(1 + WACC_p)^p} \, . \tag{5.3}$$

The free cash flow FCF is defined as the difference between EBIT and expenses for tax, depreciation and net capital adjusted for working capital changes (Hawawini and Viallet 2002):

$$FCF = EBIT - Tax\ expenses + Depreciation\ expenses$$
$$- Net\ capital\ expenditures - \Delta\ Working\ capital \, . \tag{5.4}$$

The free cash flow of each period is discounted by the weighted average cost of capital ($WACC$), which represents the minimum rate of return that must be generated in order to meet the return expectations of shareholders (Hawawini and Viallet 2002).

The key question is how to quantify value contributions that arise from changes of working capital or SC cost over a defined period of time periods $p = 1, \ldots, P$. As we see from formula (5.4), changes of working capital as well as EBIT relevant changes of SC cost affect the FCF and thus contribute to company value. Therefore the value contribution VA^W or VA^C generated by the respective value drivers over a time horizon of periods $p = 1, \ldots, P$ is the sum of the value contributions, or precisely value contributing FCF effects, VA_p^W or VA_p^C of each period discounted by $WACC_p$:

$$VA^W = \sum_{p=1}^{p} \frac{VA_p^W}{(1 + WACC_p)^p} \, . \tag{5.5}$$

$$VA^C = \sum_{p=1}^{p} \frac{VA_p^C}{(1 + WACC_p)^p} \, . \tag{5.6}$$

To quantify those value contributions of each period, the respective FCF effects are calculated under consideration of three propositions:

1. In the case that the development of an SC value driver (working capital or SC cost) is proportionate to sales development, the resulting value contribution is credited against sales development. Only in the case that an SC value driver develops disproportionate to sales, the resulting value contribution is credited against the respective SC value driver.

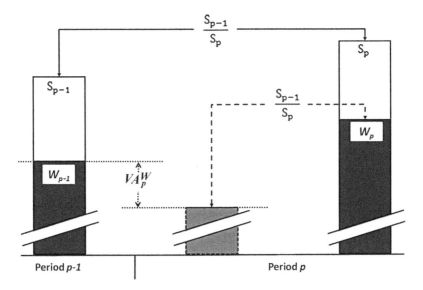

Fig. 5.1 Value contribution resulting from a disproportionate working capital development

2. Changes in working capital are one-time effects and thus result in a value contribution in only one period.
3. Changes of SC cost are recurring effects and thus result in value contributions in all subsequent periods.

The first proposition is illustrated in Fig. 5.1 based on the example of working capital development.

To realize the second proposition, the value contribution VA_p^W arising from working capital development in a time period p is defined by the difference of working capital W_p at the end of period p and working capital W_{p-1} at the beginning of period p adjusted for sales development $\frac{S_{p-1}}{S_p}$ in period p:

$$VA_p^W = W_{p-1} - \frac{S_{p-1}}{S_p} \cdot W_p . \tag{5.7}$$

Similar approaches apply to quantify effects from supply chain cost under consideration of the third proposition. The value contribution arising from changes of SC cost C_p in a period p is defined by the difference of SC cost C_0 of period 0 and SC cost C_p of period p adjusted for sales development $\frac{S_0}{S_p}$ and tax rate T_p:

$$VA_p^C = \left(C_0 - \frac{S_0}{S_p} \cdot C_p \right) \cdot (1 - T_p). \tag{5.8}$$

Table 5.2 Illustrative example for quantification of value contribution

	Scenario		1. Constant sales			2. Growing sales		
	p		0	1	2	0	1	2
	S_p	m €	10,000	10,000	10,000	10,000	20,000	30,000
Case A	W_p	m €	1,600	1,600	1,600	1,600	3,200	4,800
	VA_p^W	m €	–	0	0	–	0	0
	VA^W	m €	–	0	0	–	0	0
	C_p	m €	7,000	7,000	7,000	7,000	14,000	21,000
	VA_p^C	m €	–	0	0	–	0	0
	VA^C	m €	–	0	0	–	0	0
Case B	W_p	m €	1,600	1,500	1,500	1,600	3,000	4,500
	VA_p^W	m €	–	+100.0	0	–	+100.0	0
	VA^W	m €	–	+90.9	+90.9	–	+90.9	+90.9
	C_p	m €	7,000	6,900	6,900	7,000	13,800	20,700
	VA_p^C	m €	–	+65.0	+65.0	–	+65.0	+65.0
	VA^C	m €	–	+59.1	+112.8	–	+59.1	+112.8

5.3.1 Illustrative Example

Let a fictitious company of 10,000 m € sales have a working capital of 1,600 m € and SC cost of 7,000 m € at a WACC of 10.0% and tax rate of 35.0%.[2] Two example cases A and B are considered for developments of working capital and SC cost, each case split in two scenarios for sales development (1. at constant sales and 2. at growing sales). Table 5.2 depicts the results of the model for this example.

Case A: The developments of the two SC value drivers, working capital and SC cost, are proportionate to the sales development. Therefore they do not result in value contribution which is credited against those value drivers (as required by proposition 1), although in scenario 2 the absolute figures for both SC value drivers grow.

Case B: A value adding disproportionate working capital development in period $p = 1$ is saved in period $p = 2$ without additional value contribution (as required by proposition 2). The disproportionate development of SC cost in period $p = 1$ results in value contributions in both periods $p = 1$ and $p = 2$ (as required by proposition 3).

5.4 Case Example from Industry

To illustrate and discuss the proposed quantitative model, its properties and functionality are shown based on an example of a single company. Henkel KGaA from FMCG industry is selected as a case example, because all required data is published

---

[2]Note: In this chapter, all figures are rounded to maximum one decimal digit.

Table 5.3 Case example from Henkel KGaA

p	UOM	2003	2004	2005	2006	2007	2008
S_p^a	m €	9,436	10,592	11,974	12,740	13,074	14,131
C_p^a	m €	4,965	5,615	6,533	6,963	7,013	8,190
W_p^a	m €	1,845	1,840	1,693	1,699	1,500	1,651
Inventory[a]	m €	1,053	1,196	1,232	1,325	1,283	1,482
Receivables[a]	m €	1,581	1,743	1,794	1,868	1,694	1,847
Payables[a]	m €	789	1,099	1,333	1,494	1,477	1,678
$WACC_p^a$	%	8.0	7.0	7.0	7.0	7.0	7.5
T_p^a	%	35.0	35.0	35.0	30.0	30.0	30.0
VA_p^{C}[b]	m €	–	−24	−119	−135	−68	−353
VA^{C}[b]	m €	–	−23	−127	−236	−288	−534
VA_p^{W}[b]	m €	–	206	342	96	237	−28
VA^{W}[b]	m €	–	192	491	570	751	732
VA^{Total}	m €	–	170	365	333	463	198

[a] Source: annual report of respective period
[b] Calculated with described formulas

Table 5.4 SC cost and working capital ratios at Henkel KGaA

p	UOM	2003	2004	2005	2006	2007	2008
SC cost ratio	%	52.6	53.0	54.6	54.7	53.6	58.0
Working capital ratio	%	19.6	17.4	14.1	13.3	11.5	11.7

in the annual reports (Henkel 2004–2009) of this company. Working capital figures were calculated from balance sheet data, for simplicity reasons SC cost are limited to cost of goods sold (COGS) figures taken from P&L statements, figures for tax rate and WACC are published in the respective annual reports, too. The input data and results of the quantitative model are depicted in Table 5.3.

The total value contribution VA^{Total}, i.e. the sum of value contributions VA^{W} and VA^{C} from each SC value driver, is positive. Hence, SCM at Henkel KGaA added value to the company. Two other observations of this case can easily be made and examined further by a root cause analysis and a simulation scenario:

1. In no period of time was any value generated by SC cost.
2. Value was generated by working capital in each period of time except in 2008.

Analyzing the developments of SC cost ratio, i.e. SC cost in % of sales, and working capital ratio, i.e. working capital in % of sales, helps to explain why value was added or lost by the developments of those value drivers (see Table 5.4). The SC cost ratio shows a continuous and deteriorating trend, because the level of 52.6 % in 2003 was never achieved in the subsequent periods 2004–2008. Hence no value was added from SC cost. The working capital ratio on the contrary develops continuously and significantly improving between 2003 and 2007, this achieved decline significantly adds value. A comparably small increase of working capital ratio in 2008 does not substantially influence the value contribution achieved so far.

Table 5.5 Results of the simulation scenario for SC cost

p	UOM	2003	2004	2005	2006	2007	2008
S_p	m €	9,436	10,592	11,974	12,740	13,074	14,131
C_p	m €	4,965	5,615	6,533	6,963	**6,572**	**7,072**
VA_p^C	m €	–	−24	−119	−135	**155**	**170**
VA^C	m €	–	−23	−127	−236	**−118**	–
SC cost ratio	%	52.6	53.0	54.6	54.7	**50.3**	**50.0**

A simulation scenario derived from this case example helps to illustrate and to discuss value adding developments of SC value drivers. This simulation scenario answers the question how SC cost should have developed in 2007 and 2008 to avoid the value loss of −534 m €. Similar approaches are possible for working capital. Based on defined target value contributions va_p^C for 2007 and 2008, the figures of target SC cost c_p which are needed to achieve those value contributions can be calculated by rearranging formula (5.8):

$$c_p = \frac{S_p}{S_0} \cdot (C_0 - va_p^C \cdot (1 - T)^{-1}) . \tag{5.9}$$

By 2006 a value contribution of −236 m € from SC cost was achieved, hence this value loss would be compensated by achieving +118 m € value contribution from SC cost in each of the last two periods. Applying formula (5.9), the required target SC cost c_p can be calculated to obtain the simulation scenario depicted in Table 5.5 (figures obtained from simulation **highlighted**).

The case example and the derived simulation scenario illustrate important characteristics of value-adding SC value driver developments:

1. Continuous improvements and sustainable developments of SC value drivers foster value creation: Alternating improvements and deteriorations in SC value driver developments cannot guarantee overall value achievements.

   Illustrated by the case example: Although in 2007 the SC cost improved slightly compared to 2006, this improvement was not sufficient to compensate losses from earlier periods. Furthermore the improvement was not strong enough to achieve the SC cost ratio from 2003 and hence did not add any value.
2. Timing aspects have to be considered: Improvements of SC value drivers achieved in later phases cannot guarantee to fully compensate deteriorations from earlier phases.

   Illustrated by simulation scenario: The deterioration of SC cost in early periods 2003–2006 (SC cost ratio in 2006 deteriorated vs. 2003 by 2.1pp) can only be compensated by a disproportionately high reduction in the late periods 2007 and 2008 (SC cost ratio improvement vs. 2003 by 2.6 pp in 2008 needed to compensate value losses from earlier periods).

5.5 Conclusion

This chapter contributes to the development of frameworks and approaches to value-based SCM. A model is proposed to quantify impacts of SC cost and working capital on shareholder value. This model is mathematically derived from the DCF model and hence substantiates the link between SC value drivers and shareholder value. The financial comparability of EBIT relevant changes of SC cost and asset relevant changes of working capital by one aggregated figure is ensured. A case example of a company from FMCG industry illustrates how to use published data to efficiently measure shareholder value impacts of SC value drivers.

Further research opportunities are offered by the possibility to extend the empirical evaluations to other companies or industries. Furthermore the model can be applied or extended to evaluate specific SC value driver components. The performance of the working capital components inventory, trade receivables and trade payables as well as the value contributions of function-specific cost, e.g. for material acquisition or production, can be analyzed. Besides, the model can be extended to other financial SC value drivers, such as fixed asset performance. The context of SC risk management and value creation allows for further research, especially regarding influences of SC risks on SC cost or WACC. Beyond this, a holistic value-based SCM concept must consider non-financial value drivers, such as SC risk, intangibles or intellectual capital, and inter-company aspects to reflect the network approach of SCM.

Chapter 6
Benchmarking Companies from the Fast Moving Consumer Goods Industry

Abstract The research question addressed is to which extent supply chain management (SCM) creates value from cost and working capital. The chapter provides an empirical evaluation including insights on important criteria for value creation. In a secondary data analysis, ten leading fast moving consumer goods (FMCG) companies are benchmarked regarding the value created from cost of goods sold (COGS) and working capital within the time horizon 2003–2008. The study applies benchmarking methodology and a discounted cash flow (DCF) based model for quantifying value contributions. It is shown that SCM is realized in a value-adding way with different emphasis on COGS or working capital. Monetary working capital components (trade payables, trade receivables) have a high relevance for value creation. Continuous improvements and long lasting developments of value drivers are more appropriate for value creation than alternating improvements and deteriorations. Timing aspects of value driver developments have to be considered for value creation. The value of the chapter stems from empirical comparison of value created by working capital and COGS and from evidence of important criteria for value creation. Further analysis based on cost components as well as benchmarking with different or extended content, such as fixed asset performance or cross-industry benchmarking, leave room for future research.[1]

---

[1]This chapter has been previously published as a paper (Brandenburg M, Seuring S (2010a) The influence of supply chain cost and working capital on company value: benchmarking companies from the fast moving consumer goods industry. Logist Res 3(4):233–248) and is reprinted in this dissertation by courtesy of © Springer Verlag, Berlin Heidelberg. The content of this chapter has been presented at the 22nd NOFOMA conference held in Kolding, Denmark, June 10–11, 2010.

M. Brandenburg, *Quantitative Models for Value-Based Supply Chain Management*,   85
Lecture Notes in Economics and Mathematical Systems 660,
DOI 10.1007/978-3-642-31304-2__6, © Springer-Verlag Berlin Heidelberg 2013

6.1   Introduction

During the last decades supply chain management (SCM), which can be seen as the "integration of business processes from end users through original suppliers that provides products, services and information that add value for customers" (Cooper et al. 1997, p. 2), has gained significant relevance in academic research (Gunasekaran and Kobu 2007; Melnyk et al. 2009; Mentzer et al. 2001; Sachan and Datta 2008), and it is an accepted insight that SCM has a strong influence on the value of a company (Brandenburg and Schilling 2010; Christopher and Ryals 1999; Lambert and Pohlen 2001; Walters 1999). This coherence between SCM and company value, which can be named value-based SCM, consists of four drivers of value creation: sales growth, operating cost reduction and efficiency of (fixed and working) capital (Christopher and Ryals 1999). Conceptual frameworks for value-based SCM are proposed by different research papers (Brandenburg and Schilling 2010; Lambert and Pohlen 2001; Walters 1999).

The subsequent question in value-based SCM is how to measure, analyze and compare the overall impacts on company value which arise from changes in these SCM-related value drivers. Sales impacts are mainly substantiated by the influence of SCM on service level (Corsten and Gruen 2003; Yang et al. 2009). Influences from SCM on cost (Keebler et al. 1999; papers in Seuring and Goldbach 2001), (working) capital productivity (Lambert and Burduroglu 2000; Schilling 1996; Walters 2006) or working capital components (e.g. inventory) (Capkun et al. 2009; Williams and Tokar 2008) can also be evaluated directly in a quantitative way. Furthermore a quantitative model is suggested to measure impacts of SC cost and working capital on company value (Brandenburg and Seuring 2010b).

To shed further light on value-based SCM, this chapter focuses on two research questions:

- Can empirical evidence be found that overall developments of SCM-related value drivers, in particular cost and working capital, have an impact on company value?
- What decisive criteria for value creation from these drivers can be identified empirically?

One approach to empirically assess the performance of value drivers is benchmarking (Hanman 1997), particularly if related to SCM (Basnet et al. 2003). Hence, to answer the research questions a benchmarking study is performed which analyzes the developments of cost of goods sold (COGS) and working capital and the resulting value contributions over a mid-term horizon. This study provides empirical evidence of important criteria for turning value driver developments into value creation and an empirical analysis of value contributions achieved by working capital components. The benchmarking group comprises companies from the same sector in order to increase their comparability regarding structural and operational characteristics. The focus is put on manufacturing companies from the fast moving consumer goods (FMCG) industry. FMCG manufacturers produce a large number of different products in global supply networks consisting of plants with various combinations of "make-and-pack" processes as well as contract manufacturers and service providers for warehousing and logistics (Honkomp et al. 2000). Despite this complexity, different FMCG manufacturers and their supply chains often show similar characteristics (see e.g. Meyr and Stadtler 2008).

The remainder of this chapter is structured as follows. A literature review in Sect. 6.2 is followed by an introduction of the research methodology in Sect. 6.3. Section 6.4 comprises the benchmarking study followed by a summarizing discussion in Sect. 6.5. The chapter concludes with findings, limitations and future prospects for further research in Sect. 6.6. A supplementary table is given in Sect. 12.2 of this thesis.

6.2 Literature Review

This section comprises an overview of relevant literature on value-based SCM, SCM in FMCG industry and benchmarking. First, the terminology is clarified by introducing and explaining appropriate definitions for the areas SCM and value-based management (VBM), from which the area value-based SCM is derived. Twelve papers on value-based SCM are reviewed to illustrate the variety of research directions in this area. The selected manuscripts also provide a basis for the positioning of this chapter to current research, which is discussed in Sect. 6.5. Fourteen different papers on SCM in FMCG industry, which adumbrate the status of current research on this topic, are briefly discussed to outline structural and process-related characteristics of FMCG manufacturers and their supply chains. Eighteen papers on benchmarking are chosen to delineate developments of this methodology and its applications in academic research on SCM.

6.2.1 Terminology

While the definition of supply chain management is still a hotly discussed topic, here the one given by Mentzer et al. (2001, p. 7) is taken up:

> 1. A systems' approach to viewing the supply chain as a whole, and to managing the total flow of goods inventory from the supplier to the ultimate customer;
> 2. a strategic orientation toward cooperative effort to synchronise and converge intra-firm and inter-firm operational and strategic capabilities into a unified whole; and
> 3. a customer focus to create unique and individualised sources of customer value, leading to customer satisfaction.

This definition contains a close link to an operational comprehension of supply chain management, which can be measured by assessing related value components. VBM is defined as a "management accounting system linking value-maximization to strategic objectives, a coherent set of performance measures, and compensation through cause-and-effect-chains" (Chenhall 2005; Lueg and Schäffer 2010, p. 5;

Young and O'Byrne 2001). In this respect, SCM is comprehended to manage operational processes and assess this in value-based measures. This is elaborated further in the literature review section.

6.2.2 Value-Based Supply Chain Management

A thorough review of academic literature on VBM is given by Lueg and Schäffer (2010), hence only selected papers are mentioned here to outline the broadness of this area. Rappaport (1998) brought the idea of VBM in context to the term shareholder value, which stipulates all parts of a company to be managed in such a way that the equity value is sustainably increased. A survey and discussion of valuation concepts is provided by Damodaran (2005). Different approaches for valuation, amongst others economic value added (EVA) (Stewart 1991), cash flow return on investment (CFROI) (Madden 1998), cash value added (CVA) (Ottosson and Weissenrieder 1996) and earned economic income (Grinyer 1985), have been developed and increased the popularity of VBM in academic science and managerial practice (Copeland et al. 2005; de Wet 2005; Malmi and Ikäheimo 2003). One well known valuation approach is the discounted cash flow (DCF) model, which is broadly accepted in academic research (Brealey et al. 2008; Hawawini and Viallet 2002; Ross et al. 2002).

Existing literature emphasizes that the question of value-based SCM has been of considerable interest for academic research for the last 10 years (Melnyk et al. 2009). A thorough literature review would exceed the extent of this chapter. Hence, an overview of selective literature indicating the heterogeneity of approaches derived from VBM and concepts for value-based SCM is depicted in Table 6.1 and briefly interpreted: SCM concepts in the reviewed papers vary from functional (Lambert and Burduroglu 2000; Sridharan et al. 2005) or company specific (Hendricks and Singhal 2003, 2005b; Losbichler and Rothböck 2006)   perspective to network considerations (Christopher and Ryals 1999; Hofmann and Locker 2009; Otto and Obermaier 2009) (see column "SCM approach" in Table 6.1). Value-based SCM is most often linked to EVA and shareholder value (Brandenburg and Schilling 2010; Brandenburg and Seuring 2010b; Christopher and Ryals 1999; Hofmann and Locker 2009; Lambert and Pohlen 2001; Losbichler and Rothböck 2006; Otto and Obermaier 2009) (see column "VBM approach"). Concepts and value drivers in SCM focused in the reviewed papers range from single functions (Lambert and Burduroglu 2000), operational SC activities and processes (Hofmann and Locker 2009; Lambert and Pohlen 2001; Otto and Obermaier 2009) to SC strategy (Christopher and Ryals 1999) (see column "Concept, value driver"). Empirical aspects are reflected differently (see column "Empirical aspect") – some rather theoretical papers give no or few references to industrial examples (Christopher and Ryals 1999; Lambert and Burduroglu 2000; Lambert and Pohlen 2001; Otto and Obermaier 2009; Sridharan et al. 2005), some papers comprise case studies from one or few companies (Brandenburg and Seuring 2010b; Hofmann and Locker 2009),

Table 6.1 Overview on papers dealing with value-based supply chain management

Paper	SCM approach	VBM approach	Concept, value driver	Empirical aspects
Christopher and Ryals (1999)	Company network with internal processes and external interfaces	Shareholder value, mainly EVA	SCM affects revenue, cost, fixed capital, working capital	Twelve observations from industrial or consulting practice
Lambert and Burduroglu (2000)	Functional (logistics)	Different approaches, shareholder value as most comprehensive	Logistics impact on revenue, cost, fixed capital, working capital	None
Lambert and Pohlen (2001)	Eight cross-company processes add customer and stakeholder value	Shareholder value, EVA	Eight key processes mapped to shareholder value	None
Hendricks and Singhal (2003, 2005b)	Company-internal SC	Market value of a firm (stock price)	Impacts of production or delivery delays on stock price	519 respectively 827 observations from industrial practice
Sridharan et al. (2005)	Functional (IT for SCM)	Market value of a firm (stock price)	Effects from implementation of IT for SCM on stock price	Three company case studies
Losbichler and Rothböck (2006)	Company-internal SC	Shareholder value, EVA	Value-driven SC management accounting framework	Working capital performance of 6,925 European firms
Capkun et al. (2009)	Company-internal SC	Gross profit, operational profit	Inventory performance	US manufacturing companies 1980–2005
Hofmann and Locker (2009)	Inter-organizational management of flows of goods and information	Shareholder value, EVA	SCM processes linked to EVA categories via key performance indicators (KPI)	Case study from packaging industry
Otto and Obermaier (2009)	Inter-organizational network	Shareholder value, DCF	Adjustments of processes, behavior, resources	None
Brandenburg and Schilling (2010)	Dyadic SC	Shareholder value, DCF	Value impacts of dynamics and uncertainties	Case example from FMCG industry
Brandenburg and Seuring (2010b)	Company-internal SC	Shareholder value, DCF	Value impacts of SC cost and working capital	Illustrative industry example

some papers extensively evaluate several hundreds of observations (Capkun et al. 2009; Hendricks and Singhal 2003, 2005b; Losbichler and Rothböck 2006).

Although it is taken for granted that SCM influences the cash flow and hence the shareholder value of a company (Christopher and Ryals 1999; Hendricks and Singhal 2003), little empirical evidence exists that effective SCM is linked to shareholder value creation (Hendricks and Singhal 2003). Further research potential addresses the need of cost effective ways to measure shareholder value impacts (Lambert and Burduroglu 2000) and improvements regarding data used for evaluation (Hofmann and Locker 2009). To help filling this gap, Brandenburg and Seuring (2010b) suggest a model based on the DCF method to quantify value impacts of changes of working capital and SC cost. This model is in line with an approach proposed by Otto and Obermaier (2009).

6.2.3 Supply Chain Management in the Fast Moving Consumer Goods Industry

SCM in FMCG industry shows a considerable complexity which is driven by a large number of facilities and products as well as the resulting flows through inter-organizational and international networks comprising suppliers, manufacturers, distributors, retailers and service providers (Mukhopadhyay and Barua 2003).

These flows of information, goods and financial resources in networks of FMCG industry and the arising complexity are in focus of different research papers. The flow from suppliers to manufacturers is dealt with in a case study from Sandholm et al. (2006), who apply an optimization engine to improve strategic sourcing at The Procter & Gamble Company, a major FMCG manufacturer. Dekker et al. (2009) evaluate four different distribution concepts to optimize the flow between FMCG manufacturers and retailers' warehouses. The material flow across multiple echelons of an SC is analyzed in a case study from Schilling et al. (2010), who identify uncertainties and dynamics as major complexity drivers for FMCG industry. By applying discrete-event simulation (DES), they evaluate different options for SC design in new product introduction at a cosmetics manufacturer in order to decide upon the best SC setting with regards to financial aspects and product availability. The importance and impacts of shelf availability and out of stock situations in FMCG industry are evaluated and discussed by Corsten and Gruen (2003). The complexity drivers demand uncertainties and dynamics are analyzed by Wong et al. (2005) in a longitudinal SC study of toy manufacturers and retailers. Brandenburg and Schilling (2010) integrate DCF and DES to assess value impacts of these complexity drivers in a case example of new product introduction in an SC from FMCG industry. Danne and Häusler (2010) evaluate impacts of assortment complexity in consumer goods SC and propose a decision support system to evaluate assortment dependent cost positions for a production and distribution network.

The characteristics of production processes and production plant networks in FMCG industry are analyzed in academic research. Günther et al. (2006) propose a block planning approach for optimized scheduling of make-and-pack processes on different facilities of a production plant. They introduce the optimization approach, outline aspects of integration with standard planning systems and give empirical illustration by a case study from a cosmetics manufacturer. Günther (2008) describes the application of block planning in a plant at a case study from the beverage industry. Tahmassebi (1998) focuses on control and management of multiple plants in an SC network and suggests a probabilistic model for strategic redesign and operation of existing chains and new product introduction. Duffy (2004) describes approach and impact of re-engineering an SC network in a case study from The Gillette Company. Method and benefits of SC optimization are furthermore presented by Camm et al. (1997), who apply a mathematical model to restructure the plant network of The Procter & Gamble Company in North America.

6.2.4 Benchmarking

Since its appearance in the 1980s, benchmarking itself has passed four stages of evolution – from benchmarks to benchmarking, from product performance to process evaluation, from financial analysis to customer satisfaction and from operational to strategic benchmarking (Maire et al. 2005). Benchmarking has developed to a broad field of academic research (see Dattakumar and Jagadeesh 2003, for a related literature review). Fong et al. (1998) define benchmarking as the "process of continually comparing a company's performance on critical customer requirements against that of the best in industry (direct competitors) or class (companies recognized for their superiority in performing certain functions) to determine what should be improved" (Fong et al. 1998; Vaziri 1992, p. 408). The proposed process comprises a planning phase for decision upon benchmarking content and data collection, an analysis phase to determine current performance gaps and future performance levels, an integration phase for target setting and an action phase for development and implementation of optimization actions.

Benchmarking is often applied in the area of SCM (Wong and Wong 2008), and different benchmarking concepts are designed or applied to evaluate and compare SC performance. Hanman (1997) for instance applies benchmarking methodology to evaluate the supply chain performance of more than 100 organizations and to identify best practices in logistics, purchasing and supply, inventory management and warehousing as well as customer service. Gilmour (1999) proposes a framework for benchmarking operational and strategic aspects of logistics. Many SC benchmarking studies can be found which focus on a certain function, region or industry (e.g. Basnet et al. 2003; Keebler and Plank 2009; Mollenkopf and Dapiran 2005; Tuominen et al. 2009). Blanchard et al. (2008) focus on one company[2] only to identify best practices in SCM.

---

[2] Wal-Mart Stores, Inc.

Benchmarking the working capital performance, which can be measured by the metric cash-to-cash (C2C) cycle (Schilling 1996), has gained particular interest in the context of SCM. Farris II and Hutchison (2002) discuss the C2C cycle and identify optimization levers. In a longitudinal study based on secondary data from Research Insights database, Farris II and Hutchison (2003) analyze 5,884 different companies regarding the performance of working capital and working capital components between 1986 and 2001. These firms are clustered to industries which are classified by median performance of each working capital component. Farris II and Hutchison (2003) observed that in 27 out of 31 industries the working capital performance was improved, mainly by reducing inventory or prolonging payment periods to suppliers, and that inventory reduction offers the highest financial improvement potential in working capital. Randall and Farris II (2009a) provide a method to identify and quantify profitability improvement levers of collaborative working capital management and illustrate the benefits of this collaboration. In another paper, Randall and Farris II (2009b) illustrate the application of C2C cycle for benchmarking by three case studies. In a longitudinal study based on secondary data from Amadeus database, Losbichler and Rothböck (2006) analyze the development of the performance of working capital and its components in 6,925 European companies between 1995 and 2004. They observe that, although individual industries and companies optimized their C2C cycle, on an overall perspective working capital has been moved within European supply chains: The inventory reduction potential is not fully capitalized, and manufacturing companies seem to optimize their working capital at their suppliers' expenses. In an empirical evaluation, Obermaier and Donhauser (2009) benchmark 100 German companies from seven different industry classes regarding their inventory development between 1993 and 2005. They identify improvements in inventory performance in four out of six industry classes and conclude that overall the resulting impact on financial performance of a firm is limited.

6.3 Research Methodology

This section shows how the benchmarking method is applied to answer the two research questions of this chapter. The application of the benchmarking approach proposed by Fong et al. (1998) is outlined. Furthermore the definition of the benchmarking content and the procedures for data collection and preparation are described. An emphasis is put on the introduction of the DCF-based model applied for quantifying value impacts and on limitations of the research method.

6.3.1 Benchmarking Method

To empirically evaluate value contributions arising from SCM, benchmarking, defined as "the process of identifying the highest standards of excellence for products, services or processes" (Bhutta and Huq 1999, p. 254), is applied in the sense of a performance benchmarking, i.e. "the comparison of performance measures for the purpose of determining how good our company is as compared to others" (Bhutta and Huq 1999, p. 257). The benchmarking study is based on a benchmarking process consisting of four phases proposed by Fong et al. (1998). This chapter focuses on the planning and analysis phases and omits the integration and action phases, which are rather applicable for managerial purposes in industrial practice.

6.3.2 Benchmarking Content

This external benchmarking study compares ten leading companies from FMCG industry regarding the value contributions they achieved in the time horizon 2003–2008 from working capital and COGS comprising various costs in the process of transformation from raw material to finished product, e.g. labor costs and manufacturing overhead (Hawawini and Viallet 2002). The benchmarking group is selected based on an analysts' industry research report (Smith 2004), which evaluates companies of a significant relevance for FMCG industry.

6.3.3 Data Collection and Preparation

This benchmarking study is performed as a secondary data analysis, i.e. based on published data from annual reports of the respective companies and Bloomberg data prepared by and accessible at Stern School of Business, New York University (Damodaran 2009).

The value contributions arising from changes in COGS or working capital, defined as the sum of inventories and trade receivables reduced by trade payables, are quantified by a DCF-based model introduced by Brandenburg and Seuring (2010b). This model is briefly explained in the following:

The value contribution VA_p^W arising from working capital development in a time period p is defined by the difference of working capital W_p at the end of period p and working capital W_{p-1} at the beginning of period p adjusted for sales development $\frac{S_{p-1}}{S_p}$ in period p:

$$VA_p^W = W_{p-1} - \frac{S_{p-1}}{S_p} \cdot W_p . \tag{6.1}$$

The value contribution arising from changes of COGS in a period p is defined by the difference of cost $COGS_0$ of period 0 and cost $COGS_p$ of period p adjusted for sales development $\frac{S_0}{S_p}$ and tax rate T_p:

$$VA_p^{COGS} = (COGS_0 - \frac{S_0}{S_p} \cdot COGS_p) \cdot (1 - T_p) . \qquad (6.2)$$

To calculate the value contribution VA^W or VA^{COGS} generated by the respective value drivers over a time horizon of periods $p = 1, \ldots, P$, the value contributions VA_p^W and VA_p^{COGS} of each period p are discounted by weighted average cost of capital $WACC_p$ and the terms $VA_p^W \cdot (1 + WACC_p)^{-p}$ and $VA_p^{COGS} \cdot (1 + WACC_p)^{-p}$ are summed up.

The calculation formula for $WACC$ (see e.g. Brealey et al. 2008; Hawawini and Viallet 2002; Ross et al. 2002) comprises ratios of debt D (derived from the respective book values) and equity E (defined as market capitalization) and furthermore cost of debt k_D, cost of equity k_E and tax rate T:

$$WACC = k_D \cdot \frac{D}{D + E} \cdot (1 - T) + k_E \cdot \frac{E}{D + E} . \qquad (6.3)$$

To ensure comparability, all WACC values used for this benchmarking study (see Table 12.1 in Sect. 12.2) were calculated based on data from Bloomberg L. P.

To analyze developments of working capital components within the benchmarking group in the considered horizon, days sales outstanding (DSO), days sales of inventory (DSI) and days payables outstanding (DPO) are applied. These commonly used metrics (see e.g. Farris II and Hutchison 2002; Lambert and Pohlen 2001) are calculated cumulative for all companies of the benchmarking group and aggregated to the C2C cycle, which measures the working capital performance (Pfohl and Gomm 2009):

$$DSO = \frac{\text{Trade receivables}}{\text{Sales}} \cdot 365 . \qquad (6.4)$$

$$DSI = \frac{\text{Inventory}}{COGS} \cdot 365 . \qquad (6.5)$$

$$DPO = \frac{\text{Trade payables}}{COGS} \cdot 365 . \qquad (6.6)$$

$$C2C = DSO + DSI - DPO . \qquad (6.7)$$

6.3.4 Limitations of the Benchmarking Study

This benchmarking study aims at comparing a larger number of companies regarding the value contributions achieved by SCM. Availability and comparability of data is a crucial factor of such empirical evaluation, because access to comparable data from various firms is often limited to company publications such as annual reports. Hence this benchmarking study is based on secondary data, which is published by the enterprises and comparably easy to access.

This approach limits the content of the benchmarking study. Assessing the impacts of SCM on the value drivers sales and fixed assets empirically would for instance require detailed information as to which share of the fixed assets is SCM-related and to which extent sales developments are influenced by SCM. As this information cannot be made available by secondary data, this benchmarking study is limited to COGS, working capital and working capital components. The analysis of SCM-related figures from annual reports does not enable further evaluation of how these figures in turn are influenced by operational SCM activities. Such analysis would require company internal data. To ensure the comparability of the operational SCM level of the explored firms, the benchmarking group focuses manufacturing companies from the same sector: ten major cosmetics manufacturers from FMCG industry.

Two other aspects have to be considered regarding the level of detail of this benchmarking study. More detailed data would be needed to empirically study conflictive effects of cash and cost aspects, e.g. between cost decrease and trade payables optimization or between inventory reduction and decreasing cost of production or warehousing, or to consider impacts of acquisitions or divestments. Besides, accounting figures from annual or quarterly reports could face window dressing effects.

6.4   Benchmarking Study from the Fast Moving Consumer Goods Industry

This section is structured according to the first two steps of the benchmarking process suggested by Fong et al. (1998), benchmarking planning and benchmarking analysis. The first sub-section gives information how the definition of the benchmarking content and the data collection and preparation are realized. The second subsection comprises the description and analysis of the empirical results obtained by the benchmarking study. A correlation analysis of developments of COGS and working capital and the resulting value impacts will show that value impacts arising from developments of these value drivers can be verified empirically. A more detailed analysis of the benchmarking results and an example on company level will illustrate two relevant aspects which have to be taken into account for such an empirical verification. Furthermore four detailed comparisons of value driver developments and resulting value impacts will demonstrate the relevance of timing and continuity for value creation. A benchmarking analysis of working capital components will point out the relevance of working capital for value creation and identify which aspects were emphasized by the FMCG manufacturers. An empirical sensitivity analysis of WACC figures will substantiate that value impacts of WACC changes can be neglected.

6.4.1 Benchmarking Planning

6.4.1.1 Benchmarking Content

Compared to the analysts' research report (Smith 2004), adjustments were needed in some cases: Due to acquisition by The Procter & Gamble Company in 2005, Gillette Co. had to be excluded from this benchmarking group. Due to limited comparability of their published data, L'Oreal S. A. following French accounting standards until 2004 and Hindustan Lever Ltd. following Indian accounting principles could not be considered in this benchmarking group. Kimberly-Clark Corporation was added to the benchmarking group under consideration of its size and relevance for the FMCG industry to facilitate a representative benchmarking group.

For simplicity reasons, three letter abbreviations will be used for the names of the companies of the benchmarking group: Avon Products Inc. (AVO), Beiersdorf AG (BDF), Colgate-Palmolive Company (CPA), The Estée Lauder Companies Inc. (ELA), Henkel KGaA (HEN), Kao Corporation (KAO), Kimberly-Clark Corporation (KMB), The Procter & Gamble Company (PRG), Reckitt Benckiser Group plc (RCU), The Unilever Group (UNI).

6.4.1.2 Data Collection and Preparation

Working capital figures were calculated from balance sheet data by adding trade receivables and inventory reduced by trade payables. COGS figures are taken from P&L statements. The calculation results for the *WACC* values of each company are listed in Table 12.1 in Sect. 12.2 of this thesis. The calculation itself is omitted in this chapter, but follows the above outlined approach (Hawawini and Viallet 2002).

National currencies were converted based on official exchange rates as per December 31, 2008 (1 € = 1.3977 US\$ = 0.96 GB£ = 126.4 JP¥). Exchange rate effects are not considered in this benchmarking study to facilitate like-for-like analysis.

The value contributions of each company are calculated by applying the quantitative model described in Sect. 6.3.3, the calculation results are depicted in Table 6.2. To ensure comparability, the analysis considers working capital ratio (working capital in % of sales) and COGS ratio (COGS in % of sales) and furthermore value contributions related to sales. The columns "Chg. of ratio" comprise the changes of working capital ratio or COGS ratio between 2003 and 2008 measured in percentage points (pp), the columns "Value contribution of sales" contain the resulting value contribution effect measured in m € and as % of sales 2003.

Table 6.2 Value contributions from COGS and working capital in the FMCG industry

Company	Sales 2003 m €	COGS effects Chg. of ratio (pp)	Value contr. m €	Value contr. of sales (%)	Working capital effects Chg. of ratio (pp)	Value contr. m €	Value contr. of sales (%)	Total effects Value contr. m €	Value contr. of sales (%)
AVO	4,920	−1.1	−48	−1.0	−3.3	158	3.2	111	2.3
BDF	4,435	−2.6	192	4.3	−8.2	330	7.4	522	11.8
CPA	7,085	−1.3	57	0.8	−0.7	51	0.7	108	1.5
ELA	3,661	−0.9	55	1.5	1.4	−52	−1.4	3	0.1
HEN	9,436	5.3	−603	−6.4	−7.9	723	7.7	120	1.3
KAO	6,845	−0.2	−29	−0.4	0.9	−61	−0.9	−89	−1.3
KMB	10,265	4.0	−838	−8.2	−0.2	21	0.2	−817	−8.0
PRG	31,035	−2.3	2,267	7.3	1.1	−328	−1.1	1,938	6.2
RCU	3,868	−6.0	394	10.2	1.7	−64	−1.7	330	8.5
UNI	42,693	3.0	−1,874	−4.4	−2.4	844	2.0	−1,030	−2.4
Avg.	12,424	−0.2	−43	0.4	−1.8	162	1.6	120	2.0

6.4.2 Benchmarking Analysis

6.4.2.1 Correlation Between Value Driver Developments and Value Contribution

An analysis of the correlation between overall[3] development of COGS and working capital (see columns "Chg. of ratio" in Table 6.2) and the resulting value contribution (see columns "Value contribution" in Table 6.2) helps to answer the question if it can be shown empirically that overall developments of SCM-related value drivers influence the company value. For this purpose, the calculated benchmarking figures are analyzed. Linear regression analysis shows strong correlations between the developments of each value driver and the respective achieved value contribution, which is visualized in the scatter plot depicted in Fig. 6.1. The x-axis depicts the change of value driver development (columns "Chg. of ratio" of Table 6.2), the y-axis depicts the resulting value contribution (columns "Value contribution of sales" of Table 6.2). The regression coefficient for the correlation between COGS change and value contribution from COGS is −0.948, the regression coefficient for the correlation between working capital change and value contribution is −0.999.

As a first finding it can be stated that overall developments of SCM-related value drivers are strongly linked to company value. Although in general this correlation is expected, exceptional cases can be observed and analyzed on company level. AVO and KAO both lost value from COGS (−1.0 % and −0.4 % respectively, see Table 6.2), although both companies achieved offverall reductions of COGS (−1.1 pp and −0.2 pp respectively, see Table 6.2). An analysis of the developments

---

[3]Overall development in this context is defined as the change of the figure of 2008 compared to the figure of 2003.

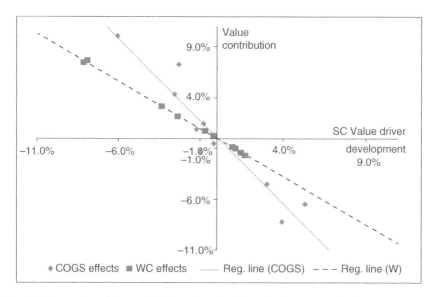

Fig. 6.1 Scatter plot with regression lines for value driver developments and value contributions

Table 6.3 Developments of COGS and resulting value contributions at AVO and KAO

Company	Metric	UOM	2003	2004	2005	2006	2007	2008
AVO	COGS ratio	%	38.0	37.6	38.5	39.2	39.7	36.9
	VA_p^{COGS}	m €	0	14	−15	−39	−54	35
	VA^{COGS}	m €	0	13	0	−31	−72	−48
KAO	COGS ratio	%	42.3	41.9	43.2	44.0	40.9	42.0
	VA_p^{COGS}	m €	0	16	−39	−72	56	9
	VA^{COGS}	m €	0	15	−20	−84	−36	−29

of the COGS ratios and the resulting value contributions, which are depicted in Table 6.3 for both companies, helps to explain this observation.

AVO achieved slight reductions of COGS in 2004 which resulted in initial value creation. In the periods 2005–2007, the COGS ratio developed continuously deteriorating above the initial level of 2003. In both cases this resulted in value loss, the initial value creation from 2004 was already fully compensated in 2005. The additional losses in the subsequent periods 2006 and 2007 were not compensated by the late and comparably slight value creating improvement of COGS ratio in 2008.

KAO achieved an initial value creation from a slight decrease of COGS ratio in 2004. In the subsequent periods 2005 and 2006, the COGS ratio deteriorated considerably and developed above the initial level from 2003. The results were losses of value in both periods 2005 and 2006, which were not fully compensated by later improvements. In 2007 and 2008, the overall value contribution VA^{COGS} was still negative although the value impacts VA_p^{COGS} in these periods were positive.

A second finding is that the development of a value driver in the intermediate periods has an impact on the overall value creation.

Another observation is that all companies of the benchmarking group achieved overall reductions of at least one value driver (see columns "Chg. of ratio" in Table 6.2), but not all companies achieved overall value contributions from these developments (see columns "Total effects" in Table 6.2). An analysis of the overall changes and resulting value impacts of both value drivers for each company helps to explain this observation.

BDF and CPA created value from both value drivers. ELA, PRG and RCU managed to overcompensate value losses resulting from working capital by positive value impacts from COGS. At AVO and HEN, the positive value impacts from working capital improvement outranged value losses resulting from COGS. KAO lost value from both value drivers, COGS and working capital. At KMB and UNI, the value losses resulting from COGS exceeded the value gains obtained by working capital developments.

As a third finding it can be stated that the combined value impacts resulting from developments of both value drivers have to be taken into account.

A first answer to the research questions can be concluded from these observations and analyses: Value contributions from COGS and working capital can be substantiated empirically by the overall developments of these value drivers. The developments of the value drivers in the intermediate periods of the considered time horizon have to be taken into account as well as the combined value impacts stemming from both value drivers.

6.4.2.2 Relevance of Timing and Continuity for Value Contribution

Analyzing the value driver developments and resulting value contributions in greater detail will illustrate the relevance of timing and continuity of value driver developments for value creation. Four examples will provide empirical support for the following two hypotheses:

1. Continuous improvements and long lasting developments of value drivers foster value creation: Alternating improvements and deteriorations in value driver developments do not guarantee overall value achievements.
2. Timing aspects have to be considered: Improvements of value drivers achieved in later phases do not guarantee to fully compensate deteriorations from earlier phases.

Example 1 focuses on effects from working capital development at HEN and BDF and illustrates the relevance of both timing and continuity of value driver developments. It can be observed (see Table 6.2) that HEN created more value (+7.7 % of sales) from working capital development than BDF (+7.4 % of sales) despite the fact that the overall reduction of working capital ratio at BDF (−8.2 pp) was stronger than at HEN (−7.9 pp). An analysis of the developments of the working

Table 6.4 Developments of working capital and resulting value contributions at BDF and HEN

Company	Metric	UOM	2003	2004	2005	2006	2007	2008
BDF	Working capital ratio	%	22.3	20.2	18.8	15.4	16.2	14.0
	VA_p^W	m €	0	90	63	162	−39	119
	VA^W	m €	0	85	140	274	244	330
HEN	Working capital ratio	%	19.6	17.4	14.1	13.3	11.5	11.7
	VA_p^W	m €	0	206	342	96	237	−28
	VA^W	m €	0	191	487	565	742	723

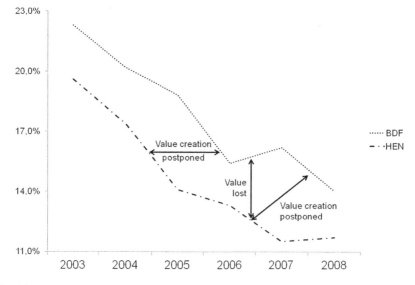

Fig. 6.2 Development of working capital ratios at BDF and HEN

capital ratio and the resulting value contributions (see Table 6.4) identifies two
explanatory reasons.

- HEN realized a more stable value creation by continuously reducing its working
  capital ratio with only one minor exception (by +0.2 pp increase from 11.5 % in
  2007 to 11.7 % in 2008). BDF on the contrary faced a considerable intermediate
  increase in working capital ratio (by +0.8 pp from 15.4 % in 2006 to 16.2 % in
  2007), by which more value was lost at an earlier point of time.
- HEN created value faster than BDF, because HEN achieved reductions of
  comparable magnitude one period earlier (by −3.3 pp from 17.4 % in 2004 to
  14.1 % in 2005 and by −1.8 pp from 13.3 % in 2006 to 11.5 % in 2007) than
  BDF (by −3.4 pp from 18.8 % in 2005 to 15.4 % in 2006 and by −2.2 pp from
  16.2 % in 2007 to 14.0 % in 2008).

These observations indicate the relevance of continuous and long lasting working
capital developments and the importance of timing aspects for value creation. This
finding is illustrated graphically in Fig. 6.2.

Table 6.5 Developments of COGS and resulting value contributions at AVO and ELA

Company	Metric	UOM	2003	2004	2005	2006	2007	2008
AVO	COGS ratio	%	38.0	37.6	38.5	39.2	39.7	36.9
	VA_p^{COGS}	m €	0	14	−15	−39	−54	35
	VA^{COGS}	m €	0	13	0	−31	−72	−48
ELA	COGS ratio	%	26.1	25.5	25.5	26.1	25.2	5.2
	VA_p^{COGS}	m €	0	14	14	0	21	21
	VA^{COGS}	m €	0	13	25	25	41	55

Taking into account that developments of COGS create recurring impacts on company value, the relevance of timing and continuity occur more clearly in the following examples which focus COGS.

In example 2, effects from COGS developments at AVO and ELA are compared to illustrate the relevance of continuous value driver developments. It can be observed (see Table 6.2) that the reductions of COGS ratio achieved at AVO (−1.1 pp) and ELA (−0.9 pp) are of the same magnitude. Nevertheless, ELA turned this achievement into value (+1.5 % of sales) while at AVO value was lost (−1.0 % of sales).

An analysis of the developments of the COGS ratios and the resulting value contributions shows two reasons for this observation (see Table 6.5).

- ELA achieved a more continuous reduction of its COGS ratio compared to AVO. At ELA, the initial COGS ratio of 26.1 % in 2003 was never exceeded in the subsequent periods. Hence, in no period a negative value impact occurred. Opposed to this at AVO, the COGS ratio was significantly higher in the periods 2005–2007 than initially in 2003. This resulted in value losses at AVO which could not be overcompensated by slight achievements in 2004 and 2008.
- Although ELA did not achieve further reductions of COGS ratio in 2005 and 2008, the COGS development resulted in positive value impacts in each period. The reason for this effect is the circumstance that COGS reductions create recurring value impacts. Improvements of the COGS ratio in 2004 (−0.6 pp) and 2007 (−0.9 pp) resulted in value creation in the respective period and furthermore in the subsequent period (+14 m EUR in 2004 and 2005, +21 m EUR in 2007 and 2008).

The observations of this example illustrate the relevance of continuous and long lasting COGS developments for value creation and the impacts of recurring value effects stemming from COGS improvements.

In example 3, the relevance of timing effects is illustrated by comparing value creating COGS developments at BDF and PRG. It can be observed (see Table 6.2) that PRG created more value from COGS (+7.3 % of sales) than BDF (+4.3 % of sales), although the overall improvement of the COGS ratio at BDF (−2.6 pp) was higher than at PRG (−2.3 pp).

An analysis of the developments of the COGS ratios and the resulting value contributions helps to explain this observation (see Table 6.6). Both companies

Table 6.6 Developments of COGS and resulting value contributions at BDF and PRG

Company	Metric	UOM	2003	2004	2005	2006	2007	2008
BDF	COGS ratio	%	35.7	35.5	34.7	33.9	33.2	33.1
	VA_p^{COGS}	m €	0	7	30	54	75	77
	VA^{COGS}	m €	0	7	33	78	136	192
PRG	COGS ratio	%	51.0	48.8	49.0	48.6	48.0	48.7
	VA_p^{COGS}	m €	0	528	476	580	716	538
	VA^{COGS}	m €	0	490	900	1.364	1.896	2.267

Table 6.7 Developments of COGS and resulting value contributions at HEN and KMB

Company	Metric	UOM	2003	2004	2005	2006	2007	2008
HEN	COGS ratio	%	52.6	53.0	54.6	54.7	53.6	58.0
	VA_p^{COGS}	m €	0	−29	−144	−151	−76	−395
	VA^{COGS}	m €	0	−27	−151	−272	−329	−603
KMB	COGS ratio	%	65.8	66.4	68.1	69.7	68.8	69.8
	VA_p^{COGS}	m €	0	−44	−180	−307	−236	−321
	VA^{COGS}	m €	0	−41	−196	−442	−617	−838

show continuous improvements of the COGS, because in the periods 2004–2008 the COGS ratio never exceeds the initial level from 2003. But in the early periods 2004–2007, PRG achieved higher and earlier reductions of COGS ratio than BDF.

This example indicates the relevance of timing for value creation from COGS developments.

In example 4, the relevance of timing effects is illustrated by comparing value destroying COGS developments at HEN and KMB. It can be observed (see Table 6.2) that KMB lost more value from COGS (−8.2 % of sales) than HEN (−6.4 % of sales), although the overall deterioration of the COGS ratio at HEN (+5.3 pp) was higher than at KMB (+4.0 pp).

An analysis of the developments of the COGS ratios and the resulting value contributions helps to explain this observation (see Table 6.7). Both companies show continuous COGS deteriorations, because in the periods 2004–2008 the COGS ratio continuously developed above the initial level from 2003. Hence both companies lost value from COGS in each period. In the early periods 2004–2007 however, KMB faced stronger and earlier deteriorations of COGS ratio than HEN. Therefore, the value loss at KMB was higher than at HEN.

This example indicates the relevance of timing for value creation from COGS developments.

As a second answer to the research questions, the observations from these four company examples indicate the relevance of continuous and long lasting value drives developments and the importance of timing aspects for value creation. Although the relevance of these criteria can be seen for working capital developments, these effects occur more strongly for COGS developments.

Table 6.8 Value contributions from working capital components in the FMCG industry

Company	Sales 2003 m €	Trade receivables			Inventory			Trade payables		
		Chg. of ratio (pp)	Value contr. m €	of sales (%)	Chg. of ratio (pp)	Value contr. m €	of sales (%)	Chg. of ratio (pp)	Value contr. m €	of sales (%)
AVO	4,920	−2.3	111	2.3	−0.1	6	0.1	1.0	41	0.8
BDF	4,435	0.3	−12	−0.3	−3.6	145	3.3	4.9	197	4.4
CPA	7,085	−2.0	132	1.9	0.6	−35	−0.5	−0.7	−46	−0.7
ELA	3,661	0.7	−27	−0.7	0.8	−28	−0.8	0.1	2	0.1
HEN	9,436	−3.7	344	3.6	−0.7	64	0.7	3.5	315	3.3
KAO	6,845	1.0	−48	−0.7	1.3	−94	−1.4	1.4	81	1.2
KMB	10,265	−0.8	72	0.7	1.9	−175	−1.7	1.3	124	1.2
PRG	31,035	1.1	−307	−1.0	1.7	−589	−1.9	1.7	567	1.8
RCU	3,868	1.5	−54	−1.4	2.4	−92	−2.4	2.3	82	2.1
UNI	42,693	−1.3	431	1.0	−0.2	64	0.2	0.9	348	0.8
Avg.	12,424	−0.5	64	0.5	0.4	−73	−0.4	1.6	171	1.5

6.4.2.3 Working Capital Components

For a detailed analysis and discussion of value contributions from working capital, its components inventory, trade receivables and trade payables are compared (see Table 6.8, structure identical to Table 6.2).

It can be observed that no company deteriorated all of the working capital components. HEN, UNI and AVO improved all working capital components, but with a focus on monetary value drivers, trade payables and trade receivables. Nearly all companies, except CPA showing only slight deteriorations, improved trade payables in a value adding way (see columns "Trade payables" of Table 6.8). In nearly all cases, only companies belonging to top five sales firms[4] optimized their trade receivables, the only exceptions are PRG with deteriorations of this working capital component and AVO, which as a comparably small company achieved value-adding improvements (see columns "Trade receivables" of Table 6.8). BDF is the only company which significantly created value from inventory optimization, furthermore slight inventory achievements were realized at HEN, UNI and AVO (see columns "Inventory" of Table 6.8).

On average of all benchmarking companies (see row "Avg." of Table 6.8), improvements were achieved at trade payables (+1.6 pp improvement, +1.5 % value contribution) and trade receivables (−0.5 pp improvement, +0.5 % value contribution), while the inventory performance has deteriorated (+0.4 pp deterioration, −0.4 % value loss).

To gain further insight how FMCG companies focused working capital optimization over time, the developments of working capital components within the FMCG company group are analyzed in the considered horizon. Table 6.9 depicts

---

[4]The top five sales firms are CPA, HEN, KMB, PRG, UNI (see column "Sales 2003" of Table 6.8).

Table 6.9 Value contributions from working capital components in the FMCG industry

Metric	UOM	2003	2004	2005	2006	2007	2008
DSO	d	36	36	36	37	36	34
DSI	d	70	70	71	72	73	75
DPO	d	56	61	61	64	64	65
C2C	d	50	45	46	45	45	44

these developments of DSO, DSI and DPO, measured in days (d), and furthermore the aggregated metric of C2C cycle measured in d expressing the working capital performance.

The developments of these metrics show that the performance of trade receivables remained nearly constant across the considered horizon, while trade payables were continuously improved and the inventory performance deteriorated.

These observations can be summarized in three points:

- No company completely ignores the relevance of working capital, which has been continuously improved in FMCG industry.
- Monetary components trade payables and trade receivables are focused in working capital optimization, while the inventory performance is not considered a priority issue.
- Improvements of trade payables seem to be achievable comparably easy, while value contributions from trade receivables are realizable mainly for very large companies.

These findings provide further answers to the research questions of this chapter. The observations indicate the importance of working capital as a considerable value contributor and an important criterion of SC performance. In FMCG industry, trade payables seem to be quite easily improvable in a value-adding way, which can be explained by considering the comparably strong position of a customer in the SC. For FMCG manufacturers, the optimization of trade receivables is simplified for companies of a considerable sales volume or applying a specific business model, e.g. AVO which avoids distribution channels comprising strong retailers by distributing products to final consumers via sales representatives only. During the last 5 years, the inventory performance has moved out of focus in the FMCG industry.

6.4.2.4 Time Dependent WACC

In this benchmarking study a simplifying assumption is made by keeping WACC of each company constant over time, although WACC components (e.g. book value of dept or market capitalization) of a company and hence WACC itself can change over time. Consequently in a mathematically precise approach, WACC of each company would have to be calculated for every single period of the considered time horizon. Between 2003 and 2008 WACC components of the considered companies did not change to such an extent that it would significantly change the findings of

Table 6.10 Impacts of $WACC$ variance (± 1.0 pp) on value contributions VA^{COGS} and VA^{W}

| | VA^{COGS} (% of sales) | | | VA^{W} (% of sales) | |
| | (i) $WACC -1$ pp | (ii) $WACC +1$ pp | | (i) $WACC -1$ pp | (ii) $WACC +1$ pp |
Company (%)		(%)	Company (%)		(%)
RCU	10.5	9.9	HEN	7.8	7.5
PRG	7.5	7.1	BDF	7.6	7.3
BDF	4.5	4.2	AVO	3.3	3.1
ELA	1.6	1.5	UNI	2.0	1.9
CPA	0.8	0.8	CPA	0.8	0.7
KAO	−0.4	−0.4	KMB	0.2	0.2
AVO	−1.0	−0.9	KAO	−0.9	−0.9
UNI	−4.5	−4.2	PRG	−1.1	−1.0
HEN	−6.6	−6.2	ELA	−1.5	−1.4
KMB	−8.4	−7.9	RCU	−1.8	−1.6

the benchmarking study. Thus the aspect of time-dependent WACC is neglected to keep the balance between simplicity and precision.

An empirical sensitivity analysis indicates the feasibility of this simplification. WACC figures published by companies of the benchmarking group indicate a comparable stable WACC development in the considered horizon, e.g. HEN published the WACC figures ranging from 7.0 to 8.0 % in the annual reports 2003–2008. Thus assuming a variance of ± 1.0 pp for the WACC figures of the considered companies is a realistic magnitude. Calculating the value contribution for each company and each value driver based on (i) WACC figures reduced by 1.0 pp and (ii) WACC figures increased by 1.0 pp shows that such variance affects the value contributions of each value driver only to a negligible extent (see Table 6.10).

This approach is explained at the example of RCU.[5] Assuming $WACC$ of 6.66 % respectively 8.66 % would result in value contributions VA^{COGS} of 10.5 % respectively 9.9 % (in % of sales).

This sensitivity analysis helps answering the research questions of this chapter by providing empirical support that value impacts of time-dependent $WACC$ changes are negligible.

6.5   Summary and Discussion

Summarizing the findings of the benchmarking study from the FMCG industry, the research questions of this chapter can be answered as follows:

RQ1:   Can empirical evidence be found that overall developments of SCM-related value drivers, in particular cost and working capital, have an impact on company value?

---

[5]RCU has a $WACC$ of 7.66 %.

Answer: Value contributions from COGS and working capital can be substantiated
      empirically by the overall developments of these value drivers under
      consideration of the developments of the value drivers in the intermediate periods
      of the time horizon and the combined value impacts of both value drivers.
RQ2:   What decisive criteria for value creation from these drivers can be identified
      empirically?
Answer: This benchmarking study indicates the relevance of continuous and long
      lasting working capital developments and the importance of timing aspects for
      value creation. Working capital can be seen as a considerable value contrib-
      utor for FMCG manufacturers, which focused value creating optimization of
      monetary working capital components, especially trade payables. Value impacts
      arising from WACC changes over time were negligible.

The following brief discussion, which is based on the literature reviewed in
Sect. 6.2, will point out the positioning of this benchmarking study to existing
research on value-based SCM.

The link between SCM and shareholder value is often highlighted in SCM
literature (e.g. Lambert and Burduroglu 2000). Christopher and Ryals (1999) point
out the relevance of working capital requirements and the potential for operating
cost reductions. While benchmarking on value-based SCM is rather rare so far, this
chapter provides empirical insights on how SCM influences the company value. In
contrast to other empirical evaluations (e.g. Farris II and Hutchison 2003; Losbichler
and Rothböck 2006), this benchmarking study applies a combined analysis of
the profit-related value driver COGS and the capital-related value driver working
capital. Furthermore this chapter provides an empirical analysis of value impacts of
these SC-related value drivers.

According to Lambert and Pohlen (2001) many SC metrics fail to identify where
opportunities exist to increase shareholder value. An appropriate approach to cover
this need is the benchmarking method applied here. Furthermore it is illustrated
in this chapter how a model (Brandenburg and Seuring 2010b) can be applied on
secondary data in order to determine and compare value contributions arising from
SCM. This is in line with various methods of measuring value impacts of SCM in
order to show customers and top management the value which is being created by
SCM (Lambert and Burduroglu 2000).

The relevance of working capital for business efficiency and enterprise value as
stated by Walters (2006) is fostered by empirical evidence shown in this chapter. The
observation that manufacturing companies tend to optimize their working capital
at their suppliers' expense by increasing trade payables (Losbichler and Rothböck
2006) is reinforced for the FMCG industry by this benchmarking study. The findings
of Farris II and Hutchison (2002) that inventory reduction has priority in working
capital optimization is not fostered by the evaluation presented in this chapter, which
identifies that FMCG industry did not seem to consider inventory performance as
a priority topic. In line with other research papers (e.g. Obermaier and Donhauser
2009), this benchmarking study provides empirical support for the argument that

the performance of working capital or its components is linked to the financial performance of a firm.

Further indication from empirical analysis is provided by this chapter to support the finding of Brandenburg and Seuring (2010b) regarding the relevance of timing continuity and aspects of value driver developments as decisive criteria for value creation.

6.6 Conclusion

The benchmarking study presented in this chapter gives empirical evidence of the value impacts of developments of the value drivers COGS and working capital. Continuity and timing aspects of value driver developments are identified as important criteria for value creation, while effects of time-dependent WACC turned out to be negligible. It is shown that, although with different focus, all considered companies from FMCG industry improved SCM regarding overall cost or capital performance, but not all companies created value from these improvements. Especially the relevance of the working capital performance is identified empirically with its monetary components being in focus of the FMCG industry, while nearly all considered companies neglect the inventory performance. It is observed that trade payables optimization has been achieved by most companies while improvements of trade receivables seem to require a certain company size or a special business model.

Research in this benchmarking study was limited by availability and comparability of data from annual reports. Structural changes, such as acquisitions or divestments, could be reflected regarding their value impacts only to a limited extent. Furthermore conflictive effects of SC optimization on cost and capital performance, e.g. improvements of working capital resulting in cost increases, could not be evaluated thoroughly in this benchmarking study. An evaluation of conflicts, e.g. between sales growth and trade receivables optimization, cost-effective cash discounts and trade payables improvement or decreasing cost of production or warehousing and inventory performance, would require company-internal data.

Complementary analysis of value-based SCM in FMCG industry as well as cross-industrial benchmarking offers further research potential. A benchmarking of COGS components or other SC cost categories as well as a causal analysis on conflictive effects from cost and capital optimization would create further insights on value creation from SCM. Further empirical analyses would enrich research on value-based SCM. These comprise evaluations of other value drivers, e.g. fixed assets or non-financial SC performance issues, or cross-industrial benchmarking to identify trends specific for or independent from certain industries. Beyond this, extending the benchmarking group by suppliers, service providers, retailers and distributors of the considered companies would help evaluate if value was created in a co-operative or competitive way in SC networks from FMCG industry.

Chapter 7
Value-Based Strategic Supply Chain Planning

Abstract This chapter deals with the question how value-based aspects could be reflected in strategic supply chain (SC) planning, in particular how to determine strategic targets for SC value drivers in a long-term horizon of several years from which a framework for tactical and operational SC planning and control can be obtained. It describes an approach to value-based strategic SC planning, in which long-term targets for company value are disaggregated to annual targets for SC cost and working capital under explicit consideration of planned future sales development. A top down determination of annual targets for SC cost and working capital is combined with a bottom up validation to form a closed planning and control cycle. The planning method, which is derived from a discounted cash flow based model for quantifying value impacts from SC cost and working capital, is discussed thoroughly and illustrated by a numerical example. Aspects of integrating this approach with financial planning and tactical SC planning are outlined.[1]

7.1 Introduction

Supply chain management (SCM), i.e. the "integration of business processes from end users to original suppliers that provides products, services and information that add value to customers" (Cooper et al. 1997, p. 2), has turned out to be a competitive advantage for companies from different industries (Handfield and Nichols 1999; Mentzer et al. 2001) and hence gained significant relevance in

---

[1] This chapter has been previously published as a paper (Brandenburg M, Seuring S (2010) Value-based strategic supply chain planning. In: Kersten W, Blecker T, Lüthje C (eds) Pioneering solutions in supply chain management – a comprehensive insight into current management approaches. Operations and technology management, vol 14. Erich Schmidt, Berlin, pp 185–196) and is reprinted in this dissertation by courtesy of © Erich Schmidt Verlag GmbH & Co. KG, Berlin 2010. The content of this chapter has been presented at the Hamburg International Conference on Logistics HICL 2010 held in Hamburg, Germany, September 2–3, 2010.

M. Brandenburg, *Quantitative Models for Value-Based Supply Chain Management*, 109
Lecture Notes in Economics and Mathematical Systems 660,
DOI 10.1007/978-3-642-31304-2__7, © Springer-Verlag Berlin Heidelberg 2013

industrial practice (Lummus and Vokurka 1999). SCM is identified as a good lever to increase profitability and capital efficiency, and therefore has a direct link to and a strong impact on shareholder value (Christopher and Ryals 1999). Due to these circumstances, supply chain (SC) cost and working capital, two main drivers of company value, are of particular interest for academic research and managerial practice (Schilling 1996, papers in Seuring and Goldbach 2001).

For the last decades tremendous progress in information technology (IT) facilitated the development of advanced planning systems (APS) and increased the relevance of SC planning (Günther and Meyr 2009; Stadtler and Kilger 2008), which focuses on flows of information and material in sourcing, production and distribution on strategic, tactical and operational levels (Fleischmann et al. 2008). Thus SC planning is realized mainly in a volume-based way, although the consideration of financial flows in tactical and operational SC planning (Comelli et al. 2008; Hahn and Kuhn 2011; Kannegiesser et al. 2009) or on functional level (Walters 1999) has increased. Nevertheless the aspects of value creation and contribution are still underemphasized, and especially the need of value-based methods for strategic SC planning still exists. The circumstance that pure financial planning models neglect changes in cost or capital ratios and hence are considered too simple strengthens this need (Ross et al. 2002).

This chapter helps to fill this gap by proposing a value-based strategic SC planning concept for a long-term horizon of several years. This planning approach, which comprises a top-down planning step and a bottom-up validation step, can be applied to determine targets for SC value drivers SC cost and working capital which in turn can act as strategic framework for other business planning processes.

The remainder of this chapter is structured as follows. The next Sect. 7.2 covers a literature review followed by a description of the research methodology and the applied conceptual elements in Sect. 7.3. The subsequent Sect. 7.4 comprises the introduction and illustration of the strategic SC planning approach as well as an outline of the integration with other financial and SC planning processes. The article concludes with findings, limitations and future prospects for further research in Sect. 7.5.

7.2   Literature Review

7.2.1   Value-Based Supply Chain Management

A review on selected literature depicted in Table 7.1 shows that question of value-based SCM has been of considerable interest for academic research for the last 10 years and indicates the heterogeneity of approaches to this topic. Value-based SCM concepts vary from functional or company specific perspective to network considerations. Core concepts and identified drivers for value-based SCM, which is most often linked to shareholder value and economic value added (EVA),

Table 7.1 Value-based SCM in selected research papers

Paper	SCM approach	VBM approach	Concept, value driver	Empirical aspect
Christopher and Ryals (1999)	Processes and interfaces in company network	Shareholder value, mainly EVA	SCM affects revenue, cost, fixed and working capital	Twelve observations from industry or consulting
Lambert and Burduroglu (2000)	Functional (logistics)	Shareholder value and other approaches	Logistics impact on revenue, cost and capital	None
Lambert and Pohlen (2001)	Eight cross-company processes	Shareholder value, EVA	Processes mapped to shareholder value	None
Hendricks and Singhal (2003, 2005a)	Company-internal SC	Market value of a firm (stock price)	Impacts of production or delivery delays on stock price	519 respectively 827 observations from industry
Sridharan et al. (2005)	Functional (IT for SCM)	Market value of a firm (stock price)	Impact of SCM-IT implementation on stock price	Three company case studies
Losbichler and Rothböck (2006)	Company-internal SC	Shareholder value, EVA	Value-based SC controlling framework	Working capital performance of 6,925 firms
Hofmann and Locker (2009)	Inter-organizational management of flows of goods and information	Shareholder value, EVA	SCM processses linked to EVA categories via key performance indicators (KPI)	Case study from packaging industry
Brandenburg and Seuring (2010a,b)	Company-internal supply chain	Shareholder value, DCF	Value impacts of SC cost and working capital	(a) Illustrative example and (b) bench-marking of FMCG companies

range from single functions, operational SC activities and processes to SC strategy. Empirical aspects are reflected differently. Some rather theoretical papers give few references to industrial examples, some papers comprise case studies from one or few companies, some papers evaluate several hundreds of observations extensively.

Although it is taken for granted that SCM influences the cash flow and hence the shareholder value of a company (Christopher and Ryals 1999), little evidence exists that effective SCM is linked to shareholder value creation (Hendricks and Singhal 2003). Further research potential addresses the need of cost effective ways to measure shareholder value impacts (Lambert and Burduroglu 2000) and improvements regarding data used for evaluation (Hofmann and Locker 2009). To help to fill this gap, Brandenburg and Seuring (2010b) apply a model based on the discounted cash flow (DCF) method to quantify value impacts of changes of working capital and SC cost. Based on this model, Brandenburg and Seuring (2010a) benchmark ten firms from the fast moving consumer goods (FMCG) industry regarding the value contributions they achieved from SC cost and working capital. A brief introduction of this model, which is the basis for the planning concept presented in this chapter, can be found in the next Sect. 7.3.

7.2.2 Supply Chain Planning

The number of publications on SC planning is tremendous, hence rather than attempting to review the existing literature on this research area a reference is given to selected papers and books comprising various articles on different concepts, aspects and applications of SC planning and APS.

Stadtler (2005) gives a survey on the manifold aspects of SC planning which comprise all SC functions and processes on strategic, tactical and operational level. Günther (2005) provides a tutorial on the link between SCM, SC planning and APS, which has been fostered strongly by the tremendous improvements in IT. Papers in Günther and Meyr (2009) focus on the application of quantitative methods to SC planning, especially to demand management and inventory management or in different industries. Papers in Stadtler and Kilger (2008) cover SC planning approaches – ranging from strategic network design and demand planning to production scheduling and distribution planning – as well as implementations and applications of APS. Papers in Günther et al. (2005) address the potentials and synergies of applying quantitative methods in SCM and logistics, especially in the areas of SC planning, production logistics or logistics and traffic. Papers in Günther and van Beek (2003) comprise methodology and industrial application of advanced planning and scheduling solutions in the process industry.

The strong link between SC planning issues and SC performance is described by Lockamy and McCormack (2004) in an exploratory study based on the framework of the supply chain operations reference (SCOR) model (Supply-Chain Council 2006). Despite such evidence for the high relevance of SC planning to a company's performance, most publications on SC planning limit their focus on volume-based aspects, and corporate financial decisions remain largely qualitative (Shapiro 2007). Recent papers show increasing interest in incorporating value-based aspects in SC planning. Walters (1999) develops a framework for shareholder value planning which comprises strategic and operational value drivers and points out its implications to logistics decisions. The global evaluation approach in a company supply chain proposed by Comelli et al. (2008) considers the combined financial and physical flows in tactical production planning. An integrated planning model for chemical commodities introduced by Kannegiesser et al. (2009) is used to optimize the profitability by coordination of sales and supply decisions based on volume and value aspects. Hahn and Kuhn (2011) present a robust optimization method for value-based performance and risk optimization in supply chains. In another paper, Hahn and Kuhn (2010) develop and test a mathematical optimization model for value-based supply chain planning.

7.3 Research Methodology and Conceptual Elements

In this chapter, approaches for value-based strategic SC planning and its integration with financial planning and SC planning are proposed. These planning and integration approaches are designed by combining conceptual elements of a quantitative model for value-based SCM with existing concepts for financial planning and SC planning in a theorizing desk research method (Halldorsson and Arlbjørn 2005).

The proposed value-based strategic SC planning concept is derived from a DCF-based model to quantify value contributions from SC cost and working capital (Brandenburg and Seuring 2010b). The planning approach is illustrated by an explanatory example of a fictitious company introduced by Ross et al. (2002). Aspects of integration with other planning processes are based on a company model described by Shapiro (2007) and apply corporate financial planning concepts introduced by Ross et al. (2002) and SC planning concepts designed by Shapiro (2007). The conceptual elements, the quantitative model and the processes of SC planning and corporate financial planning are briefly introduced.

7.3.1 The Quantitative Model

The value contributions that arise from future changes of SC cost or working capital, defined as the sum of inventories and trade receivables reduced by trade payables, are quantified by a model based on the DCF method. With reference to an in-depth explanation (Brandenburg and Seuring 2010b) the introduction of this model is kept short. The value contribution VA_p^W arising from working capital development in a time period p is defined by the difference of working capital W_{p-1} at the beginning of period p and working capital W_p at the end of period p adjusted for sales development $\frac{S_{p-1}}{S_p}$ in period p:

$$VA_p^W = W_{p-1} - \frac{S_{p-1}}{S_p} \cdot W_p . \tag{7.1}$$

The value contribution VA_p^C arising from changes of SC cost in a period p is defined by the difference of SC cost C_0 of period 0 and SC cost C_p of period p adjusted for sales development $\frac{S_0}{S_p}$ and tax rate T_p:

$$VA_p^C = (C_0 - \frac{S_0}{S_p} \cdot C_p) \cdot (1 - T_p) . \tag{7.2}$$

To calculate the value contribution VA^W or VA^C generated by the respective value drivers over a time horizon of periods $p = 1, \ldots, P$, the value contributions VA_p^W or VA_p^C of each period p are discounted by weighted average cost of capital $WACC_p$ and the resulting terms $VA_p^W \cdot (1 + WACC_p)^{-p}$ or $VA_p^C \cdot (1 + WACC_p)^{-p}$ are summed up. Elaborated literature (e.g. Hawawini and Viallet 2002; Ross et al. 2002) provides an in-depth introduction of the $WACC$ concept, which is explained here only in brief. The calculation formula for $WACC$ comprises ratios of debt D and equity E, cost of debt k_D, cost of equity k_E and tax rate T:

$$WACC = k_D \cdot \frac{D}{D + E} \cdot (1 - T) + k_E \cdot \frac{E}{D + E} . \qquad (7.3)$$

The market value of equity E is defined as market capitalization and the market value of dept D is derived from the respective book values. The cost of debt k_D are calculated by adding an estimated credit risk spread to the market yield on government securities. The cost of equity k_E is determined by the capital asset pricing model (CAPM), which defines the cost of equity as the sum of a government bond rate and a market risk premium weighted by the company's equity beta (see e.g. Hawawini and Viallet 2002).

7.3.2 Supply Chain Planning and Financial Planning

The integration between SC planning and financial planning is required, especially because the perception of the relevance of SCM for financial performance is limited and strategic SC analysis is not sufficient to constitute strategic analysis of the company as a whole (Shapiro 2007). The basis for the integration approach proposed in this chapter is a company model comprising the organizational structure of owners, managers and services, a production process to generate goods and a financial process to provide financing and revenue distribution (Shapiro 2007).

For the financial process, Ross et al. (2002) outlines long-term financial planning on strategic level and short-term financial planning on tactical level. In long-term financial planning, capital budgeting, dividend policy and capital structure are fixed over a horizon of 2–5 years to maximize shareholder value. Further planning components include sales forecast, pro forma balance sheets and pro forma profit and loss (P&L) statements or economic assumptions. Constraints arise from the simplifying assumption of assets and profitability developing proportionate to sales. Short-term financial planning arranges operational financial parameters such as cash, material orders or customer credits to optimize the cash cycle consisting of inventory, trade receivables and trade payables. For the SC process, Shapiro (2007) distinguishes between strategic SC planning to identify and evaluate resource acquisition options over a horizon of 3–10 years and tactical SC planning to optimize resources adjustment and allocation to satisfy demands over a horizon of less than 1 year.

7.4   Value-Based Strategic Supply Chain Planning

The purpose of this proposed value-based strategic SC planning process is to determine target values for SC cost and working capital for each period of a multi-period planning horizon. The plan is based on an initial situation of a company at the beginning of the planning horizon, e.g. current financial situation given by P&L statement and balance sheet, and targets for sales developments and value contributions over the whole planning horizon. In a top-down planning step, targets for each SC value driver – SC cost and working capital – in each period of the considered planning horizon are determined arithmetically by applying rearranged formulas of the quantitative model. The resulting initial value-based strategic SC plan is validated in a bottom-up planning step by SC optimization projects which are selected from an SC project portfolio. Their estimated financial impacts are quantified by the quantitative model.

7.4.1   Initial Top-Down Planning

The basis for the strategic SC plan is given by an initial situation of a company at the beginning of the planning horizon. The defining business parameters of this initial situation comprise sales, SC cost, working capital, tax rate and WACC. Strategic SC plans are generated in a top-down approach consisting of three steps:

1. Planning of overall value creation and definition of ratios to disaggregate this overall value target to each period of the planning horizon and each SC value driver.
2. Planning of sales development within the considered planning horizon.
3. Determination of targets for each SC value driver in each planning period by applying rearranged calculation formulas of the quantitative model.

The expected overall value creation va^{Total} and disaggregation ratios α^W, α^C and α_p for $p = 1, \ldots, P$ (step 1) and the targeted sales development S_p in periods $p = 1, \ldots, P$ of the planning horizon (step 2) result from long-term financial planning. The interface to the financial process will be outlined in the third part of this section.

Based on these planning results, the target value contributions va_p^W and va_p^C for each period p arising from working capital and SC cost can be calculated:

$$va_p^W = va^{Total} \cdot \alpha^W \cdot \alpha_p \cdot (1 + WACC_p)^p . \tag{7.4}$$

$$va_p^C = va^{Total} \cdot \alpha^C \cdot \alpha_p \cdot (1 + WACC_p)^p . \tag{7.5}$$

By substituting VA_p^W and VA_p^C respectively by $va^{Total} \cdot \alpha^W \cdot \alpha_p$ and $va^{Total} \cdot \alpha^C \cdot \alpha_p$ respectively these formulas are derived from the terms $VA_p^W \cdot (1 + WACC_p)^{-p}$ and

Table 7.2 Parameters and expectations of Hoffmann Corporation

Parameters 2010			Expectations for planning periods 2011–2015		
Net sales	US$	10,000	Annual sales growth target (CAGR)	%	20.0
C_{2010}	US$	7,000	va^{Total}	US$	2,000
W_{2010}	US$	5,000	α^C	%	75.0
T	%	34.0	α^W	%	25.0
$WACC$	%	10.0	α_{2011}	%	10.0
			α_{2013}	%	30.0
			$\alpha_{2012}, \alpha_{2014}, \alpha_{2015}$	%	20.0

Table 7.3 Initial strategic SC plan for Hoffmann Corporation (top-down approach)

P	UOM	2010	2011	2012	2013	2014	2015
S_p	US$	10,000	12,000	14,400	17,280	20,736	24,883
va^{Total}	US$	–	200	600	1,200	1,600	2,000
va^C	US$	–	150	450	900	1,200	1,500
va^C_p	US$	–	165	363	599	439	483
c_p	US$	7,000	8,100	9,288	10,528	13,135	15,597
va^W	US$	–	50	150	300	400	500
va^W_p	US$	–	55	121	200	146	161
w_p	US$	5,000	5,934	6,976	8,131	9,582	11,305

$VA^C_p \cdot (1 + WACC_p)^{-p}$ respectively of the formulas for VA^W and VA^C of the quantitative model described in Sect. 7.3.1.

The targets for SC cost c_p and working capital w_p in each period $p = 1, \ldots, P$ can be calculated by applying rearranged calculation formulas for VA^W_p and VA^C_p of the quantitative model described in Sect. 7.3.1:

$$w_p = \frac{S_p}{S_{p-1}} \cdot (w_{p-1} - va^W_p) . \tag{7.6}$$

$$c_p = \frac{S_p}{S_0} \cdot \frac{C_0 - va^{SCC}_p}{1 - T_p} . \tag{7.7}$$

This approach is illustrated by an example of the fictitious Hoffmann Corporation (see Ross et al. 2002, p. 739 et seq.).[2] Table 7.2 contains the parameters for the year 2010 and the planning expectations for the planning periods 2011–2015.

Based on these planning assumptions, an initial strategic SC plan as depicted in Table 7.3 can be determined by applying the calculations of step 3 described above.

---

[2]Note: In this chapter, all figures are rounded to integers. Tax rate T and cost of capital $WACC$ are assumed to remain constant in all periods of the planning horizon.

Table 7.4 Bottom-up strategic SC planning scenario for Hoffmann Corporation

P	UOM	2010	2011	2012	2013	2014	2015
S_p	US$	10,000	12,000	14,400	17,280	20,736	24,883
c_p	US$	7,000	8,100	9,432	10,973	12,753	14,681
va_p^C	US$	–	165	297	429	561	726
va^C	US$	–	150	395	718	1,101	1,552
w_p	US$	5,000	6,000	6,960	8,112	9,494	11,393
va_p^W	US$	–	0	200	200	200	0
va^W	US$	–	0	165	316	452	452
va^{Total}	US$	–	150	561	1,033	1,553	2,004

7.4.2 Bottom-Up Validation of Strategic Supply Chain Plans

To ensure a closed SC planning loop, the initial strategic SC plan created in a top-down approach has to be confirmed by a bottom-up validation which is based on a project portfolio consisting of SC optimization projects with estimated financial impacts. At first, one or more SC projects of the portfolio have to be selected and scheduled in the planning horizon. Secondly, the developments of SC value drivers have to be calculated which would result from the estimated financial impacts of the scheduled projects. This generates a bottom-up strategic SC planning scenario. As a third step, the value contributions resulting from the planning scenario have to be calculated by applying the quantitative model. In the case that the SC value driver developments and their resulting value contributions match with the targets given by the top-down planning, the strategic SC plan is validated and the iteration of a closed SC planning loop ends. Else another iteration of the planning loop, which starts with top-down planning and considers the results from the bottom-up validation, is required.

Selecting and scheduling SC projects from a project portfolio to meet defined value expectations can result in complex planning problems. Hence, in more complex situations, e.g. a higher number of projects in the SC project portfolio, appropriate simulation or optimization methods can support the proposed value-based strategic SC planning.

For the illustrative example, an SC project portfolio of three SC optimization projects is assumed: The estimated financial impact of project 1 for three subsequent years is a reduction of working capital (improvement by -200 US$ p.a.) at increasing SC cost (deterioration of SC cost ratio by $+0.5$pp p.a.). The estimated financial impacts of project 2 – a continuous improvement project – are improved SC cost (decrease of SC cost ratio by -2.5 pp p.a.) in each period the project is executed. Project 3 is estimated to improve both SC value drivers in two subsequent years (reduction of working capital by -300 US$ p.a. and reduction of SC cost by -3.0 pp p.a.). Selecting project 1 scheduled to generate value impacts in periods 2012–2014 and project 2 scheduled to create value in each year generates the bottom-up strategic SC planning scenario depicted in Table 7.4.

The cumulative value contribution is 2,004 US$, thereof 1,552 US$ from SC cost and 452 US$ from working capital. Hence, the overall value expectations defined by initial SC plan can be met, even without selecting project 3 for execution.

7.4.3   Integration Aspects

On strategic level, integration aspects have to be considered at the interface between value-based strategic SC planning and long-term financial planning. Items from balance sheet and P&L statement which define the initial company situation for value-based strategic SC planning are provided by long-term financial planning. Furthermore expectations of future sales development and value creation defined by long-term financial planning are input parameters for value-based strategic SC planning. Future developments of SC cost and working capital forecasted by value-based strategic SC planning can be used as dynamic input parameters for long-term financial planning.

On tactical level, value-based strategic SC planning is integrated with short-term financial planning and tactical SC planning. Targets for working capital obtained by value-based strategic SC planning are input parameters for short-term financial planning which aims at optimally arranging working capital components within one financial year. Targets for SC cost fixed by value-based strategic SC planning determine financial constraints for resource adjustment and allocation in tactical SC planning. In a rolling planning approach, planning scenarios created by short-term financial planning and tactical SC planning determine initial situations for the subsequent period of value-based strategic SC planning.

7.5   Conclusion

In this chapter, a value-based strategic SC planning concept is designed which comprises SC cost and working capital and thus combines EBIT-related and asset-related factors of value creation on the strategic level. It is illustrated that SC contributions to company value can be planned under consideration of company-specific characteristics, in particular targeted future sales developments. In contrast to pure financial planning models, the proposed approach considers cost and capital proportions to sales as dynamic. As outlined, this planning concept can be used as a framework to integrate SC planning with financial planning and to link strategic and tactical planning processes. Hence this chapter contributes to the research on concepts for value-based SCM and helps to close the gap between existing volume-based concepts for SC planning and value-based aspects of SCM.

Limitations mainly arise from the fact that the proposed approach to strategic SC planning is purely value-based without considering volume aspects, which are usually in focus of SC planning. This circumstance leaves room for further research.

Opportunities for further research include extensions of the value-based strategic SC planning concept to cover other SC value drivers, e.g. fixed assets or SC risk, as well as the planning interfaces to other functions of a company, such as marketing planning or investment planning. Additionally, research on value-based concepts for collaborative planning between different linked companies would broaden the planning perspective to value creation on SC network level.

Chapter 8
Dynamics and Uncertainties in Tactical Supply Chain Design for New Product Introduction

Abstract The task of tactical supply chain design (TSCD) for new product introduction (NPI) is to establish product-specific supply chains that ensure cost-efficiently on time and in full availability of new high quality products over the whole product life cycle (PLC). Besides cross-regional network aspects and inter-disciplinary factors the problem complexity is driven by dynamics and uncertainties of short PLCs. This raises the questions to what extent these complexity drivers affect supply chain design scenarios and how they are linked to company value. In the conceptual part of this chapter, dynamics and uncertainties are integrated in a proposed framework for value-based SCM which is linked to a discrete event simulation model. In the empirical part of this chapter, impacts of these complexity drivers on TSCD scenarios for NPI are illustrated by a case example from the fast moving consumer goods industry.[1]

8.1 Introduction and Problem Statement

Supply chain management (SCM) can be defined as the "integration of business processes from end users to original suppliers that provides products, services and information that add value to customers" (Cooper et al. 1997, p. 2) and contributes towards establishing competitive advantages for companies across all industries (Mentzer et al. 2001). To leverage this competitive advantage, SCM is faced with challenges in the fields of configuration and operations in all stages of the product life cycle (PLC) (Seuring 2001): introduction and growth, maturity, and phase-out. Although these fields are interlinked by decision-making and resulting consequences, the particularities of each field and business specifics limit the

---

[1]This chapter is a result of a scientific collaboration with Professor Dr. Heinrich Kuhn and Dr. Robert Schilling, both Catholic University of Eichstätt-Ingolstadt, and Professor Dr. Stefan Seuring, University of Kassel (in alphabetical order).

M. Brandenburg, *Quantitative Models for Value-Based Supply Chain Management*,
Lecture Notes in Economics and Mathematical Systems 660,
DOI 10.1007/978-3-642-31304-2__8, © Springer-Verlag Berlin Heidelberg 2013

possibilities of unconstraint optimization. For example, supplier selection and product allocation decisions in supply chain (SC) configuration before product launch define material flows in the operational field later on.

To succeed in increasingly competitive markets, companies in many industries are continuously aligning their product assortments with customer requirements by introducing new products or enhanced versions of existing ones. As a consequence, PLCs shorten, while product introduction rates increase and product assortments proliferate (Pero et al. 2010). By avoiding obsolete inventories, supporting short time to market, and ensuring sufficient product availability at product launch dates (van Hoek and Chapman 2006) the SC performance can be affected positively. One of the main tasks of SCM within new product introduction (NPI) projects is to define and establish a product- or category-specific SC, i.e. allocate those new or modified products to own plants or contract manufacturers within the existing SC network, so that on time and in full availability of high quality products is ensured in a cost-efficient way over the whole PLC. Especially when introducing products with comparably short life cycles this is a critical task since there might not be enough time for major adjustments or improvements later on (Higuchi and Troutt 2004).

Furthermore, SC design in NPI must be distinguished from strategic SC design involving the reorganization of the entire SC network (Graves and Willems 2005). Strategic network design decisions usually consider the entire product assortment of a company or business unit and determine the SC network configuration comprising plants, distribution centers and suppliers. Hence, these decisions are capital-intense, occur rather infrequently, are quite difficult to revert, and have long-term impacts onto the economic performance of a company (Goetschalckx and Fleischmann 2008; Mena et al. 2009). Therefore, adjustments of the whole SC configuration are in many cases not appropriate for NPI. Conversely, product allocation decisions caused by NPI occur very frequently and can often not be reverted or adjusted with reasonable effort. As those decisions affect only parts of the SC network for the limited time of the PLC, the problem is considered tactical, thus referred to as tactical SC design (TSCD) (Schilling et al. 2010).

The complexity of TSCD decisions is driven by uncertainties and dynamics (Wilding 1998). Uncertainties in an SC arise from demand and supply related sources (Saad and Gindy 1998) comprising time and quantity of demand, availability of capacity, processing and transportation times, cost, quality specifications, due dates, priorities, and ambiguous or missing information (Blackhurst et al. 2004). In order to achieve customer satisfaction SCM must be aligned with product development and introduction processes (Pero et al. 2010). SC design decisions in NPI projects often have to be based on rough, not finalized product concepts before the development of a product has ended. Consequently, these decisions are associated with a comparably high degree of demand uncertainties, since the actual market reception of the product is neither known at this point in time nor can be forecasted adequately based on historical data (van Hoek and Chapman 2006). Moreover, up to 80 % of the arising costs are committed at this time (Ayag 2005).

Dynamics on the other hand arise for instance from order oscillations, seasonality or minimum order quantities (Villegas and Smith 2006) and may result in a bullwhip

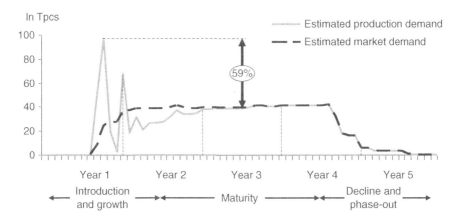

Fig. 8.1 Demand patterns of volume commitments considering pipeline filling over the projected PLC (Schilling et al. 2010)

effect (Lee et al. 1997 a,b). Ensuring product availability at product launch can also create internal dynamics within an SC, e.g. in case a significant proportion of demand is expected at or shortly after product launch and thus needs to be pre-produced and distributed while maintaining a short time to market (van Hoek and Chapman 2006).

These complexity drivers are distinctive in the fast moving consumer goods (FMCG) industry (Wong et al. 2005). FMCG are products which at high turnover and comparably low cost, can act as substantial profit contributors, e.g. cosmetics, batteries, household goods, toiletries, or paper products (Pourakbar et al. 2009). Product availability is crucial in FMCG industries since consumers have limited tolerability for out-of-stock (OOS) situations and hence most likely switch to substitute products (Marquai et al. 2010) which in turn influences repurchase rates and revenues negatively.

PLCs in the FMCG industry are characterized by dynamics from pipeline filling requirements during introduction and growth stages, obsolete stock management during phase-out, as well as uncertainties of demand across the whole PLC (Higuchi and Troutt 2004). Pipeline filling is defined as the production and distribution of a product prior to product launch to ensure sufficient product availability across all stocking points at the launch date when product demand is fostered by strong marketing campaigns (Schilling et al. 2010). During pipeline filling activities, all stocking points are filled with 30–60 % of the expected annual demand before the product is actually launched into the market (see Fig. 8.1).

Demand uncertainties affect product availability, inventory levels and effective use of capital assets and hence are of great relevance for companies in the FMCG industry (Adebanjo and Mann 2000). Beyond this, the complexity of an SC in the FMCG industry is increased by proliferating product assortments (Danne and Häusler 2010), a large number of facilities (Shapiro 2007; Siemieniuch et al. 1999) and the resulting flows of information and material (Dekker et al. 2009; Sandholm et al. 2006) through inter-organizational and international networks comprising suppliers, manufacturers, distributors, retailers and service providers (Honkomp et al. 2000; Meyr and Stadtler 2008).

Consequently, dynamics and demand uncertainties influence SC design decisions for NPI in the FMCG industry and affect SC performance over the whole PLC. The financial performance of a firm, i.e. ultimately the company value, is also influenced by SC-related impacts on the value drivers sales, cost, and working and fixed capital (Christopher and Ryals 1999). While some of these influences are directly quantifiable, e.g. those arising from working capital or SC cost (Brandenburg and Seuring 2010b), other impacts are only indirectly or qualitatively supported, e.g. poor product availability and a resulting sales loss (Corsten and Gruen 2003).

In order to select the appropriate SC design in NPI projects, potential SC options need to be evaluated regarding their financial and non-financial performance impacts, especially in the presence of demand uncertainties and internal dynamics. While financial and non-financial evaluations might not lead to unambiguous results, value-oriented evaluations integrate both perspectives. Moreover, the evaluation of dynamics and uncertainties in TSCD regarding value contribution still leaves considerable research potential. This chapter strives to contribute to closing this gap. The resulting research question of this chapter is what drives the performance of an SC option over the whole PLC. This question is elaborated based on a case example from the FMCG industry by evaluating the following aspects:

- How do the SC complexity drivers dynamics and uncertainties link to SC-related drivers of company value?
- How and to what extent do these complexity drivers affect TSCD in NPI?

The remainder of this chapter is structured as follows. The next Sect. 8.2 comprises a brief review of related scientific literature, in particular on SCM in the FMCG industry, SC design in NPI, and value-based SCM. In Sect. 8.3 an integrated framework for value-based SCM is presented. In the following Sect. 8.4, a case example from the FMCG industry is given which comprises a simulation model, different simulation scenarios, the numerical evaluation and its interpretation. This chapter ends with a discussion in Sect. 8.5 and concluding remarks on findings, limitations and further research opportunities in Sect. 8.6.

8.2 Literature Review

8.2.1 Supply Chain Management in the Fast Moving Consumer Goods Industry

The FMCG industry is of particular interest for academic research in SCM, as illustrated by van Hoek and Chapman (2006) in different examples in NPI from the fashion, consumer goods and consumer electronics industries. Especially the effects of dynamics and uncertainties in FMCG supply chains are discussed in several papers. Tahmassebi (1998) considers control and management of multiple plants in a multilevel distribution system from the FMCG industry. A stochastic model is suggested to evaluate alternatives for strategic redesign and operation of an existing SC at uncertain demand situations. Reiner and Trcka (2004) propose a simulation environment to evaluate SC configuration alternatives considering demand uncertainties. Based on a case study from the food industry, the authors observe that general statements like short SCs to reduce bullwhip effects or the utilization of point of sale (POS) data to improve a manufacturer's planning situation are not valid in every case, and conclude the need to include the context of the specific SC.

In a longitudinal SC study of toy manufacturers and retailers Wong et al. (2005) identify SCM practices for dealing with unpredictable and variable demand caused by seasonality, customer requirements, short PLCs and selling windows, as well as a substantial proportion of new products and promotional campaigns, and reveal mismatches between manufacturers and retailers.

Impacts of SCM on company value in the FMCG industry are evaluated by Brandenburg and Seuring (2010b) in a secondary data analysis of ten leading FMCG manufacturers. It is observed that all companies created value by reducing working capital or SC cost and that monetary working capital components are of considerable relevance for value creation.

8.2.2 Supply Chain Design and New Product Introduction

The areas of SC design and NPI have received considerable attention among researchers as well. In many cases SC design in NPI is considered as an optimization problem. Chauhan et al. (2004) introduce a mixed integer programming (MIP) model for strategic SC design for a new product that minimizes total costs. For the configuration of an NPI-driven SC, Graves and Willems (2005) apply a dynamic programming model to minimizes total SC costs comprising inventory holding cost, transport cost up to the customer, and cost of goods sold (COGS). Butler et al. (2006) present a robust MIP model that maximizes net profit while considering the complete PLC and furthermore uncertainties of demand. Wang and Shu (2007) propose a configuration model based on fuzzy sets to reflect and evaluate SC uncertainties. The objective of the model is to minimize total SC costs while maximizing the possibility of achieving the target fill rate.

Higuchi and Troutt (2004) apply a system dynamics simulation approach to analyze SC dynamics arising from demand variability at the example of a short life cycle product from the consumer electronics industry. The authors observe re-amplifying bullwhip effects and show that early setting of product and SC specifications is more important than later improvements after product launch.

8.2.3   Value-Based Supply Chain Management

Existing literature indicates value-based SCM is being of great interest for academic research for more than a decade (Melnyk et al. 2009). The conceptual aspects are among others considered by Christopher and Ryals (1999) who assess the framework of value-based management and shareholder value and its links to SCM. The authors identify sales, cost, and capital to be the levers of SCM that drive shareholder value by enhancing or accelerating cash flows through internal processes as well as interfaces to customers and suppliers. Lambert and Burduroglu (2000) evaluate the impact of logistics on these levers and propose a framework to measure the resulting value contribution. Shareholder value is identified as the most comprehensive measure to quantify logistics impact on company value. Moreover the need for cost effective ways to measure this impact is addressed. Lambert and Pohlen (2001) present a methodology to develop appropriate metrics for SC performance by analyzing eight identified key SC processes and their link to corporate performance. The authors propose a framework for the development of appropriate metrics for performance measurement of SC processes, identification of a firm's impact on overall SC performance and translation of SC performance into shareholder value. Employing a conceptual research method, Hofmann and Locker (2009) examine how SCM affects shareholder value and propose a value-based performance measurement system to link operating SC activities with economic value added (EVA). The performance measurement system is tested in a single case study from the packaging industry.

Quantitative approaches of value-based SCM can be differentiated between purely value-based approaches and hybrid value- and volume-based concepts. Brandenburg and Seuring (2010b) employ discounted cash flows (DCF) in a value-based model to quantify value impacts arising from changes of working capital and SC cost. Timing and continuity of value driver developments are found to be crucial for the overall value creation. To reflect value-based aspects in strategic SC planning, Brandenburg and Seuring (2010c) apply this DCF-based quantitative model to propose a combined top-down and bottom-up concept and outline integration with strategic financial planning as well as with tactical and operational SC planning. A hybrid value- and volume-based concept combining financial and physical flows in an SC is proposed by Hahn and Kuhn (2010). A robust optimization method to combine value-based performance and risk management in SCM is suggested and illustrated with a case example from the consumer goods industry. In a second paper, Hahn and Kuhn (2011) propose a holistic framework for value-based SC planning and present a tactical SC sales and operational planning model to optimize sales, operations and financial decisions for shareholder value creation by maximized EVA.

Empirical aspects of value-based SCM are considered thoroughly by Hendricks and Singhal (2003, 2005b) by evaluating 519 and 827 cases of supply chain disruptions, respectively, and their impacts on stock price. Production and delivery delays are found to have a negative influence on the stock price of a firm.

Losbichler and Rothböck (2006) analyze the development of working capital and its components in a study among 6,925 European companies between 1995 and 2004. One major observation is that working capital has been moved upstream within European supply chains with original equipment manufacturers (OEM), apparently optimizing their working capital at their suppliers' expense. In a secondary data analysis of ten leading FMCG manufacturers, Brandenburg and Seuring (2010a) evaluate the impacts of working capital and SC cost on company value. Focused on these value drivers, all companies create value through SCM with monetary working capital components having a considerable relevance for value creation.

8.3 Conceptual Framework for Value-Based Supply Chain Management

The link of uncertainties and dynamics to company value is evaluated in a theorizing desk research (Halldorsson and Arlbjørn 2005). Conceptual elements from existing literature are combined to a framework for value-based SCM to which the SC design and its complexity drivers dynamics and uncertainties are linked.

The financial performance of a firm is among others influenced by SC-related impacts on the value drivers sales, cost, and working and fixed capital (Christopher and Ryals 1999). The impact of the complexity drivers uncertainties and dynamics is not limited to SC design but also influences the value drivers of an SC and thus company value itself. These interdependencies are outlined in a framework for value-based SCM derived from existing literature. Based on this framework, performance criteria are selected and used to evaluate candidate SC options in the case example presented in this chapter.

SC design decisions must consider financial as well as non-financial performance criteria (Gunasekaran and Kobu 2007). Financial SC performance criteria comprise fixed capital, SC cost (see papers in Seuring and Goldbach 2001) and working capital (Randall and Farris II 2009a), with the latter two influencing company value in a directly measurable and quantifiable way (Brandenburg and Seuring 2010b). Non-financial performance criteria include fill rate (Gunasekaran and Kobu 2007), SC flexibility and reactivity (Bernandes and Hanna 2009), product range and assortment complexity (Danne and Häusler 2010; Gunasekaran et al. 2004), and product quality (Gunasekaran et al. 2004). These operational performance aspects again strongly influence the financial situation of a company (Reiner and Hofmann 2006): The fill rate, for instance, measures the degree of product availability which in turn directly affects the initial purchase and repurchase rate of a product and hence the revenue of a company (Marquai et al. 2010). Brand manufacturers furthermore face the challenge to reduce replenishment lead times (Chang and Makatsoris 2001), which indicates the flexibility and responsiveness of an SC (Gunasekaran et al. 2004) and again influences the financial performance of a company (Christensen et al. 2007). These interdependencies are illustrated in Fig. 8.2.

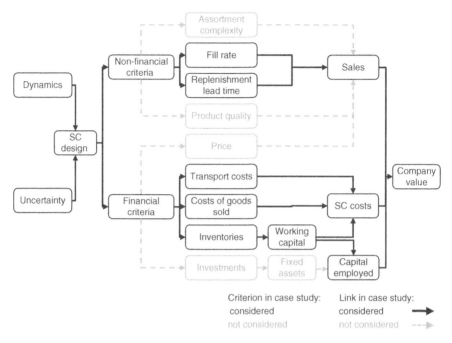

Fig. 8.2 Complexity drivers and value drivers in a framework for value-based SCM

In TSCD problems from the FMCG industry, these performance criteria are either considered in a static way, if the criterion is to a large extent independent from dynamics or uncertainties, or in a dynamic way, if dynamics and uncertainties have a strong influence on the performance criterion.

Main components of SC costs are transportation cost, inventory holding cost, and COGS. The latter reflect the direct costs and overheads associated with the physical production of products for sale (Poston and Grabinski 2001). Fixed capital aspects are considered through investments in machinery and equipment, which are required in case a (production) technology is newly allocated to a production site, established for the first time in a production network, or in case an extension of existing capacities is required. Moreover, the depreciation of the investments also needs to be reflected in product costs and therefore SC costs. Both financial performance criteria are largely independent from dynamics or uncertainties and therefore can be estimated in a static quantification approach for each considered SC option. Working capital aspects are taken into account by inventories comprising cycle, safety and transit stocks of components and finished goods, which are strongly influenced by dynamics and uncertainties (Bottani and Montanari 2010) and hence must be measured dynamically. Consequently the non-financial performance criteria also need to be evaluated dynamically. Non-financial performance criteria comprise fill rate, measuring on-time and in-full availability of products, and replenishment lead time (RLT), a driver of flexibility and reactivity of an SC. Product quality, being an order qualifier for market entry, and assortment complexity, which is rather driven by assortment strategy than by SC design decisions, are not considered as decision parameters for TSCD.

8.4   Empirical Case Example

8.4.1   Solution Approach

The analysis and discussion of a simulation-based evaluation of SC options in NPI projects, considering the complete PLC, are based onto a case example based on empirical data (Reiner 2005) from a cosmetics manufacturer introduced by Schilling et al. (2010). Decision making in TSCD for NPI can be supported by quantitative methods from operations research, which can be broadly classified into optimization models and simulation models (Biswas and Narahari 2004). Optimization models are often applied in the context of supply chain planning (Ivanov et al. 2010). Simulation models are descriptive models which permit studying the dynamic behavior of supply chains and help understanding causalities in SC performance (Shapiro 2007). Simulation techniques are often applied for the evaluation of a system's operating performance prior to its implementation (Chang and Makatsoris 2001), especially since variability of parameters (uncertainties) and interplays across time (dynamics) can be reflected (Higuchi and Troutt 2004). Taking into account the scope of this chapter, a methodological introduction and discussion of existing literature is omitted. For instance, Terzi and Cavalieri (2004) provide a comprehensive review of 80 articles, while Kleijnen (2005) discusses simulation types and methodological issues thoroughly.

Depending on the structure and capabilities of a company's SC network, generating feasible SC options can be a hard to solve problem itself (see e.g. Butler et al. 2006). However, taking into account the parameters of the various decision categories, a shortlist of candidate SC options can often be compiled comparatively easily.

The financial evaluation of cost and investments can in many cases be based on static calculations. Conversely, non-financial criteria are subject to significant impacts from dynamics and uncertainties and can only be calculated analytically if the system is assumed to be in a steady state with stationary demands (see e.g. Butler et al. 2006; Chwif et al. 2002). Due to the presented problem structure with internal SC dynamics caused by characteristic demand patterns and specific focus on the ramp-up phase, an evaluation approach based on quantitative modeling using discrete event simulation (DES) (Kleijnen 2005) is chosen to adequately reflect such effects.

Fig. 8.3 Candidate SC options

8.4.2 General Settings

The case example builds on a realistic NPI project from a global FMCG man-ufacturer (Schilling et al. 2010). For confidentiality reasons the collected data and structures, in particular cost information, have been adapted without loss of scientific relevance of problem structure and characteristics. The specific NPI project has been selected since several influences like pipeline filling, supplier capacity ramp-up and long transport lead times apply simultaneously.

The case example comprises one cosmetics product line with three language variants (stock keeping units, SKU), one for each demand region Europe, covering the majority of the demand, Latin America and Asia. Country-specific launch dates are reflected in the regions' demand patterns based on sales volume commitments for the whole PLC which are collected from local affiliates during NPI projects several months prior to a launch.

The two candidate SC options comprise three echelons with a supplier located in Asia, production centers in Europe (SC option 1) and Asia (SC option 2), and distribution centers (DC) in each of the three demand regions (see Fig. 8.3). For the supplier, restrictions regarding a fixed order quantity and a daily production capacity apply. Moreover, supplier capacity is only available from a certain point in time on with a capacity ramp-up phase at reduced capacity. In the plants no capacity constraints are considered. However, setups and production cycles are reflected by a (technically derived) fixed production quantity and a fixed production lead time of 1 week. The SC operates under a make-to-stock policy based on forecasted demands. The market demand, e.g. from wholesalers, distributors or retailers, is satisfied directly from a DC's stock in a monthly cycle. In the case that the complete demand cannot be fulfilled, backorders are allowed and delivered in the next month. The transport times in the SC network vary between 7 and 56 days. Moreover, estimated landed costs – comprising transport cost and COGS – for all three SKUs as well as packaging materials have been calculated per SC option based on production and transport cost information. These costs are used for cost evaluation and to calculate inventory values. Overall, SC option 2 yields 2 % lower landed costs per SKU than SC option 1 which is driven by lower production costs.

Table 8.1 Overview of parameters and symbols

Parameter	Description
r	Review period
t	Time period
S_t	Target inventory level in period t
SS_t	Safety stock in period t
i_t	On-hand inventory in period t
j_t	On-order inventory in period t
x_t	Inventory order in period t
y_t	Forecast demand in period t
$\sigma(y_t)$	Standard deviation of forecast demand y_t during replenishment time
lt_{sd}	Lead time from origin s to destination d
z	Normal distribution safety factor

8.4.3 Simulation Model

The model of the SC is built with the DES software ARENA^{TM} from Rockwell Automation (Rockwell Automation 2007). Various validation and verification procedures of both model and output are performed (Kelton et al. 2002; Manuj et al. 2009). The model is validated by internal cross-checks using dynamic counters as well as thorough observation of process animations. The created demand patterns and model results are validated by comparison with historical data.

The model reflects the three-echelon SC described above and can be adapted to the SC options by adjusting several parameters (see Table 8.1).

The make-to-stock policy is incorporated through a dynamic (r, S_t) inventory policy in the DCs for finished goods and plants for packaging materials. In a monthly ordering cycle (r) inventory orders are placed at the preceding echelon, i.e. plant or supplier, so that the inventory level S_t would be reached if the order was delivered at once:

$$x_t = S_t - (i_t + j_t) . \tag{8.1}$$

The dynamic re-order point S_t per period t is then calculated based on forecast demands:

$$S_t = SS_t + \sum_{i=t}^{t+lt_{sd}} y_i . \tag{8.2}$$

The safety stock level (SS_t) per SKU per period t is calculated based on a normal distribution safety factor z at a fill rate of 95 % (Silver et al. 1998):

$$SS_t = \sigma(y_t) \cdot \sqrt{lt_{sd}} \cdot z . \tag{8.3}$$

Uncertainties in the demand signal are modeled by distinguishing between the level of expectation value, representing over- and under-estimation of market

Table 8.2 Overview of scenario settings

Scenario	Demand pattern	Forecast accuracy	Contingency planning
1	Launch	100 %	–
2	pattern and	93 %	
3	pipeline	85 %	
4	filling	78 %	
5		70 %	
6		63 %	
7		55 %	
8	Launch	85 %	+30 %
9	pattern and		+20 %
10	pipeline		+10 %
11	filling		–
12			–10 %
13			–20 %
14			–30 %
15			–40 %
16			–50 %

Note: Scenario 3 and 11 are identical

demand respectively (contingency planning), and the variance, describing the random fluctuation in demand. The random fluctuations are assumed to be standard distributed at specified forecast accuracy, while contingency planning is calculated with a scenario-specific factor. In the latter case, the demand forecasts are also allowed to be adjusted automatically by the system after an assumed "learning period" of 3 months. This reflects the potential of an organization to comprehend the overall market acceptance of a particular product. Pipeline filling demand volumes prior to product launch dates are assumed to be deterministic as retailers initially need to fill up all shelf facings and stocks.

8.4.4   Simulation Scenarios

Based on the two components of demand uncertainties forecast accuracy and contingency planning, several scenarios are defined arbitrarily to conduct a structured analysis of SC complexity drivers' impacts. Scenarios 1–7 analyze SC performance under increasing demand variability, while scenarios 8–16 provide insight into the effects of a long-lasting over- and underestimation of product reception in the market (see Table 8.2).

8.4.5   Numerical Results

The simulation model has been validated by internal cross-checks and extensive analysis. Since the evaluation of the ramp-up phase of the SC options is of special

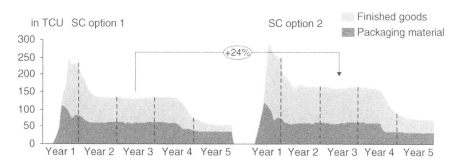

Fig. 8.4 Average inventory value profiles for both SC options (scenario 3)

interest, a terminating simulation and analysis approach is used (Kelton et al. 2002). The results presented show the monthly average values over a number of replications with random demand variations which is found to be sufficient to produce results with an error of less than 5 % at a 95 % confidence interval on total inventory values and order lead times.

Overall, the simulation experiments prove both candidate SC options to be capable of supporting the product launch with desired fill rates of 95–99 % during introduction, growth and maturity stages of the PLC. NPI projects in FMCG industries operate under tight schedules to reduce time to market to the economically feasible minimum, where pre-production and transport times in particular offer reduction potentials. Therefore indicating that an SC option is able to support a desired launch schedule on time and in full is already a valuable insight, especially in the presence of capacity constraints, comparably long transport times and significant demands peaks at the beginning of the PLC.

Differences between both candidate SC options and impacts from uncertainties and dynamics on SC performance are evaluated in detail for each performance criterion inventory, RLT, and fill rate.

The inventory level of each SC option follows similar demand-driven developments in general, with SC option 2 showing a higher peak in finished goods' inventories during pipeline filling activities. Significant transport time differences from the plants to the European markets drive inventory value levels. Due to longer transport time from the plant to Europe in SC option 2, pipeline filling inventories remain in the SC much longer. Hence, more capital is bound over a longer time (see Fig. 8.4).

On average the total inventory value of all stocks is about 24 % higher over the whole PLC in SC option 2 than SC option 1. Although transport times between production plant and supplier are longer in SC option 1, packaging goods inventory levels on average do not differ significantly (on average between 2 and 4 %). This observation is even more surprising, considering that safety stock levels for packaging materials are – depending on the selected scenario – on average 15 % higher in SC option 1 than in SC option 2. The safety stock advantage of SC option

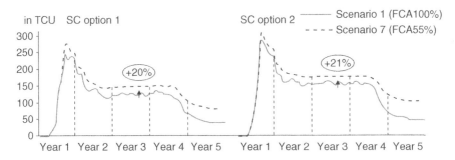

Fig. 8.5 Impacts of contingency planning on average inventory value profiles

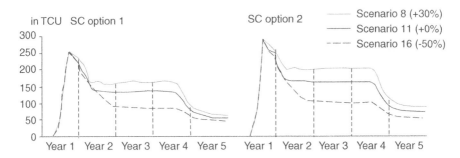

Fig. 8.6 Impacts of contingency planning on average inventory value profiles

2 is obviously compensated by higher primary finished goods' demands that drive inventories and are caused by longer RLT into the main market Europe.

Moreover it is observed that increasing demand uncertainties leads equally to higher average inventory levels in both SC options (see Fig. 8.5). In this case, a major proportion of the increase is driven by increasing safety stocks due to decreasing forecast accuracy.

A positive correlation between contingency scenario and inventory level is also observed, independent from the chosen SC option. This effect is based on the assumed "learning system" which is able to adjust the inventory levels to the observed market reception (see Fig. 8.6) within a comparably short time. Nevertheless, total inventory value of SC option 2 is on average still approx. 25 % higher than SC option 1.

For packaging materials, the RLT of SC option 2 is in the maturity stage of the PLC approximately 33 % shorter than of SC option 1. However, internal SC dynamics created by a combination of a supplier ramp-up phase, pipeline filling requirements, and country-specific launch patterns lead to a supplier capacity bottleneck prior to the crucial product introduction phase. As a result, the packaging material RLT in SC option 2 increases at the beginning of the PLC during supplier capacity ramp-up and even exceeds the packaging material RLT of SC option 1 (see Fig. 8.7).

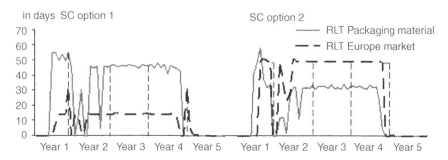

Fig. 8.7 Impacts of dynamics onto average replenishment lead times (scenario 1)

Differences in RLT from the plants to the markets are found as expected between SC option 1 and SC option 2, since processing and transport times are considered as static. A significant difference is recorded in RLTs from the plants to Europe. While SC option 1 is able to deliver within 2–3 weeks, SC option 2 requires 7–8 weeks. However, at the beginning of the PLC, RLTs to Europe double in SC option 1 as the supplier ramp-up bottleneck is carried forward and the production orders have to wait for packaging material supply at the plant (see Fig. 8.7).

With regards to RLT, thus SC flexibility, the results suggest SC option 1 to be able to react significantly faster to unforeseen demand changes than SC option 2. Although the RLT of finished goods to Europe reacts quite sensitively to the packaging material bottleneck in SC option 1, the total lead time, i.e. from supplier to Europe, is at the beginning of the PLC significantly shorter than in SC option 2. This effect can be explained by the fact that the longer lead time from the Asian plant to Europe (SC option 2) requires significantly higher packaging material volumes to be ordered earlier, thus mainly during capacity ramp-up.

From a project planning and risk management perspective the findings also indicate that SC option 2 is likely to react more sensitively to project schedule delays than SC option 1. In case of a delay, costly expediting actions such as a switch of the transport mode from ocean shipping to airfreight, would be required to hold launch timing while impairing the cost advantage of SC option 2.

Nevertheless, both SC options are able to support the product launch with desired fill rates of 95–99 % during introduction and main sales phase in all scenarios. This observation adds empirical support to the conclusion that the responsiveness of both SC designs is sufficient to cope with major underestimations of market reception.

Table 8.3 summarizes the results from the dynamic evaluation of both candidate SC options. The results indicate that at similar fill rates, SC option 1 utilizes 20 % less inventory than SC option 2 and offers a higher responsiveness due to significantly shorter RLT to the main market Europe, especially during the product launch phase. Additionally the simulation runs provide evidence that SC option 2 might react quite sensitively to delays. A structured analysis of influences from demand and market uncertainties suggests SC option 1 to maintain its performance

Table 8.3 Summary of evaluation results

Criterion	SC option 1 (plant Europe)	SC option 2 (plant Asia)
Fill rate	Similar results in both SC options	
Flexibility (RLT)	• Shorter RLT of packaging materials during product introduction • Significantly shorter average RLT from plant to Europe • Shorter total RLT from supplier to main market during product introduction phase	• Shorter average RLT of packaging materials to plant during maturity stage
Inventory		+25 % vs. SC option 1
SC cost		−2 % vs. SC option 1
Investments	No investment required in both SC options	
Risk		SC option expected to react more sensibly to project timing delays, requiring costly expediting actions

advantages even if those influences apply. However, at the same time accumulated landed costs in SC option 2 are approximately 2 % lower than in SC option 1.

While a financial cost evaluation would favor SC option 2, the non-financial evaluation suggests SC option 1 to yield better overall SC performance. As a consequence, a clear decision for the one or the other SC option is only possible if financial and non-financial criteria are either clearly prioritized or integrated into one metric. By linking volume-based simulation results and static financial information in the value-based SCM framework, SC designs can be assessed based on their value contribution. Potential revenue impacts per period are linked to fill rates, while cost impacts are calculated based on landed costs and capital costs for inventories. However, as capital costs constitute only a minor share of total SC-related costs, a cost advantage of 2 % in landed costs is very challenging to compensate through capital cost savings caused by lower inventories. Moreover, with COGS-shares of net sales in the FMCG industry of 35–42 % (Brandenburg and Seuring 2010a), the impact of lost sales is likely to dominate value contribution calculations. Therefore, SC option would be recommended from a value contribution perspective.

8.5 Discussion

The presented approach to value-based SCM is in line with the framework introduced by Christopher and Ryals (1999) comprising sales, cost and capital and the metrics for the NPI process according to Lambert and Pohlen (2001). While Lambert and Burduroglu (2000) focus on value contributions arising from logistics only, this chapter considers international and cross-functional SC aspects of value creation. Moreover the case example provides empirical support for the statement that delays in an SC have a negative impact on company value, as observed by Hendricks and Singhal (2003, 2005b). Furthermore this example shows that cost and inventory are considerable value drivers in the FMCG industry, as pointed out by Brandenburg and Seuring (2010b). Additionally the applied simulation approach adds to hybrid value- and volume-based quantitative methods in value-based SCM, as suggested by Hahn and Kuhn (2010, 2011).

In contrast to other quantitative approaches applying normative optimization techniques to SC design problems in NPI (Chauhan et al. 2004; Graves and Willems 2005), the desciptive DES is employed in this case example. While optimization approaches are able to consider demand uncertainties (see Butler et al. 2006; Wang and Shu 2007), their ability to cope with dynamics is limited. Like Higuchi and Troutt (2004) the presented approach considers dynamics and uncertainties simultaneously and addresses the problem arising from introducing products with short PLCs and high product availability requirements. In the case of Higuchi and Troutt (2004), dynamics are caused externally by shadow demands which occur due to a significant under-estimation of a product's market reception. Pipeline filling activities are intended to mitigate this effect, but on the other hand create internal dynamics in the SC as shown in this chapter.

Although other papers discuss the relevance of uncertainties (see Blackhurst et al. 2004; Wilding 1998) and dynamics (see e.g. Villegas and Smith 2006), the contribution of this chapter is to consider both complexity drivers in a combined value-based and volume-based evaluation. Additionally, the illustration and discussion of pipeline filling aspects enriches the current research on NPI (see e.g. Butler et al. 2006; Higuchi and Troutt 2004) as well as the consideration of such self-created SC dynamics in SC planning.

8.6 Conclusion

This chapter analyzes the performance drivers of an SC design over the whole PLC. Based on conceptual research, first elements of a framework for value-based SCM are proposed which link the SC complexity drivers dynamics and uncertainties to SC related drivers of company value. Beyond this, the impacts of these complexity drivers on TSCD decisions in NPI are evaluated in a simulation case example from the FMCG industry, taking into account the specific requirements of the PLC, especially before and during product launch. The simulation study illustrates the impacts of both non-financial and financial criteria of SC performance onto the financial situation of a company.

Limitations of the proposed framework for value-based SCM arise from the fact that links between SCM and other aspects of value-based management, e.g. the impact of SC risk on weighted average cost of capital, are not considered. Furthermore, this framework is not related to various aspects of strategic and operational SCM. A major limitation of the simulation model is that processing durations for transportation and production are assumed static. As a consequence, the RLT is independent from uncertainties. Moreover, expediting actions are not considered. Thus, cost aspects arising from project delays cannot be evaluated.

Further research is suggested on operational as well as on tactical level. On operational level, different aspects of pipeline filling, e.g. its impact from self-induced demand peaks on production planning can be studied. On tactical level, the modeling and analysis approach can be extended to reduce time to market or evaluate flop scenarios. Moreover, additional research is suggested whether and how these FMCG-specific issues need to be incorporated as frame conditions into strategic SC design problems for the FMCG industry. Some elements of the conceptual framework for value-based SCM, e.g. price effects on sales or fixed assets, are not considered in this chapter. Furthermore the framework can be directly integrated into a simulation model in order to quantify value-impacts of different TSCD options or to quantify the value of risk created by obsolete inventory in case of product flop scenarios. Beyond this, possibilities and impacts of marketing decisions during NPI, e.g. regional launch postponements to react to global supply bottlenecks, can be evaluated based on this case example.

Chapter 9
Value Impacts of Dynamics and Uncertainties in Tactical Supply Chain Design

Abstract Highly competitive consumer markets resulting in growing product launch rates amplify the relevance of tactical supply chain design (TSCD) for new product introduction (NPI). The complexity of TSCD decisions is enhanced by dynamics and uncertainties in supply chains. Beyond this, increasing profitability expectations of capital markets lead to the question how dynamic and uncertain TSCD options for NPI can be assessed regarding their value impacts. This paper proposes a hybrid value- and volume-based evaluation and quantification approach, in which a discrete event simulation model is combined with the discounted cash flow method. The suggested approach is illustrated based on a realistic case example from the fast moving consumer goods industry.[1]

9.1 Introduction

Supply chain management (SCM) can be understood as the "integration of business processes from end users to original suppliers that provides products, services and information that add value to customers" (Cooper et al. 1997, p. 2), which contributes towards establishing competitive advantages for companies across all industries (Mentzer et al. 2001). One potential source for increased competitiveness is a deeper integration of supply chain (SC) design and new product introduction (NPI) (Pero and Sianesi 2009), especially since growing pressures from customers

---

[1]This chapter has been previously published as a paper (Brandenburg M, Schilling R (2012) Value impacts of dynamics and uncertainty in tactical supply chain design for new product introduction. In: Geiger M, Geldermann J, Voß S (eds) Wirtschaftsinformatik, Entscheidungstheorie und - praxis (Business informatics, decision theory and practice). Shaker, Aachen, pp 23–46) and is reprinted in this dissertation by courtesy of © Shaker Verlag GmbH, Aachen 2012. The content of this chapter has been presented at the workshop of the "Gesellschaft für Operations Research e. V.", working groups "Wirtschaftsinformatik" and "Entscheidungstheorie und -praxis", held in Hamburg, Germany, March 30–April 1, 2011.

M. Brandenburg, *Quantitative Models for Value-Based Supply Chain Management*,   139
Lecture Notes in Economics and Mathematical Systems 660,
DOI 10.1007/978-3-642-31304-2_9, © Springer-Verlag Berlin Heidelberg 2013

and competitors as well as shortening product life cycles (PLC) force companies to increase the rate of new product launches into the market (Caridi et al. 2009).

On the one hand, a short PLC often limits the possibility to adjust the SC design regarding its performance after the product has been launched in the market (Higuchi and Troutt 2004). On the other hand, SC design for NPI must be distinguished from strategic SC design (Graves and Willems 2005), which is a capital intense and hardly revertible reorganization of the entire SC network with long-term impacts onto economic performance of a company (Goetschalckx and Fleischmann 2008; Melnyk et al. 2009). Hence, SC design issues already have to be taken into account in the early phase of a PLC. This requirement results in the task of tactical SC design (TSCD) for NPI, which can be formulated as to define and establish a product- or category-specific supply chain, i.e. allocate these new or modified products to own plants or contract manufacturers within the existing SC network in such a way that on time and in full availability of high quality products is ensured in a cost-efficient way over the whole PLC (Schilling et al. 2010).

The complexity of TSCD, which to a considerable extent is caused by NPI activities itself (Caridi et al. 2009), is amplified by uncertainties and dynamics (Wilding 1998). Dynamics can arise from order oscillations, seasonality or minimum order quantities (Villegas and Smith 2006). In NPI situations, internal SC dynamics can be created by pipeline filling requirements when significant proportions of demand are expected at or shortly after product launch. As a result, considerable product quantities must be produced and distributed before product launch (van Hoek and Chapman 2006). Uncertainties in an SC arise from demand and supply related sources (Saad and Gindy 1998) comprising time and quantity of demand, availability of capacity, processing and transportation times, cost, quality specifications, due dates, priorities, and ambiguous or missing information (Blackhurst et al. 2004). In NPI situations, SCM should be aligned with product development (Pero et al. 2010) as SC design decisions often have to be based on rough, not finalized product concepts before the development of a product has ended and thus before the market reception of a product is known or can be forecasted adequately based on historical data (van Hoek and Chapman 2006).

The circumstance that up to 80 % of the arising costs of a product are committed before product development ends (Ayag 2005) underlines the economic relevance of TSCD decisions. Considering the aspect that SCM is linked to company value (Christopher and Ryals 1999), the question arises how the impacts of TSCD options, dynamics and uncertainties in NPI situations can be assessed and quantified in a value-based way.

This question is elaborated in a case example from the fast moving consumer goods (FMCG) industry (Schilling et al. 2010). FMCG are products, e.g. cosmetics, batteries, household goods, toiletries, or paper products, which at high turnover and comparably low cost, can act as substantial profit contributors (Pourakbar et al. 2009). In particular in FMCG industry, the above mentioned characteristics of short PLC with dynamics during introduction and growth stages (Higuchi and Troutt 2004) and uncertainties of demand across the whole PLC

(Adebanjo and Mann 2000) as well as high requirements on product availability (Corsten and Gruen 2003; Marquai et al. 2010) apply.

The remainder of this chapter is structured as follows: The next Sect. 9.2 comprises a review on relevant literature, especially on SC design in NPI and value-based SCM, followed in Sect. 9.3 by a short illustration of the solution approach applied in this chapter. The subsequent Sect. 9.4 contains the case example comprising the problem statement and the description of the simulation model as well as the analysis and interpretation of the numerical results. The chapter concludes with a brief discussion and remarks on findings and future research perspectives in Sect. 9.5.

9.2 Literature Review

9.2.1 Supply Chain Design and New Product Introduction

Qualitative research on SC design for NPI emphasizes the necessity to align these two processes. Caridi et al. (2009) evaluate impacts of product and process innovations to SC in a study of multiple cases from 18 manufacturing companies. The authors conclude that higher innovation in NPI strengthens the need to implement changes in the SC and increases the managerial complexity. They furthermore show how NPI influences the SC structure, supply features and the distribution of innovated products. Based on a desk research from existing literature, Pero and Sianesi (2009) design a framework for the alignment of NPI and SCM and define appropriate metrics based on cost, time and number of products. In a case example it is illustrated that misalignments of created variety, transported variety and customer demanded variety can worsen the SC performance. Pero et al. (2010) assess how SCM and NPI are related to each other and how companies can increase their SC performance by aligning both processes appropriately. For this alignment, the authors suggest a framework that is tested in five case examples and conclude that SC design depends on modularity and level of product innovativeness. They furthermore show that SC complexity should be adjusted to the degree of innovation of a product and that mis-engineering of an SC can cause mis-alignments between SCM and NPI.

In quantitative research, SC design in NPI is often considered an optimization problem. Chauhan et al. (2004) introduce a mixed integer programming (MIP) model that minimizes total costs in strategic SC design for a new product. For the NPI-driven configuration of an SC, Graves and Willems (2005) apply a dynamic programming model to minimize cost for inventory holding, transportation and costs of goods sold (COGS). Butler et al. (2006) present a robust MIP model that maximizes net profit while considering the complete PLC and furthermore uncertainties of demand. Wang and Shu (2007) propose a configuration model based on fuzzy sets to reflect and evaluate SC uncertainties. The objective of the model is to minimize total SC costs while maximizing the possibility of achieving the target fill rate. Higuchi and Troutt (2004) apply a system dynamics simulation approach to analyze SC dynamics arising from demand variability in a case of a short life cycle product from consumer electronics industry. The authors observe reamplifying bullwhip effects and show that early setting of product and SC specifications is more important than later improvements after a product launch.

Value-based quantitative approaches or in-depth analyses of the link between SC design in NPI and value aspects have not been found in the reviewed literature.

9.2.2   Value-Based Supply Chain Management

Existing literature indicates value-based SCM is being of considerable interest for academic research for more than a decade (Melnyk et al. 2009). The conceptual aspects are among others considered by Christopher and Ryals (1999) who identify sales, cost, and capital as levers of SCM that drive company value by enhancing or accelerating cash flows. Quantitative approaches for value-based SCM can be differentiated between purely value-based approaches and hybrid value- and volume-based concepts. Brandenburg and Seuring (2010b) use discounted cash flows (DCF) in a value-based model to quantify value impacts arising from changes of working capital and SC costs and illustrate the relevance of timing and continuity of value driver developments for the overall value creation. To reflect value-based aspects in strategic SC planning, Brandenburg and Seuring (2010c) apply this DCF-based quantitative model in a combined top-down and bottom-up planning approach and outline aspects of integration with strategic financial planning as well as with tactical and operational SC planning. Hahn and Kuhn (2010, 2011) suggest hybrid value- and volume-based concepts combining financial and physical SC flows by integrating value-based SC performance and SC risk management in a robust optimization method (Hahn and Kuhn 2011) or by linking value-based SC planning to tactical SC sales and operations planning in a model to optimize sales, operations and financial decisions for maximized EVA (Hahn and Kuhn 2010).

Empirical aspects of value-based SCM are considered thoroughly by Hendricks and Singhal (2003, 2005b), who evaluate 519 and 827 cases respectively of supply chain disruptions regarding their impacts on stock price and conclude that production and delivery delays negatively influence the stock price of a firm. Losbichler and Rothböck (2006) analyze the development of working capital and its components in a study among 6,925 European companies between 1995 and 2004 to illustrate the relevance of working capital for value creation. This finding is supported by Brandenburg and Seuring (2010a), who evaluate the impacts of working capital and COGS on company value in a secondary data analysis of ten leading FMCG manufacturers.

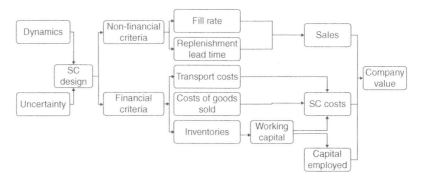

Fig. 9.1 Complexity drivers in a value-based SCM framework

9.3 Solution Method

The research methodology uses a quantitative model based on empirical data (Reiner 2005). The proposed model reflects a hybrid approach, which combines volume-based discrete event simulation (DES) of TSCD options with a value-based SCM framework and a discounted cash flow (DCF) approach to calculate value impacts. Based on a case study of a cosmetics manufacturer from FMCG industry introduced by Schilling et al. (2010), the value-based simulation and evaluation of TSCD options in NPI projects considering dynamics and uncertainties over the complete PLC is analyzed and discussed.

Simulation models are descriptive models which permit the evaluation of the dynamic behavior of supply chains and causalities in SC performance (Shapiro 2007). Simulation techniques are often applied to assess a system's operating performance prior to its implementation (Chang and Makatsoris 2001), especially since variability of parameters (uncertainties) and interplays across time (dynamics) can be reflected (Higuchi and Troutt 2004). The simulation model applied in this paper describes the behavior of a TSCD option in each period of the whole PLC by providing figures on transportation cost and COGS, inventories, and fill rate. Hence, a simulation run creates data which, as illustrated in Fig. 9.1, can be linked to SC-related drivers of the company value, sales, cost and capital (Christopher and Ryals 1999). Transportation cost and COGS are the main components of SC cost (see papers in Seuring and Goldbach 2001), and inventory is the only non-monetary component of working capital (Losbichler and Rothböck 2006). Fill rate measures product availability, which in turn is directly linked to sales, because consumers of FMCG most likely switch to substitute products when a product is unavailable (Marquai et al. 2010).

With the data obtained by the simulation model, the SC-related cash flow of a TSCD option can be calculated, which in turn allows for quantifying value impacts of TSCD options by applying a DCF method to SCM (Brandenburg and Seuring 2010b). Based on several SC scenarios defined by different degrees of dynamics

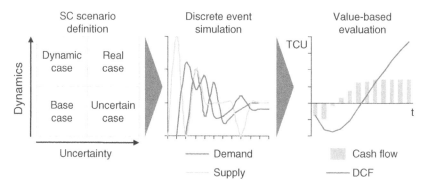

Fig. 9.2 Value-based evaluation of simulation scenarios

and uncertainties, value impacts arising from these complexity drivers are analyzed. The hybrid value- and volume-based solution method is illustrated in Fig. 9.2.

9.4   Case Example

9.4.1   General Setting

The case example builds on a realistic NPI project from a global FMCG manufacturer (Schilling et al. 2010). For confidentiality reasons the collected data and structures, in particular cost information, have been adapted without loss of academic relevance of problem structure and characteristics.

The case example comprises one cosmetics product line with three language variants (stock keeping units, SKU), one for each demand region Europe (EU), covering the majority of the demand, Latin America (LA) and Asia. The two candidate TSCD options comprise three echelons with a supplier located in Asia, production plants in Europe (TSCD option EU) and Asia (TSCD option Asia) respectively, and distribution centers (DC) in each of the three demand regions Europe, Asia and South America (see Fig. 9.3). For the supplier, restrictions regarding a fixed order quantity and a daily production capacity apply. Moreover, supplier capacity is only available from a certain point in time and reduced during a ramp-up phase. In the plants, no capacity constraints are considered. However, set up activities and production cycles are reflected by a (technically derived) fixed production quantity and a fixed production lead time of 1 week. The SC operates under a make-to-stock policy based on forecasted demands. The market demand, e.g. from wholesalers, distributors or retailers, is satisfied directly from a DC's stock in a monthly cycle. In case the demand cannot be fulfilled on time and in full, backorders are not allowed and result in lost sales.

Fig. 9.3 Candidate TSCD options

Table 9.1 Overview of the transport durations in days [d]

Source	Sink		
	EU	LA	Asia
EU	7	42	42
LA	42	56	7

The transport times in the SC network are assumed deterministic and static for each transport relation from supplier to each possible plant location and from there to each demand region, but they vary between 7 and 56 days depending on the respective transport relation (see Table 9.1).

For all three SKUs and packaging materials, option-specific landed costs – defined as sum of transport cost and COGS – are determined. These are used for cost comparison between the two TSCD options and to calculate inventory values. Due to lower production cost, TSCD option Asia yields 2 % lower landed costs per SKU than TSCD option EU.

Dynamics arise from launch patterns and pipeline filling requirements. Country-specific launch patterns are derived from commitments on launch dates and annual sales volume for each year of the whole PLC which are collected before the actual product launch. Pipeline filling requirements of 50 % of the annual demand and initial safety stock production result in peak demands of up to 60 % above comparably stable demands in year 3 (see Fig. 9.4).

Uncertainties stem from forecast errors and contingency situations defined by a wrongly estimated overall market reception of a product. Forecast errors describe the inaccuracy of tactical or operational demand planning for the near future, i.e. the next few weeks or months. Misestimated overall market reception is a rather strategic error which occurs if the cumulated sales potential of a product is over- or underestimated. The former case can lead to an oversized SC with deficient utilization of capacities or even to a PLC which terminates shortly after launch with abruptly crashing demands. In the latter case, the capacity of the SC can turn into a permanent bottleneck resulting in product unavailability and finally lost sales and unleveraged market potential. The information processes and logical flows

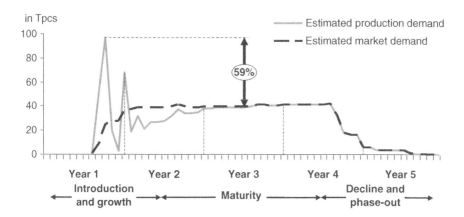

Fig. 9.4 Demand patterns of volume commitments considering pipeline filling over the projected PLC (Schilling et al. 2010)

of demands and orders are assumed to have static and non-delayed durations of negligible extent.

9.4.2   Simulation Model and Value-Based Evaluation Approach

The model of the SC is built with the DES software ARENA™ from Rockwell Automation (2007). Various validation and verification procedures of both model and output are performed (Kelton et al. 2002; Manuj et al. 2009). The model is verified externally to ensure that the real world system is reflected appropriately and furthermore validated internally to prevent from mathematical errors within the model that occur during implementation (Billington and Davis 1992; Simchi-Levi et al. 2005). The external verification that helps to adequately model the real world SC for these products is realized by comparing created demand patterns and simulation results with undisclosed data of the real case (Schilling et al. 2010). The internal validation that helps to eliminate technical implementation errors, such as mathematically wrong calculation schemes or infinite loops, was carefully ensured during the implementation of the model (Kleijnen 2005).

The model reflects the three-echelon SC described above and can be adapted to the TSCD options by adjusting several parameters (see Table 9.2).

The make-to-stock policy is incorporated through a dynamic (r, S_t) inventory policy in the DCs for finished goods and plants for packaging materials. In a monthly ordering cycle (r) inventory orders are placed at the preceding echelon, i.e. plant or supplier, so that the inventory level S_t would be reached if the order was delivered at once:

$$x_t = S_t - (i_t + j_t) . \qquad (9.1)$$

Table 9.2 Overview of inventory parameters and symbols

Parameter	Description
r	Review period
t	Time period
S_t	Target inventory level in period t
SS_t	Safety stock in period t
i_t	On-hand inventory in period t
j_t	On-order inventory in period t
x_t	Inventory order in period t
y_t	Forecast demand in period t
$\sigma(y_t)$	Standard deviation of forecast demand y_t during replenishment time
lt_{sd}	Lead time from origin s to destination d
z	Normal distribution safety factor

The dynamic re-order point S_t per period t is then calculated based on forecast demands:

$$S_t = SS_t + \sum_{i=t}^{t+lt_{sd}} y_i \, . \tag{9.2}$$

The safety stock level (SS_t) per SKU per period t is calculated based on a normal distribution safety factor z at a fill rate of 95 % (Silver et al. 1998):

$$SS_t = \sigma(y_t) \cdot \sqrt{lt_{sd}} \cdot z \, . \tag{9.3}$$

Uncertainties in the demand signal are modeled split in the two components level of expectation value, representing over and under-estimation respectively of market demand (contingency planning), and variance, describing the random fluctuation in demand. The random fluctuations are assumed to be standard distributed at specified forecast accuracy. The forecast errors are modeled by a stochastic time series of forecasted quantities which is obtained by combining a deterministic time series of actual demand quantities with a time series of stochastic independent, normal distributed random variables, each with an expectation value of one minus the average forecast error. To model contingency planning, the stochastic time series of forecasted quantities is scaled by a scenario-specific factor that represents the misestimates of the overall market reception of the product (as illustrated in Fig. 9.5).

In this contingency case, the demand forecasts are also allowed to be adjusted automatically by the system after an assumed "learning period" of 3 months. More precisely, in case that the forecasted quantities develop above respectively below the actual demand quantity for more than three subsequent months, the forecast is automatically adjusted for a contingency-related parameter that results from the ratio of forecasted and actual quantities. This reflects the potential of an organization to comprehend the overall market acceptance of a particular product. Pipeline filling

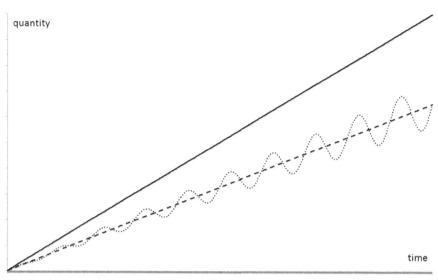

—— actual demand – – demand adjusted for contingency factor ⋯⋯ forecasted demand

Fig. 9.5 Actual demand, demand adjusted for contingency factor and forecasted demand

Table 9.3 Overview of cash flow parameters and symbols

Parameter	Description
cf_t	Net cash flow in period t
ci_t	Cash-in in period t
co_t	Cash-out in period t
d_t	Demand in period t
ls_t	Lost sales in period t
tp	Transfer price
p_t	Packaging material received in period t
fg_t	Finished goods produced and shipped in period t
pc	Packaging costs incl. transport
tc	Total production costs of finished goods incl. transport
ncc	Non-cash items of total finished goods production costs
q	Capital costs

demand volumes prior to product launch dates are assumed to be deterministic as retailers initially need to fill up all shelf facings and stocks.

The value contribution of a TSCD option is measured using the net present value (NPV) of SC-related discounted cash flows. The parameters required for this calculation are listed in Table 9.3.

Due to dynamics and differences in SC design, different TSCD options require cash expenditures or generate payments at different points in time. To measure the value-contribution of cash flows related to the SC only and exclude marketing and sales effects like pricing or media investments, the revenue is calculated based on a transfer price (tp) which is paid by the sales division in the market to the

SC organization. Incoming payments (ci_t) result from successful deliveries to a customer:

$$ci_t = (d_t - ls_t) \cdot tp . \tag{9.4}$$

Cash expenditures (co_t) are incurred at the time of consumption, i.e. when packaging materials are delivered or finished goods are produced and shipped. The calculation formula reflects that total production costs (tc) comprise non-cash items (ncc) such as depreciation and that the time of finished goods production and packaging supply diverge:

$$co_t = p_t \cdot pc + fg_t \cdot (tc - ncc - pc) . \tag{9.5}$$

The net cash flow cf_t per period t is then calculated directly as the difference of cash-in ci_t and cash-out co_t:

$$cf_t = ci_t - co_t . \tag{9.6}$$

For a horizon of T monthly time buckets, the NPV V is calculated by applying the DCF method (Brealey et al. 2008):

$$V = \sum_{t=0}^{T} \frac{cf_t}{(1 + \frac{q}{12})^t} . \tag{9.7}$$

9.4.3 Simulation Scenarios

To conduct a structured analysis of value impacts, several scenarios are defined arbitrarily and clustered to four different cases based on the two complexity drivers dynamics and uncertainties. The *base case* refers to a scenario with deterministic and static demands, i.e. demand development is assumed at the stable level of year 3 across the complete PLC (see Fig. 9.4). In the *dynamic case*, the demand pattern considers regional launch patterns as well as initial pipeline filling (see Fig. 9.4). Impacts from increasing demand variability with resulting forecast errors and effects from contingency situations, such as long-lasting over- and underestimation of product reception in the market, are taken into account in the *uncertain case* (as illustrated in Fig. 9.5). The *real case* incorporates impacts from dynamics as well as uncertainties. Defined scenarios of each case are listed in Table 9.4; the reference scenario of each case is **highlighted**, additional illustrative scenarios are written in *italics*.

9.4.4 Numerical Results

The simulation model has been validated by internal cross-checks and extensive analysis. Since the evaluation of the ramp-up phase of the SC options is of special interest, a terminating simulation and analysis approach is used (Kelton et al. 2002). The results presented show the monthly average values over a number of replications

Table 9.4 Overview of scenario settings

Case	Scenario	Demand pattern	Forecast accuracy	Contingency planning
Base case	**1**	**Static demand**	**100 %**	**100 %**
Dynamic case	**3**	**Launch pattern & pipeline filling**	**100 %**	**100 %**
Uncertain case	**109**	**Static demand**	**60 %**	**120 %**
	110			*100 %*
	111			*80 %*
	112			*60 %*
	200	*Launch pattern &*	*100 %*	*100 %*
	201	*pipeline filling*	*80 %*	
	202		*60 %*	
	203		*40 %*	
Real case	**209**	**Launch pattern &**	**60 %**	**120 %**
	210	**pipeline filling**		*100 %*
	211			*80 %*
	212			*60 %*

Table 9.5 Overview of simulation results per SC option and scenario

	Base case [1]		Dynamic case [3]		Uncertain case [109]		Real case [209]	
Parameter	EU	Asia	EU	Asia	EU	Asia	EU	Asia
Sum of cash flows (TCU)	294.5	204.5	219.2	157.5	237.6	152.9	191.3	117.1
NPV (TCU)	213.8	139.0	156.5	99.8	165.7	90.3	130.0	62.8
Payback period (months)	21	31	23	35	26	41	29	40
Service level (%)	99.3	99.9	99.4	99.2	96.6	97.4	98.1	98.2
Average landed costs (CU/pcs)	1.06	1.02	1.06	1.02	1.06	1.02	1.06	1.02

TCU '000 Currency Units, *CU* Currency Unit

with random demand variations which is found to be sufficient to produce results with an error of less than 5 % at a 95 % confidence interval on total inventory values and order lead times. The simulation results for each case and both TSCD options are depicted in Table 9.5.

Overall, the simulation experiments indicate that both candidate TSCD options are capable of supporting the product launch with comparable fill rates of more than 95 % during introduction, growth and maturity stages of the PLC. Furthermore, both TSCD options result in similar average landed cost of the products.

In contrast to these similarities, both TSCD options differ considerably with regards to cash flows and resulting NPVs which indicate that TSCD option EU is advantageous. Hence, the simulation results support the statement that TSCD has an accelerating and enhancing influence on cash flows. This observation is illustrated by Fig. 9.6. The NPV development of TSCD option EU outperforms the

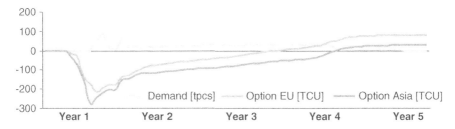

Fig. 9.6 Demand profile and NPV developments of both TSCD options (scenario 203)

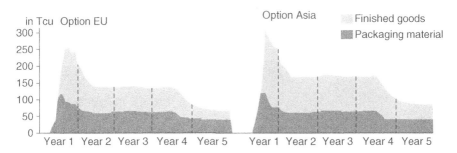

Fig. 9.7 Developments of inventory values in both TSCD options (scenario 203)

NPV development of TSCD option Asia throughout the whole PLC, i.e. cash flows are enhanced, and results in a shorter payback period, i.e. cash flows are accelerated.

An analysis of the inventory profiles of both TSCD options taking into account structural specifics helps to explain this finding. Both TSCD options result in inventory developments which follow demand profiles in a similar way as depicted in Fig. 9.7.

Inventory for regular market demands, pipeline filling, and safety stocks is built up in the product introduction phase and requires cash expenditures that can be considered an investment into the market. TSCD option Asia shows a higher peak in finished goods inventories during pipeline filling activities, which is caused by considerable differences in transportation times from the respective plant locations to the main market in Europe. Due to longer transportation times from the plant to Europe in TSCD option Asia, pipeline filling inventory remains in the SC for a significantly longer time and at a higher level, i.e. more capital is employed for a longer period. Consequently, SC option Asia requires a longer period to amortize the initial investment into inventories and to contribute value by generating a positive NPV.

A comparison between resulting cash flows and NPVs of dynamic case and base case (see Table 9.5) indicates that SC dynamics can have negative value impacts. For TSCD option EU, the base case achieves a cumulated cash flow of 294.5 TCU and an NPV of 213.8 TCU while the dynamic case realizes a cumulated cash flow of 219.2 TCU and an NPV of 156.5 TCU. The NPV developments for base case and

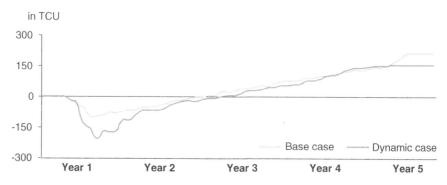

Fig. 9.8 NPV developments for base case and dynamic case (TSCD option EU)

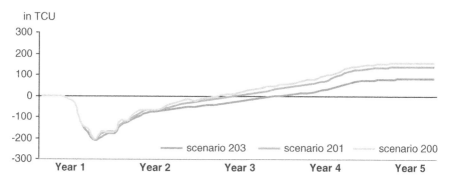

Fig. 9.9 NPV developments in different scenarios of the uncertain case (TSCD option EU)

dynamic case (see Fig. 9.8) show that required cash expenditures during pipeline filling are significantly higher in the dynamic case. Furthermore the NPV of the base case keeps outperforming the NPV development of the dynamic case and shows a strong increase at the end of the PLC. Hence value impacts of dynamics arise over the whole PLC. These findings are independent of the considered TSCD option; similar observations can be made for TSCD option Asia.

A comparison between resulting cash flows and NPVs of uncertain case and base case (see Table 9.5) shows that uncertainties in the SC can result in value deteriorations. For TSCD option EU, the uncertain case achieves a cumulated cash flow of 237.6 TCU and an NPV of 165.7 TCU, i.e. both values are significantly lower than the corresponding values of the base case. The impacts of uncertainties can be assessed further by analyzing NPV developments (see Fig. 9.9) of scenarios 203 (higher uncertainties), 201 (lower uncertainties) and 200 (no uncertainties).

The NPV development of a scenario with lower uncertainties outperforms the NPV development of a scenario with higher uncertainties. Furthermore it can be observed that the value impacts arising from uncertainties show their effects in a later phase of the PLC.

Extending the comparison to the real case (see Table 9.5) exemplifies that a combination of dynamics and uncertainties amplifies the value impacts of these complexity drivers. In both TSCD options, the real case shows the lowest values for cash flow and NPV.

9.5 Discussion and Conclusion

In this chapter, a method is proposed to evaluate and quantify value impacts of dynamic and uncertain TSCD options for NPI. This adds to research on how to align SCM with product development (Caridi et al. 2009; Pero and Sianesi 2009; Pero et al. 2010). In contrast to Higuchi and Troutt (2004), who also apply simulation techniques to TSCD in NPI, this paper furthermore considers the aspect of value creation. The resulting value- and volume-based simulation method complements similar hybrid SC optimization models suggested by Hahn and Kuhn (2010, 2011). In this chapter, the DCF method is applied to quantify value impacts of SCM. This is in line with other research papers (e.g. Brandenburg and Seuring 2010b), but compared to Brandenburg and Seuring (2010a), who use secondary data and hence apply an indirect cash flow calculation scheme, a direct cash flow calculation based on single business transactions in the SC can be applied in the approach of this chapter.

In a case example from FMCG industry it is shown that the consideration of value impacts can be an important decision factor in TSCD. This supports findings of other empirical research on the link between SCM and company value (e.g. Hendricks and Singhal 2003, 2005b). Moreover, the accelerating and enhancing influence of SCM on cash flow, which is conceptually explained by Christopher and Ryals (1999), is empirically illustrated. This chapter adds to academic research on the link between SCM and company value by illustrating negative value impacts arising from the complexity drivers dynamics and uncertainties. In the context of NPI it becomes clear that TSCD decisions can be seen similar to investments which generate cash flows.

The evaluation of TSCD scenarios with shorter PLCs, e.g. a product that flops in the market, leaves opportunities for future research on SCM in the context to NPI. Furthermore, the consideration of uncertainties on supply side or dynamic process durations for physical or logical flows would allow for assessing additional drivers of the complexity of TSCD. The applicability of the value-based simulation method to strategic SC design offers perspectives on methodology research. Empirical research applying the suggested approach can be broadened to other SC partners in FMCG industry, e.g. by evaluations from a retailer's perspective, or to different industries showing similar characteristics of short PLCs and high innovation rates, e.g. the electronics industry. The link of SCM to marketing and sales allows for broadening the research field from value-added by SCM to holistic company value approaches.

Chapter 10
Impacts of Supply Chain Management on Company Value

Abstract Supply chain management (SCM) plays a crucial role in achieving competitive advantage thereby influencing company value. Nevertheless holistic models that allow for quantifying these value impacts of SCM are missing so far. Efficient approaches to calculate and compare value contributions from supply chain (SC) value drivers are needed. This chapter proposes a model to efficiently calculate and compare value contributions from four SC value drivers that affect the profitability and asset performance: sales, SC cost, working capital and fixed assets. Thereby, financial performance metrics are linked on a strategic level to the operational layer of SCM. Properties and characteristics of the quantitative model, which is based on the discounted cash flow concept, are illustrated by an industrial example. In this context, the importance of acceleration, enhancement and volatility of cash flows for value creation is systematically explored.[1]

10.1 Introduction

Supply chain management (SCM), known as the "integration of business processes from end users through original suppliers that provides products, services and information that add value for customers" (Cooper et al. 1997, p. 2), has become a competitive advantage for companies from various industries (Christopher 2005;

---

[1]Related papers containing some elements of this chapter have been previously published (Brandenburg M, Seuring S (2011) Quantifying impacts of supply chain management on company value. In: Sucky E, Asdecker B, Dobhan A, Haas S, Wiese J (eds) Logistikmanagement – Herausforderungen, Chancen und Lösungen Bd. II. Logistics management – Challenges, chances and solutions, vol II. University of Bamberg Press, pp 117–142 and Brandenburg M (2012) Impacts of supply chain management on company value. In: Grubbström RW, Hinterhuber H (eds) 17th international Working Seminar on Production Economics. Pre-prints Vol. 2, Congress Innsbruck, Innsbruck/Austria, pp 101–114). The content of this chapter has been presented partially at the "Logistikmanagement LM11" held in Bamberg, Germany, September 28–30, 2011 and at the "17th international Working Seminar on Production Economics" in Innsbruck/Austria, February 20–24, 2012.

Mentzer et al. 2001). It is accepted that SCM has a strong impact on the value of a company (Hendricks and Singhal 2003; Lambert and Burduroglu 2000). Christopher and Ryals (1999) identify four SC-related value drivers: sales, SC cost, working capital and fixed assets. Therefore SCM can be brought into the context to value-based management (VBM) and the term shareholder value, which is defined as "a management accounting system linking value-maximization to strategic objectives, a coherent set of performance measures, and compensation through cause-and-effect-chains" (Chenhall 2005; Lueg and Schäffer 2010, p. 5; Young and O'Byrne 2001). This is comprehended as value-based SCM.

Improvements focusing on the four financial SC value drivers most often show conflicting effects on cost and capital respectively. Methods to improve working capital components (inventory, trade payables, trade receivables) for instance can result in cost increases (e.g. by negative effects on cash discount or production cost) and hence reduce the profitability of a company. Additional sales can result in an increase of working capital, e.g. caused by additional inventory resulting from pipeline filling effects when a new product is introduced in the market (Schilling et al. 2010) or by compromises on customers' payment terms. One key question is how value contributions from SC value drivers can be quantified and how financial comparability of profitability-related changes of sales or SC cost and capital-related relevant changes of fixed assets or working capital can be ensured. Other aspects of interest deal with the question which criteria are relevant for value creation and how financial performance figures linked to company value can be brought into context with operational SCM activities.

To answer these questions, the chapter aims at presenting a holistic quantitative model based on a discounted cash flow (DCF) approach. It is suggested to calculate value contributions arising from the four SC value drivers – sales, SC cost, working capital and fixed assets – by one aggregated figure. Besides, important criteria for value impacts stemming from characteristic developments of these SC value drivers are systematically explored, in particular the relevance of accelerated, enhanced and volatile value impacts are pointed out. It will furthermore be outlined how this model can be embedded into a framework for value-based SCM which links financial performance metrics on strategic level to the operational level of SCM.

The remainder of this chapter is structured as follows. In the next Sect. 10.2, an overview on scientific literature on value-based management (VBM) and value-based SCM is given, which is followed by a brief note on methodological aspects in Sect. 10.3. The subsequent Sect. 10.4 comprises the definition and analysis of the proposed quantitative model. The calculation scheme is defined for each value driver and illustrated by numerical examples. Based on an industrial case of a fast moving consumer goods' (FMCG) manufacturer, questions of relevant criteria for value creation are pointed out and answered in a systematical exploration and substantiated by mathematical proofs. Next, the integration aspects are discussed based on a framework for value-based SCM in Sect. 10.5. A summarizing discussion in the following Sect. 10.6 clarifies the positioning of this chapter to extant research and related literature. The chapter concludes with summarized findings and future prospects for research in the last Sect. 10.7. Section 12.3 comprises mathematical proofs for the lemmata stated in this chapter.

10.2   Literature Review

10.2.1   Value-Based Management

The idea of VBM is strongly linked to the term shareholder value, which stipulates all parts of a company to be managed in such a way that the equity value is sustainably increased (Rappaport 1998). Different valuation approaches, such as economic value added (EVA) (Stewart 1991), cash flow return on investment (CFROI) (Madden 1998), cash value added (CVA) (Ottosson and Weissenrieder 1996) or earned economic income (Grinyer 1985), have been developed and increased the popularity of VBM in academic research and managerial practice (Copeland et al. 2005; Damodaran 2005; de Wet 2005; Malmi and Ikäheimo 2003). One well known valuation approach is the discounted cash flow (DCF) model, which is broadly accepted in academic research (Brealey et al. 2008; Hawawini and Viallet 2002; Ross et al. 2002). A comprehensive review of literature on VBM is given by Lueg and Schäffer (2010). They classify related research as discussing capabilities, contingency factors, performance outcomes and competency. Compared to these four categories, this chapter contributes towards performance outcomes of SCM contributing to company value.

10.2.2   Value-Based Supply Chain Management

The question of how SCM affects company value has gained considerable interest for scientific research on strategic SCM (Schnetzler et al. 2004). Existing literature of the last 10 years comprises empirical studies, conceptual frameworks and quantitative models for value-based SCM.

Empirical research often focuses SCM influences on market value or stock price of a firm. Hendricks and Singhal assess the impact of SC disruptions on stock price empirically in an ex post analysis of 519 (2003) and 827 (2005b) respectively observations from industrial practice. This observation is substantiated empirically by estimating the association of SC glitches with operating performance based on a sample of 885 incidences announced by publicly traded firms (Hendricks and Singhal 2005a). Sridharan et al. (2005) empirically explore the correlation between implementation of IT for SCM and market value of a firm. A more focused analysis is provided by Capkun et al. (2009), in which the influences of inventory management on profit are assessed empirically at US manufacturing companies between 1980 and 2005. An empirical evaluation of SC-related value impacts in globally operating FMCG manufacturers between 2003 and 2008 is provided by Brandenburg and Seuring (2010a).

Conceptual models and qualitative frameworks represent the majority of academic papers on value-based SCM. Christopher and Ryals (1999) point out the influence of SCM on company value in a conceptual model, which was developed as

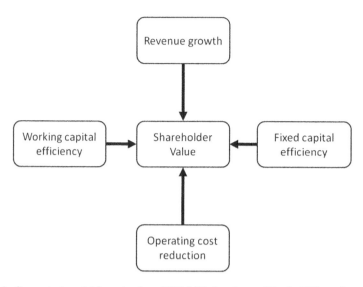

Fig. 10.1 Conceptual model for value-based SCM (Christopher and Ryals 1999, p. 4)

a reaction to the insight that a profitable company can destroy value by neglecting cost of capital and risk factors. For this model, a supply chain is comprehended as a consumer-oriented network of linked organizations which produce value in the form of products and services. Four basic drivers of company value – namely revenue growth, operating cost reduction, fixed capital efficiency and working capital efficiency – are identified and brought into relation with shareholder value (see Fig. 10.1). Qualitative arguments substantiate that each of these value drivers is directly and indirectly affected by SCM. In accordance with Srivastava et al. (1998), accelerating cash flows, enhancing cash flows, reducing volatility and vulnerability of cash flows and residual value of the business are pointed out as important criteria for value creation. The timing aspects associated with the first two criteria are discussed in the context of company-focused and relational SCM. Under consideration that future competition will shift from company level to supply chain level, it is concluded that SCM will develop to a discipline of relationship management which has a considerable impact on company value for all members of an SC.

The four drivers introduced by Christopher and Ryals (1999) allow a holistic comprehension of value-based SCM and have been taken up in subsequent research. Lambert and Burduroglu (2000) provide qualitative arguments for the impact of logistics on company value measured by EVA and discuss various metrics for value impacts of SCM. These metrics range from non-financial indicators for customer satisfaction and purely cost-or profitability-oriented metrics to shareholder value, which is stated to be the most comprehensive measure. Hofmann and Locker (2009) combine the four SC value drivers and the EVA model to a framework for value-based SC performance measurement and outline how impacts of operational SC performance on company value can be calculated. The transfer of this concept to managerial practice is illustrated in a case example from the packaging industry. Other approaches that apply EVA for value-based SCM are suggested e.g. by Lambert and Pohlen (2001) for a model to integrate eight key processes of SCM with company value or by Losbichler and Rothböck (2006) for a conceptual framework for value-based SC performance management. The application of DCF concepts for SCM is elaborated by Hofmann (2006) or Otto and Obermaier (2009) who propose inter-organizational frameworks for value-based SCM on network level.

Although it is taken for granted that SCM influences the cash flow and hence the shareholder value of a company (Srivastava et al. 1998), holistic quantitative models which link SCM to company value in a measurable way are found rather seldom. Most quantitative models concentrate on specific processes or factors of value-based SCM. An approach which combines DCF with a discrete-event simulation model to assess the value impacts of SCM is proposed by Brandenburg and Schilling (2012). The authors analyze effects of uncertainties and dynamics in tactical SC design for new product introduction based on a case example from FMCG industry. Hahn and Kuhn (2010) integrate the EVA concept into a decision model for value-based SC planning in a mid- and short-term horizon, which hence is limited to current assets and current liabilities as decision factors. Brandenburg and Seuring (2010c) suggest a quantitative model for value-based SC planning on strategic level, which focuses on value impacts of SC cost and working capital and their dynamic ratios to sales. A calculation scheme to determine value impacts of SC cost and working capital is proposed by Brandenburg and Seuring (2010b).

10.3   Methodological Aspects

10.3.1   Research Question and Methodology

This chapter contributes to academic research on value-based SCM by focusing on three research questions:

1. How to calculate value contributions of SCM in such a way that the financial comparability of profitability-related changes of sales and cost with capital-related changes of fixed assets and working capital is ensured?
2. What important criteria for value creation can be identified and substantiated?
3. How can operational SCM activities and processes be linked to company value?

To answer these research questions, a holistic quantitative model (Bertrand and Fransoo 2002) is designed in a theorizing desk research (Halldorsson and Arlbjørn 2005) by combining the DCF concept with a conceptual framework for value-based SCM introduced by Christopher and Ryals (1999). Based on this model, the importance of criteria for value creation stated by Srivastava et al. (1998) is investigated in an axiomatic research approach (Meredith et al. 1989): it is systematically attempted to find mathematical evidence for the relevance of the criteria acceleration, enhancement and volatility of cash flows for value creation. In a conceptual modeling approach (Meredith 1993) it is outlined how the quantitative model can be integrated with a framework for value-based SCM which links company value to the operational level of SCM.

10.3.2   Conceptual Elements

10.3.2.1   Value

In this chapter, the term company value will be perceived from a finance perspective: "In finance, the value of a firm is its ability to generate financial cash flows" (Ross et al. 2002, p. 28). In finance theory, net cash flows of a firm are multiplied by appropriate present-value factors to determine the value of a company, which hence is simply the sum of the present values of the individual net cash flows (Ross et al. 2002, p. 94). Derived from this approach, an impact of SCM on company value exists if SCM influences the present values of the cash flows of a firm.

10.3.2.2   Sales

It is an accepted fact that SCM can have a significant influence on sales volume, although it is not possible to calculate the exact correlation between service driven by SCM and sales (Christopher 2005). A positive causality is indicated by Corsten and Gruen (2003) who examined consumer reactions to out of stock situations in retail SC and observed that product inavailability caused sales losses of 3.9 % worldwide and finally resulted in direct and indirect losses to manufacturers and retailers. The impact of logistics service on product availability and thus sales is substantiated by Marquai et al. (2010). Other SC-related influences on sales stem from replenishment lead times or the complexity of the product assortment (Schilling et al. 2010).

10.3.2.3   Supply Chain Cost

Research in SC cost management ranges from concepts, instruments and models (see e.g. papers in Seuring and Goldbach 2001) to the link to other conceptual approaches, e.g. value based pricing (Christopher and Gattorna 2005) or logistics cost management (Suang and Wang 2009). SC cost comprise direct cost including cost for acquisition of material and labor, activity-based cost caused by administration activities arising from the organizational framework and transaction cost stemming from interactions with other companies in the SC (Seuring 2001):

$$SC \; cost \; = Direct \; cost$$
$$+Activity\text{-}based \; cost$$
$$+Transaction \; cost \; . \qquad (10.1)$$

Furthermore, SC risks can have a considerable influence on SC cost and SC performance (Lee 2008; Ritchie and Brindley 2007; Winkler and Kaluza 2006).

10.3.2.4 Working Capital

SC strategy and logistics management are linked to requirements of working capital (Christopher 2005), which has a strong influence on the liquidity position and the economic value of a company (Schilling 1996). In some definitions working capital comprises other components such as cash, prepaid expenses or accrued expenses (see e.g. Hawawini and Viallet 2002; Ross et al. 2002). For simplicity reasons, these components are neglected in the working capital definition applied in this chapter. Working capital is defined as the sum of inventories and trade receivables reduced by trade payables (Brealey et al. 2008, p. 145):

$$Working \; capital \; = Inventory$$
$$+Trade \; receivables$$
$$-Trade \; payables \; . \qquad (10.2)$$

10.3.2.5 Fixed Assets

Fixed assets are assets which have a life that is longer than 1 year and which can be differentiated between tangible assets including property, plant and equipment (PPE) and intangible assets comprising patents, trademarks, copyrights and good-will (Hawawini and Viallet 2002, p. 44). Capital expenditures describe the amount of cash which is invested to acquire tangible assets (Hawawini and Viallet 2002, p. 26) while depreciation expenses determine the calculatory cost of the periodic and systematic value-reduction process of a tangible asset (Hawawini and Viallet 2002, p. 52).

10.3.2.6 Value-Based Supply Chain Management Models

SC models can be differentiated between descriptive models which help to understand functional relationships and normative models by which decision problems are optimally solved (Shapiro 2007). Furthermore, SC models can be distinguished between conceptual models which qualitatively summarize and extend a number of different works on the same topic (Meredith 1993) and quantitative models which are suitable for developing, analyzing or testing causal relationships between control variables and performance variables in a measurable way (Bertrand and Fransoo 2002). According to these categorizations, the model proposed by Christopher and Ryals (1999) can be seen as a conceptual descriptive one. The chapter at hand aims at developing this further to a quantitative descriptive model and at extending it to a framework for value-based SCM which links company value to the operational SCM level.

10.3.2.7   Discounted Cash Flow Model

The DCF concept is the basis for the proposed quantitative model (see e.g. Brealey et al. 2008; Hawawini and Viallet 2002; Ross et al. 2002). DCF determines the company value V, which is generated during time periods $p = 1, \ldots, P$, by the sum of the discounted free cash flows FCF_p (Brealey et al. 2008, p. 37):

$$V = \sum_{p=1}^{p} \frac{FCF_p}{(1 + WACC_p)^p} \,. \tag{10.3}$$

The free cash flow FCF is defined as the difference between earnings before interest and taxes ($EBIT$) and expenses for tax, depreciation and net capital adjusted for working capital changes (Brealey et al. 2008, p. 145):

$$
\begin{aligned}
FCF = \; & EBIT - Tax\ expenses \\
& + Depreciation\ expenses \\
& - Net\ capital\ expenditures \\
& - \Delta\ Working\ capital \,. \tag{10.4}
\end{aligned}
$$

The free cash flow of each period is discounted by the weighted average cost of capital ($WACC$), which represents the minimum rate of return that must be generated in order to meet the return expectations of shareholders (Hawawini and Viallet 2002).

10.4   The Quantitative Model

10.4.1   Model Introduction

The key question is how to quantify value contributions that arise from changes of the four SC-related value drivers working capital, SC cost, sales and fixed assets over a defined horizon of time periods $p = 1, \ldots, P$. As we see from formula (10.4), changes of working capital W as well as $EBIT$ relevant changes of sales S or supply chain cost C affect the free cash flow FCF and thus contribute to company value. Furthermore, fixed assets A influence depreciation expenses as well as capital expenditures and hence have an impact on FCF. Therefore the value contribution VA^W, VA^C, VA^S or VA^A generated by the respective value drivers over a time horizon of periods $p = 1, \ldots, P$ is the sum of the value contributions, or more precisely value contributing FCF effects, VA_p^W, VA_p^C, VA_p^S and VA_p^A of each period discounted by $WACC$:

$$VA^W = \sum_{p=1}^{p} \frac{VA_p^W}{(1 + WACC_p)^p} . \tag{10.5}$$

$$VA^C = \sum_{p=1}^{p} \frac{VA_p^C}{(1 + WACC_p)^p} . \tag{10.6}$$

$$VA^S = \sum_{p=1}^{p} \frac{VA_p^S}{(1 + WACC_p)^p} . \tag{10.7}$$

$$VA^A = \sum_{p=1}^{p} \frac{VA_p^A}{(1 + WACC_p)^p} . \tag{10.8}$$

To quantify the value contributions of each period, the respective FCF effects are calculated under consideration of six characteristics:

1. Holistic approach: All value impacts of SCM can be related to exactly one of the four SC value drivers.
2. Ceteris paribus approach: Value impacts of sales growth are quantified under the assumption that its ratios to SC cost and working capital remain unchanged, i.e. the performance improvements of SC cost or working capital are excluded from sales effects. In the case that the development of working capital or SC cost is proportionate to sales development, the resulting value contribution is credited against sales development. Only in the case that working capital or SC cost develops disproportionate to sales, the resulting value contribution is credited against the respective SC value driver.
3. One-time effects of working capital: Changes of working capital create one-time effects on free cash flow and thus result in a value contribution in only one period.
4. Recurring effects of SC cost: Changes of SC cost create recurring effects on free cash flow and thus result in value contributions in all subsequent periods.
5. Recurring effects of sales: Changes of sales create recurring effects on free cash flow and thus result in value contributions in all subsequent periods.
6. Direct and indirect effects of fixed assets: Fixed asset positions are driven by capital expenditures and depreciation expenses, which affect the FCF and hence are directly linked to company value. Besides, fixed asset investments can enable sales growth or reductions of cost or working capital. Therefore, fixed assets influence company value furthermore indirectly.

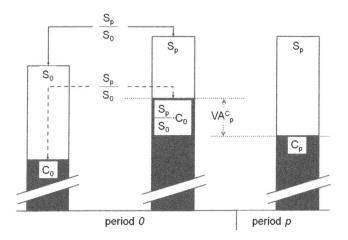

Fig. 10.2 Ceteris paribus assumption for SC cost

The ceteris paribus approach is illustrated in Fig. 10.2 based on the example of value contributions from SC cost development: The initial level of SC cost C_0 of period 0 (left column) is adjusted for sales development $\frac{S_p}{S_0}$ (mid column) and reduced by the level of SC cost C_p in period p (right column) to obtain the value contribution VA_p^C of SC cost in period p.

10.4.1.1 Value Impacts of Supply Chain Management

The first characteristic is considered by defining the value impact VA_p^{SCM} of SCM as the sum of the value impacts VA_p^W VA_p^C VA_p^S and VA_p^A of the four SC value drivers:

$$VA_p^{SCM} = VA_p^S + VA_p^C + VA_p^W + VA_p^A \tag{10.9}$$

10.4.1.2 Value Impacts of Working Capital

The value contribution VA_p^W arising from working capital development in a time period p is defined by the difference of working capital W_p at the end of period p and working capital W_{p-1} at the beginning of period p adjusted for sales development $\frac{S_p}{S_{p-1}}$ in period p:

$$VA_p^W = \frac{S_p}{S_{p-1}} \cdot W_{p-1} - W_p \ . \tag{10.10}$$

10.4.1.3   Value Impacts of Supply Chain Cost

Similar approaches as for working capital impacts apply to quantify effects from supply chain cost under consideration of the fourth characteristic. The value contribution VA_p^C stemming from changes of SC cost C_p in a period p is defined by the difference of SC cost C_0 of period 0 and SC cost C_p of period p adjusted for sales development $\frac{S_p}{S_0}$ and tax rate T_p of the respective period p:

$$VA_p^C = (\frac{S_p}{S_0} \cdot C_0 - C_p) \cdot (1 - T_p) . \tag{10.11}$$

10.4.1.4   Value Impacts of Sales

The value contribution VA_p^S caused by sales development in period p is defined as the difference of sales S_p in period p and initial sales S_0 in period 0 reduced by sales proportionate changes $(\frac{S_p}{S_0} - 1) \cdot C_0$ of initial SC cost C_0, expenses for tax T_p and sales proportionate changes of working capital $(\frac{S_p}{S_{p-1}} - 1) \cdot W_{p-1}$.

$$VA_p^S = (S_p - S_0 - (\frac{S_p}{S_0} - 1) \cdot C_0)) \cdot (1 - T_p) - (\frac{S_p}{S_{p-1}} - 1) \cdot W_{p-1} .$$

10.4.1.5   Value Impacts of Fixed Assets

Direct impacts on company value VA_p^A caused by fixed assets in period p are quantified by depreciation expenses D_p adjusted for tax rate T_p and reduced by additional capital expenditures E_p.

$$VA_p^A = D_p \cdot (1 - T_p) - E_p . \tag{10.12}$$

Furthermore indirect effects of fixed assets can arise from positive impacts which investments have on sales, cost or working capital.

10.4.2   Numerical Examples

The following generic scenarios help to explain the basic approach of the quantitative model and to point out relevance and impacts of its underlying assumptions. A case example based on secondary data of a manufacturing company illustrates how value contributions arising from SC cost and working capital can be determined by the quantitative model. Furthermore, this example is appropriate to raise the question what relevant criteria for value creation can be identified or proven.

10.4.2.1 Generic Scenarios

To illustrate this model, two generic scenarios are considered in the following. A simple scenario 1 from sales growth, cost optimization and working capital reduction in six periods is considered. The business development for this scenario 1 and the resulting value impacts are depicted in the left hand side of Table 10.1.

- In period $p = 0$ the company situation is characterized by annual sales $S_0 = 100\,\text{m}\,€$ at SC cost of $C_0 = 35\,\text{m}\,€$ and working capital of $W_0 = 25\,\text{m}\,€$.
- In period $p = 1$ the working capital is reduced to $W_1 = 20\,\text{m}\,€$.
- In period $p = 2$ a decrease of SC cost to $C_2 = 30\,\text{m}\,€$ is obtained.
- In period $p = 4$ a sales growth of 20 % is generated by improved service level. This sales growth increases working capital and SC cost proportionately by 20 %, too.
- The tax rate $T = 20\,\%$ and cost of capital $WACC = 10\,\%$ remain constant in all periods $p = 1, \ldots, 6$.

This example illustrates the characteristics 2–5 of the model:

- One time effects of working capital development: The working capital reduction in period 1 creates a one-time effect ($VA_p^W = 0$ for all $p \neq 1$).
- Recurring effects of developments of sales and SC cost: The sales increase in period 4 and the SC cost reduction in period 2 create recurring effects in all subsequent periods ($VA_p^S = 0$ for all $p \geq 4$ and $VA_p^C = 0$ for all $p \geq 2$).
- Ceteris paribus approach: Although working capital shows an absolute increase in period 4, this increase does not result in a loss of value. The reason is that working capital grew proportionate to sales by +20 %.
- The overall value impact of SCM is positive ($VA^{SCM} = 27.9\,\text{m}\,€$).

To illustrate direct and indirect value impacts of fixed assets, a modified scenario 2 is assumed with an investment which enables additional sales growth. The business development for this scenario 2 and the resulting value impacts are depicted in the right hand side of Table 10.1.

- For the realization of an investment, capital expenditure of $E_1 = 12$ in period $p = 1$ is required which is depreciated in a straight-line in the three subsequent periods ($D_i = 4$ for all $i \in \{2, 3, 4\}$).
- In the periods $p = 2, 3, 4$, the investment enables an additional sales growth of +10 % compared to the first scenario.
- In these periods, the working capital and SC cost grow proportionate to sales by +10 % compared to the first scenario.

This example illustrates the characteristics of value contributions resulting from fixed assets:

- The cumulated direct value impacts of fixed asset investments develop negative ($VA^A < 0$).

Table 10.1 Illustrative example

p	Scenario 1						Scenario 2					
	0	1	2	3	4	5	0	1	2	3	4	5
S_p	100.0	100.0	100.0	100.0	120.0	120.0	100.0	100.0	110.0	110.0	132.0	120.0
C_p	35.0	35.0	30.0	30.0	36.0	36.0	35.0	35.0	33.0	33.0	39.6	36.0
W_p	25.0	20.0	20.0	20.0	24.0	24.0	25.0	20.0	22.0	22.0	26.4	24.0
D_p	—	—	—	—	—	—	—	—	4.0	4.0	4.0	—
E_p	—	—	—	—	—	—	—	12.0	—	—	—	—
VA_p^C	—	—	4.0	4.0	4.8	4.8	—	—	4.4	4.4	5.3	4.8
VA^C	—	—	3.3	6.3	9.6	12.6	—	—	3.6	6.9	10.5	13.5
VA_p^W	—	5.0	—	—	—	—	—	5.0	—	—	—	—
VA^W	—	4.5	4.5	4.5	4.5	4.5	—	4.5	4.5	4.5	4.5	4.5
VA_p^S	—	—	—	—	6.4	10.4	—	—	3.2	5.2	12.2	12.8
VA^S	—	—	—	—	4.4	10.8	—	—	2.6	6.6	19.9	22.9
VA_p^A	—	—	—	—	—	—	—	−12	3.2	3.2	3.2	—
VA^A	—	—	—	—	—	—	—	−10.9	−8.3	−5.9	−3.7	−3.7
VA_p^{SCM}	—	5.0	4.0	4.0	11.2	15.2	—	−7.0	10.8	12.8	20.7	17.6
VA^{SCM}	—	4.5	7.9	10.9	18.5	27.9	—	−6.4	2.6	12.2	26.3	37.3

All figures in m €

- The indirect value impacts of fixed asset stemming from additional sales result in a positive overall value contribution, because VA^{SCM} increases by 9.4 m € (from 27.9 m € in the first scenario to 37.3 m € in the second scenario).
- In this investment scenario, the overall value contribution of SCM shows a typical development of an investment project (Brealey et al. 2008, p. 125; Bauer 2011, p. 191): A negative free cash flow in the early periods is overcompensated by a continuously growing free cash flow in the subsequent periods and results in a positive overall value contribution. In this scenario, VA^{SCM} declines to −6.4 m € in period $p = 1$ and then increases continuously to +37.3 m € in period $p = 5$.

10.4.2.2 Case Example

To illustrate the proposed quantitative model, its properties and functionality are shown for SC cost and working capital based on an example of a single company. Henkel KGaA, a globally operating FMCG manufacturer, is selected as the example case, because all required data is published in the annual reports (Henkel 2000–2010) of this company. Over a horizon of time periods p from 2000 to 2010, the value contributions stemming from SC cost and working capital are calculated. Working capital figures W_p were calculated from balance sheet figures trade receivables R_p, inventory I_p and trade payables P_p. For simplicity reasons SC cost C_p are limited to cost of goods sold (COGS) figures taken from profit and loss (P&L) statements. COGS reflect the direct cost and overhead associated with the

Table 10.2 Case example – Henkel KGaA

p	UOM	2000	2001	2002	2003	2004	2005	2006	2007	2008	2009	2010
S_p [a]	m €	12,779	13,060	9,656	9,436	10,592	11,974	12,740	13,074	14,131	13,573	15,092
C_p [a]	m €	6,999	7,264	5,103	4,965	5,615	6,533	6,963	7,013	8,190	7,411	8,078
W_p [a]	m €	2,896	1,735	1,760	1,845	1,840	1,693	1,699	1,500	1,651	1,054	1,045
R_p [a]	m €	2,302	1,591	1,545	1,581	1,743	1,794	1,868	1,694	1,847	1,721	1,893
I_p [a]	m €	1,711	1,081	1,073	1,053	1,196	1,232	1,325	1,283	1,482	1,218	1,460
P_p [a]	m €	1,117	937	858	789	1,099	1,333	1,494	1,477	1,678	1,885	2,308
T_p [a]	%	38.1	40.7	35.1	35.0	35.0	35.0	30.0	30.0	30.0	29.0	26.4
$WACC_p$ [a]	%	8.0	8.0	8.0	8.0	7.0	7.0	7.0	7.0	7.5	8.0	7.0
VA_p^{C} [b]	m €	–	−66	120	132	121	16	10	103	−315	16	138
VA^{C} [b]	m €	–	−61	42	147	239	251	258	322	145	153	224
VA_p^{W} [b]	m €	–	1,225	−477	−125	231	387	102	244	−30	532	127
VA^{W} [b]	m €	–	1,134	725	626	802	1,078	1,146	1,298	1,281	1,547	1,611
VA^{SCM} [b]	m €	–	1,073	767	773	1,041	1,329	1,404	1,620	1,426	1,700	1,835

[a] Data source: annual report of respective period
[b] Figures calculated with described formulas

physical production of products for sale (Poston and Grabinski 2001). Figures for tax rates T_p and cost of capital $WACC_p$ are published in the respective annual reports, too. The input data from the annual reports and calculation results obtained by the quantitative model are depicted in Table 10.2.

It can be seen that overall Henkel KGaA created value $VA^{SCM} = 1,835\,\text{m}€$ from SCM, and that value impacts $VA^{W} = 1,611\,\text{m}€$ of working capital were significantly higher than value contributions $VA^{C} = 224\,\text{m}€$ from SC cost. Analyzing this example in greater detail illustrates the incidence of recurring cost effects and the ceteris paribus assumption in practice. This observation indicates the relevance of performance levels for assessing value impacts of SC cost and working capital.

Observations of working capital illustrate the ceteris paribus approach and the relevance of performance levels for value creation:

1. In 2006, the working capital showed a slight absolute increase compared to 2005 (by 6 m €, i.e. 0.4 %, from 1,693 to 1,699 m €). In the same period, sales increased more strongly (by 6.4 % from 11,974 to 12,740 m €). Hence the working capital performance improved and value was created ($VA_{2006}^{W} = 102\,\text{m}€$).

2. In 2007, the working capital decreased absolutely (from 1,699 to 1,500 m €) at increasing sales (from 12,740 to 13,074 m €). This resulted in a value contribution of $VA_{2007}^{W} = 244\,\text{m}€$.

3. In 2008, the absolute increase of working capital (by 151 m €, i.e. 10.1 %, from 1,500 to 1,651 m €) was overproportionate compared to sales growth (by 8.1 % from 13,074 to 14,131 m €). This led to a loss of value ($VA_{2008}^{W} = -30\,\text{m}€$).

4. In 2009, working capital and sales both showed an absolute decline, but working capital decreased more strongly (by 597 m €, i.e. −36.2 %, from 1,651

to 1,054 m €) than sales (by -3.9% from 14,131 to 13,573 m €). Hence the working capital performance was improved and value was created ($VA_{2009}^W = 532$ m €).

A detailed analysis of SC cost developments shows the relevance of recurring cost effects and the importance of SC cost performance:

1. In 2006, SC cost showed an absolute increase compared to 2005 (by 430 m €, i.e. 6.6 %, from 6,533 to 6,963 m €), which was slightly higher than the sales growth in that period (by 6.4 % from 11,974 to 12,740 m €). But due to the fact that related to sales, the SC cost level in 2006 (54.7 % of sales) was still better than in the initial period 2000 (54.8 % of sales), the SC cost development resulted in value creation ($VA_{2006}^C = 10$ m €).
2. In 2007, SC cost absolutely increased compared to 2006 (by 50 m €, i.e. 0.7 %, from 6,963 to 7,013 m €) and even in comparison to the initial period 2000 (by 14 m €, i.e. 0.2 %, from 6,999 m €). But this increase was underproportionate to sales growth between 2000 and 2007 (by 2.3 % from 12,779 to 13,074 m €) and hence resulted in value contribution ($VA_{2007}^C = 103$ m €).

These observations indicate that focusing on the absolute development of an SC value driver is not sufficient to assess the resulting value impacts. Instead, the developments have to be seen in context to and brought into relation to the developments of other SC value drivers.

This finding raises the question if criteria exist which are decisive for value creation and if such criteria can be identified and proven. This aspect, which reflects the second research question of this chapter, will be dealt with in the next subsection.

10.4.3 Important Criteria for Value Creation

In this section, important criteria for value creation will be identified, assessed and proven in an axiomatic research. Srivastava et al. (1998) state that the value of any strategy is inherently driven by an acceleration of cash flows, an increase of cash flows and a reduction of volatility of future cash flows. Based on the quantitative model, the validity of these statements in context to value-based SCM will be systematically explored by mathematical evidence or counter examples. Mathematical proofs for all lemmata are given in Sect. 12.3 of this thesis.

10.4.3.1 Terminology

For the mathematical exploration of this section, an appropriate terminology is needed and hence now briefly introduced. In the following let $C := (C_p)_{p=1}^P$, $W := (W_p)_{p=1}^P$ and $S := (S_p)_{p=1}^P$ be time series of SC cost, working capital and sales in a horizon of periods $p = 1, \ldots, P$.

The SC cost **performance level** is defined as the ratio $\lambda^C(C_p) := \frac{C_p}{S_p}$ of SC cost C_p to sales S_p in period p. Analogous the working capital performance level is defined as the ratio $\lambda^W(W_p) := \frac{W_p}{S_p}$ of working capital W_p to sales S_p in period p.

The SC cost development C (and working capital development W respectively) is called **deterioration-free**, iff the corresponding time series $(\lambda^C(C_p))_{p=1}^P$ of SC cost performance levels (and $(\lambda_p^W(W_p))_{p=1}^P$ of working capital performance levels respectively) is monotonically decreasing, i.e. $\lambda^C(C_p) \geq \lambda^C(C_{p+1})$ for all $p \in \{1, \ldots, P\}$ (respectively $\lambda^W(W_p)) \geq \lambda^W(W_{p+1})$ for all $p \in \{1, \ldots, P\}$).

The SC cost development C (and working capital development W respectively) has a **continuous improvement**, iff it is deterioration-free and is strictly decreasing in at least one period p, i.e. $\lambda^C(C_p) > \lambda^C(C_{p+1})$ (and $\lambda^W(W_p) > \lambda^W(W_{p+1})$ respectively) for at least one $p \in \{1, \ldots, P\}$.

The SC cost development C is called **enhanced** compared to a time series of an SC cost development $K := (K_p)_{p=1}^P$ iff $\lambda^C(C_p) < \lambda^C(K_p)$ for at least one $p \in \{1, \ldots, P\}$ and $\lambda^C(C_p) \leq \lambda^C(K_p)$ for all $p \in \{1, \ldots, P\}$. The working capital development W is called enhanced compared to a time series of a working capital development $V := (V_p)_{p=1}^P$ iff $\lambda^W(W_p) < \lambda^W(V_p)$ for at least one $p \in \{1, \ldots, P\}$ and $\lambda^W(W_p) \leq \lambda^W(V_p)$ for all $p \in \{1, \ldots, P\}$.

The SC cost development C is called **accelerated** compared to a time series of an SC cost development $K := (K_p)_{p=1}^P$ iff $\lambda^C(C_q) \leq \lambda^C(K_p)$ for at least one pair $p, q \in \{1, \ldots, P\}, q < p$ and $\lambda^C(C_p) \leq \lambda^C(K_p)$ for all $p \in \{1, \ldots, P\}$. The working capital development W is called accelerated compared to a time series of a working capital development $V := (V_p)_{p=1}^P$ iff $\lambda^W(W_q) \leq \lambda^W(V_p)$ for at least one $p, q \in \{1, \ldots, P\}, q < p$ and $\lambda^W(W_p) \leq \lambda^W(V_p)$ for all $p \in \{1, \ldots, P\}$.

10.4.3.2   Model Consistency

The mathematical exploration of relevant criteria for value creation is based on the proposed quantitative model. Hence it is crucial to ensure that this quantitative model maps reality, i.e. represents the interplay and effects of SC value drivers in an appropriate way. To provide evidence that this prerequisite is fulfilled, the model is calibrated with standard DCF models by the following lemma:

Lemma 10.1. *In the case that all value impacts of a company are caused by SCM, the proposed quantitative model calculates the same value added to a company as the standard DCF model.*

The basic idea of this proof is to show that ceteris paribus (i.e. value impacts which do not stem from SCM are neglected) the sum $VA_p^S + VA_p^C + VA_p^W + VA_p^A$ of the value impacts VA_p^W, VA_p^C, VA_p^S and VA_p^A of the four SC value drivers working capital, SC cost, sales and fixed assets is equal to the change ΔFCF_p of free cash flow of a company in period p.

Having substantiated the consistency of the quantitative model, the relevance of each criterion will now be explored based on this model for each SC value driver.

10.4.3.3   Accelerating and Enhancing Value Impacts

The relevance of timing for cash flow and resulting value contributions has been elaborated in academic research. Christopher and Ryals (1999) state that the sooner cash is received, the greater will be the net present value of these cash flows. Timing aspects are seen as success factors, especially in cases of responsiveness to market requirements or when a new product is launched in the marketplace (Srivastava et al. 1998). In this context, the value impact of accelerated or enhanced sales growth is evaluated first.

Lemma 10.2. *Amplifying a monotonically increasing and value creating sales development generates additional value.*

The mathematical proof for this lemma is straightforward by calculating that higher and faster growing sales result in additional value. As can be seen from the prerequisites of this lemma, the development of sales levels in each period of the considered time horizon and the interplay with other value drivers have to be taken into account. In scenarios which show intermediate sales decline or value losses, an overall value creation is not guaranteed and a mathematical analysis of such a scenario would have a higher complexity. Similar conclusions can be made for accelerating or enhancing SC cost performance improvements.

Lemma 10.3. *Accelerating or enhancing improvements of SC cost performance in a deterioration-free SC cost development increases the resulting value contribution.*

The prerequisite of a deterioration-free SC cost development indicates that positive value impacts cannot be guaranteed by accelerating SC cost developments which show intermediate value losses. In case that an intermediate cost deterioration is expedited, an acceleration might be counterproductive for value creation

The question if accelerating or enhancing working capital improvements results in additional value cannot be answered without considering developments of sales and cost of capital. Although the basic assumption that reduced working capital requirements increase company value is taken for granted (Farris II and Hutchison 2002), the interplay of working capital with other value drivers, e.g. sales, or parameters such as cost of capital has to be taken into account. Lemma 10.4 shows that accelerating or enhancing the working capital performance can increase the value contribution. With additional prerequisites for *WACC* and sales growth rate, this statement can be proven mathematically.

Lemma 10.4. *In cases of constant WACC which is not exceeded by the sales growth rate and a deterioration-free improvement of working capital performance, an accelerated or enhanced improvement of the working capital performance results in higher value contributions.*

Overall these three lemmata show that value impacts of SCM can be increased by accelerating or enhancing cash flows, although the proof of this statement for working capital requires additional prerequisites.

10.4.3.4   Volatility of Value Impacts

Srivastava et al. (1998) state that a reduction in vulnerability and volatility of future cash flows can have a positive impact on cost of capital and hence on company value. In this context it will be tested if more continuous or less volatile developments of SC value drivers result in higher value contributions. Regarding the volatility it is not possible to formulate a general statement for SC value drivers. For each SC value driver – sales, cost, capital – it is possible to find scenarios in which a development with increased volatility results in higher value contributions.

Lemma 10.5. *Increasing the volatility of sales, SC cost or working capital developments can result in higher value contributions compared to more smooth developments.*

Simple scenarios which proof Lemma 10.5 are given in Sect. 12.3.6 of this thesis. The basic idea of these scenarios is that improvements achieved in an earlier period overcompensate deteriorations of a later period which hence is discounted at a higher factor. Nevertheless, aspects of continuity are considerable criteria for value impacts of sales, SC cost and working capital. This can be seen by the following lemma:

Lemma 10.6. *Deterioration-free developments of SC cost performance or working capital performance do not result in value losses. Constant developments of SC cost performance or working capital performance do not create value, while continuous improvements of SC cost performance or working capital performance result in value creation.*

Note: As a prerequisite for value creation, it would be sufficient to ensure that the initial level ($\lambda^C(C_0)$) of cost performance is not exceeded in any subsequent period i.e. $\lambda^C(C_p) \leq \lambda^C(C_0)$ for all $p \in \{1, \ldots, P\}$. This weaker prerequisite for SC cost makes this lemma stronger. For working capital performance, it is not possible to obtain a stronger statement by relaxing the prerequisite to $\lambda^W(W_p) \leq \lambda^W(W_0)$ for all $p \in \{1, \ldots, P\}$.

10.4.3.5   Overall Findings on Criteria for Value Creation

Based on the quantitative model, the relevance of acceleration and enhancement of value impacts from SCM is substantiated by mathematical proofs. It is furthermore illustrated that, especially for assessing working capital impacts, the interplay with other value drivers and parameters must be considered. Beyond this, the continuity of value driver developments is identified as important criterion for value creation. On the contrary, the relevance of volatility reduction for value creation could not be validated. The findings of the exploration of important criteria for value creation are summarized in Table 10.3.

Table 10.3 Value creation criteria

Criterion	SC cost	Working capital	Sales
Acceleration	$\checkmark$	$(\checkmark)$	$\checkmark$
Enhancement	$\checkmark$	$(\checkmark)$	$\checkmark$
Volatility	$\neg$	$\neg$	$\neg$
Continuity	$\checkmark$	$\checkmark$	$\checkmark$

$\checkmark$ = criterion fully validated for this value driver
$(\checkmark)$ = criterion partially validated for this value driver
$\neg$ = criterion not validated for this value driver

10.5 Integration Aspects

To answer the third research question how to link operational SCM activities and processes to company value, the integration of the proposed quantitative model into a framework for value-based SCM is outlined. This framework is derived from the conceptual model proposed by Christopher and Ryals (1999) in three steps:

As a first step, the value drivers are categorized. Sales and SC cost both influence the profitability measured by EBIT, which in turn has an impact on company value. Working capital and fixed assets can be grouped to capital employed, which comprises short-term debt, long-term debt and equity capital (Hawawini and Viallet 2002, p. 71) and affects company value (Brandenburg and Schilling 2012).

As a second step, value driver components and additional links can be added to the conceptual model proposed by Christopher and Ryals (1999). The value driver components were introduced to each value driver in Sect. 10.3.2. Components of the value drivers SC cost, working capital and fixed assets are financial criteria which are directly linked with a quantifiable impact on the respective value driver. Assortment complexity, service level or replenishment lead time are non-financial components which influence sales in an indirect and not quantifiable way (Schilling et al. 2010). Further links are added to the framework to express the indirect influence of fixed assets on the value drivers sales, SC cost or working capital, which has been addressed in the introduction of this conceptual element (see page 161). These impacts can be substantiated e.g. by considering that investments in machinery can be required for new product introduction (Schilling et al. 2010). The resulting extended framework for value-based SCM is depicted in Fig. 10.3.

As a third step, operational SCM activities and processes are linked to the framework by their impact on the value driver components. Direct cost for instance are caused by the production of a product, whereas activity-based cost are caused by activities that administer and steer the manufacturing and distribution processes and hence cannot be directly related to products (Seuring 2001). Besides, transaction cost encompass all activities to manage the relationships to customers and suppliers (Seuring 2001). Furthermore, improvements of operational SCM processes can affect one or more value driver components and hence increase company value. One example is the positive impact of supplier managed inventory on direct cost and inventory levels, which is elaborated in supply chains of original equipment manufacturers (van Nyen et al. 2009).

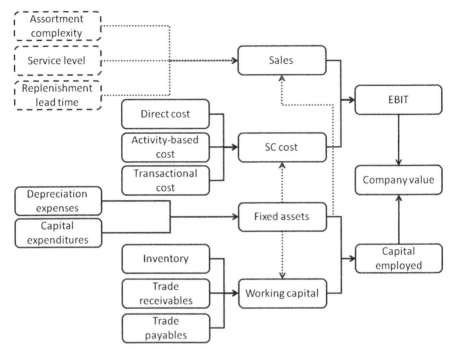

Fig. 10.3 Framework for value-based SCM, *solid box* = financial criterion, *dotted box* = non-financial criterion, *solid line* = direct or quantifiable impact, *dotted line* = indirect or not quantifiable impact

10.6   Summary and Discussion

In summary, the research questions of this chapter can be answered as follows:

1. How to calculate value contributions of SCM in such a way that the financial comparability of profitability-related changes of sales and cost with capital-related changes of fixed assets and working capital is ensured?
   Based on a conceptual model for value-based SCM and the DCF method, a quantitative model is designed to calculate and compare SC-related impacts of sales, SC cost, working capital and fixed assets on company value. Properties and functionality of the model are illustrated numerically by two generic scenarios and an industrial case example of an FMCG manufacturer.
2. What important criteria for value creation can be identified and substantiated?
   Based on the quantitative model, the relevance of accelerating and enhancing value impacts of SCM is mathematically proven. Further mathematical evidence shows that value can be generated by continuous improvements of SC value drivers.

3. How can operational SCM activities and processes be linked to company value?
   A conceptual model for value-based SCM is extended to a framework for value-based SCM to which operational SCM activities and processes can be linked.

The following brief discussion, which is based on the papers reviewed within Sect. 10.2 of this chapter, will point out the positioning of this chapter to extant scientific literature on value-based SCM.

The conceptual model for value-based SCM introduced by Christopher and Ryals (1999) is developed further in two directions by the quantitative model proposed in this chapter. The purely conceptual model is enhanced by a quantitative aspect which allows for calculating and comparing value impacts of profitability-related SC value drivers and capital-related factors. This adds to research done by Lambert and Burduroglu (2000) who discuss the linkage between EVA and SCM impacts on sales, cost and capital. An industrial case example illustrates that value impacts of SCM can be determined based on secondary data. This helps covering the need for efficient ways to measure shareholder value impacts as addressed by Lambert and Burduroglu (2000). Furthermore, the conceptual model of four SC value drivers is extended by value driver components and an outlined integration with operational SCM activities and processes. This approach is in line with a framework developed by Lambert and Pohlen (2001) to link eight SC processes to company value.

The chapter at hand contributes to academic research by providing a holistic quantitative model for value-based SCM in contrast to other quantitative descriptive models for this area, which focus only selected value drivers or analyze the coherence of company value and specific aspects of SCM, and hence cannot be considered holistic. The calculation scheme to quantify value impacts suggested by Brandenburg and Seuring (2010b), for instance, is focused on SC cost and working capital only. Their approach for value-based strategic SC planning (Brandenburg and Seuring 2010c) faces similar limitations and furthermore is directed to strategic planning aspects of SCM. A value-based SCM model designed by Brandenburg and Schilling (2010), which combinates the DCF method and discrete event simulation, additionally covers SCM impacts on sales, but is mainly suitable to evaluate SC design options or new product introduction scenarios.

Limitations of this chapter, which leave room for further research, mainly arise from conceptual constraints and required empirical substantiation. Value impacts of SC risk management were not considered explicitly in the quantitative model. For the value-based SCM framework, qualitative arguments are needed to substantiate the correlation between SCM performance and sales increase. Furthermore, the link between the framework comprising the quantitative model and operational SCM activities and processes is only outlined, but not exhaustively elaborated. To ensure consistency between the quantitative model and industrial practice, the model has been calibrated with standard DCF methods by a mathematical approach. A thorough empirical analysis would help to validate this consistency. Furthermore empirical research is needed to substantiate the findings of the systematic exploration of important criteria for value creation. Further research directions for value-based SCM arise when taking into account the inter-organizational or network perspective.

10.7 Conclusion

In this chapter, a conceptual model for value-based SCM introduced by Christopher and Ryals (1999) has been developed further. A quantitative model is proposed to efficiently calculate and compare value impacts of sales, SC cost, working capital and fixed assets. Based on this model, important criteria for value creation are systematically elaborated and the relevance of timing aspects for value creation are proven mathematically. In particular it is shown that accelerating or enhancing value impacts of SC cost or working capital results in additional value. Furthermore it is proven that value can be generated by continuous developments of SC value drivers. To link operational SCM activities and processes to company value, a framework for value-based SCM comprising the quantitative model is designed, and the integration of the four SC value drivers and their components with the operational SCM level is outlined.

Chapter 11
Conclusion

Abstract This chapter concludes the thesis at hand. In the first section of this chapter, the findings of this dissertation are summarized to give answers to the three research questions of this thesis. The second section of this chapter comprises a thorough discussion of research design and results to position this dissertation to related scientific literature. This discussion links the presented research into previous research in the field as outlined in the Chaps. 2–4. The last section of this chapter outlines limitations and future prospects for scientific research on value-based SCM.

11.1 Summary and Findings

The three research questions[1] this thesis deals with aim at extending a qualitative conceptual framework for value-based SCM by quantitative models, identifying and substantiating relevant criteria and influencing factors on company value and linking financial performance figures with tactical and operational SCM activities. Grounded on a conceptual framework for value-based SCM and a thorough analysis of the applied terminology and the status of research in this area, these questions are elaborated on by quantitative modeling in the Chaps. 5–10. The conceptual framework introduced in Sect. 3.4.2 (see Fig. 3.3 on page 63) is designed by combining the shareholder value network introduced by Rappaport (1998) with

---

[1]RQ1: How are value contributions of SCM quantified in such a way that profitability-related changes of sales or SC cost and capital-related changes of fixed assets or working capital are financially comparable? RQ2: Which criteria and influencing factors are relevant for value creation? RQ3: How are financial performance figures to measure company value brought into context with tactical and operational SCM activities? See Sect. 3.1.

M. Brandenburg, *Quantitative Models for Value-Based Supply Chain Management,*   177
Lecture Notes in Economics and Mathematical Systems 660,
DOI 10.1007/978-3-642-31304-2__11, © Springer-Verlag Berlin Heidelberg 2013

a company model proposed by Shapiro (2007) that comprises financial processes accomplished by Damodaran (2011a) and operational processes characterized by Stock and Boyer (2009).

A structured content analysis of 65 reviewed papers given in Chap. 4 illustrates terminological aspects and methodological designs for academic research on value-based SCM. This literature review shows a balance between empirical and theorizing research on this area. Empirical research is mainly based on case studies, while theorizing research emphasizes conceptual models and qualitative frameworks for value-based SCM. The majority of the reviewed manuscripts are categorized as explanatory, explorative or descriptive, hence research on this area has an observant character. In most cases, value-based SCM is grounded on shareholder value, however, non-financial aspects and efficiency criteria are reflected as well in different papers. Most papers focus value aspects on firm level and assess value impacts stemming from overall SCM, logistics or purchasing. Only few publications suggest research that goes beyond the validation of findings. These papers propose to elaborate on benefits and metrics of SCM, especially with disaggregated views on the logistics and finance perspectives or by broadening of the value comprehension to ecological or social aspects. Besides, assessing normative structures in decision making and value impacts in the inter-organizational context are arrogated.

To answer the first research question[2] of this thesis, different quantitative models are proposed in Chaps. 5, 9 and 10 to determine the value impacts of SCM stemming from profitability- or capital-related value drivers, tactical SC design decisions or SC dynamics and uncertainties. An AD model introduced in Chap. 5 is suitable to efficiently quantify and financially compare recurring value effects of SC cost and one time value impacts of working capital. In a theorizing desk research, this model is mathematically derived from the DCF concept and illustrated in a case example of an FMCG manufacturer. The research perspectives addressed in this chapter, which are taken up in the subsequent Chaps. 6, 9 and 10 of this thesis, aim at validating this model by empirical research or at extending this model by further financial and non-financial value drivers. The extension by the SCM-related value drivers sales and fixed assets is focused in Chap. 10, which describes how the DCF effects are mathematically partitioned to the share of value contribution achieved by each of the four profitability- or capital-related value drivers of SCM. This approach and its applicability to managerial practice are illustrated by numerical examples and an industrial case example of a cosmetics manufacturer. The quantification of value impacts arising from non-financial value drivers or SC design is reflected in Chap. 9. By integrating DCF valuation methods with a DES model, a hybrid volume- and value-based AS model is obtained which is applied to an empirical case example for NPI at a cosmetics manufacturer. This case example illustrates that SC dynamics and uncertainties are negatively associated with company value and that a combination

---

[2]RQ1: How are value contributions of SCM quantified in such a way that profitability-related changes of sales or SC cost and capital-related changes of fixed assets or working capital are financially comparable? See Sect. 3.1.

of both influences amplifies value losses. Furthermore, it can be concluded that decision making in tactical SC design can accelerate and enhance cash flow from operations. Hence, value contributions of tactical SC design options that result in lower inventory levels and higher non-financial performance can outperform value impacts of cost-advantageous design options.

Answers to the second research question[3] are provided by Chaps. 6, 8 and 10. In a benchmarking study of ten globally operating manufacturers from FMCG industry presented in Chap. 6, the value impacts of SC cost and working capital are analyzed based on secondary data from published financial statements and the quantitative AD model introduced in Chap. 5. This study empirically validates the AD model presented in Chap. 5 and supports the conjecture that developments of the SCM-related value drivers SC cost and working capital negatively correlate with company value. Besides, it is observed in this benchmarking study that working capital improvements in the FMCG sector were predominantly achieved by optimizing monetary components, mainly trade payables, while considerable inventory reductions and related value impacts are not detected. Furthermore, it can be concluded that the sensitivity of cost of capital can be negligible for value creation. Most notably, this benchmarking study empirically substantiates qualitative arguments of Srivastava et al. (1998) to explain that acceleration, enhancement or reduced volatility of cash flows can add value. In Chap. 10, this substantiation is complemented by a systematical exploration of the coherence between these factors and company value. Mathematical proofs show that continuous improvements of SC cost, working capital or sales positively affect company value. Furthermore, mathematical proofs partially validate the relevance of accelerating or enhancing cash flows for value creation. Evidence is given for the conjecture that accelerating or enhancing sales growth or SC cost reduction adds value, while positive value impacts stemming from accelerated or enhanced working capital reductions cannot be proven mathematically without additional constraining prerequisites. No evidence was found for the conjecture that reducing the volatility of value driver developments increases company value. On the contrary, this Chap. 10 comprises counter examples for this statement. Chapter 8 elaborates on the relevance of non-financial criteria for value creation. In a theorizing desk research, tactical SC design as well as SC dynamics and uncertainties are embedded in a value-driver hierarchy which is based on profitability- and capital-related value drivers of SCM. The links in this conceptual framework are explained by qualitative arguments and empirically tested in a quantitative AS model that illustrates how dynamics and uncertainties affect non-financial value drivers during TSCD of an FMCG network. This case example exemplifies that TSCD decisions can influence inventory levels, RLT and the robustness of an SC. In particular it is illustrated how short- and long-term uncertainties in SC affect inventory level and how pipeline filling can cause self-created dynamics of demand profiles which in turn influence RLT and stock levels,

---

[3]RQ2: Which criteria and influencing factors are relevant for value creation? See Sect. 3.1.

especially in the beginning of the PLC. Overall it has been argued for that delayed
NPI can negatively affect company value.

The third research question[4] of this thesis is focused by a value-based strategic
SC planning approach proposed in Chap. 7 to determine targets for SCM-related
value drivers over a long-term horizon of several years. In a desk research grounded
on the quantitative AD model introduced in Chap. 5 and a company model described
by Shapiro (2007), financial planning and SC planning are integrated to strategic
value-based SC planning. This value-based SC planning model helps to bridge the
research gaps in reflecting value aspects in SC planning and dynamic ratios of cost
or capital to sales in financial planning by outlining how value contributions of
SCM can be planned top down and validated bottom up under consideration of
firm growth and dynamic ratios of SC cost and working capital to sales. Hence, this
model can be categorized AN. The third research question is furthermore reflected in
the extended conceptual frameworks described in Chaps. 8 and 10. The value-driver
hierarchy introduced in Chap. 8 explains how company value and its profitability-
and capital-related drivers can be linked to decision making for tactical SC design
and NPI. The conceptual framework outlined in Chap. 10 exemplifies how company
value is influenced by operational SCM activities.

11.2 Discussion

Rather than going into depth, e.g. by thoroughly detailing the quantification of value
impacts for one particular value driver from strategic to operational level, or into
length, e.g. by considering value impacts or value transfer on an inter-organizational
level between various members in an SC, this thesis assesses value impacts of SCM
in breadth by simultaneously considering profitability- and capital-related drivers of
company value and besides influences of non-financial factors on company value.
This breadth is reflected in the research design, as different approaches are applied
for theory-driven and empirical research, and in the underlying comprehension of
SCM, because strategic, tactical and operational aspects of SCM as well as both
dimensions of the product-relationship-matrix (Seuring 2009) are considered in
this thesis. The strongest inspiration for the research of this thesis was given by
Christopher and Ryals (1999), who were among the first to link SCM to company
value by the four financial value drivers sales, cost, working capital and fixed assets.
The conceptual model for value-based SCM proposed by Christopher and Ryals
(1999) is complemented by quantitative models presented in Chaps. 5–10. To the
best of the author's knowledge, this is the first time that such a holistic perspective
on value-based SCM is taken. These aspects will be discussed in greater detail by
positioning this thesis to extant related literature reviewed in Chaps. 2–4. In this

[4]RQ3: How are financial performance figures to measure company value brought into context with
tactical and operational SCM activities? See Sect. 3.1.

discussion, the theory-driven and the empirical research approach of this dissertation will be focused as well as the SCM comprehension and its considered financial and non-financial value drivers.

The research conception of the thesis at hand reflects a balance of empirical and theorizing approaches in scientific research which is indicated by related literature (see Chap. 4). However, the research methodology applied in this dissertation differs from scientific mainstreams. Rather than focusing on conceptual frameworks, which the majority of theorizing manuscripts deal with (see Sect. 2.3.2 and findings of Chap. 4), the axiomatic research in this thesis comprises quantitative models. In contrast to Kannegiesser et al. (2009) or Hahn and Kuhn (2010, 2011) who suggest normative quantitative models for value-based SC planning, this thesis furthermore proposes descriptive quantitative models. The AD and AS models introduced in Chaps. 5, 9 and 10 are suitable to determine the magnitude of value impacts stemming from SCM while the AN model outlined in Chap. 7 can be applied for value-based strategic SC planning. Thereby this dissertation contributes to research on value-based SCM in different ways. The AD models introduced in Chaps. 5 and 10 are suitable to efficiently quantify and measure value contributions of SCM as arrogated e.g. by Hofmann and Locker (2009). In contrast to other quantitative approaches (see e.g. Brandenburg and Menke 2008; Hofmann and Locker 2009; Losbichler and Rothböck 2006), the model presented in Chap. 10 allows for simultaneously assessing value impacts of sales, SC cost, working capital and fixed assets and furthermore enables a financial comparison of the value influences arising from each of these value drivers. Furthermore, this model is suitable to substantiate the relevance of timing and volatility of cash flow effects for value creation by mathematical evidence. Srivastava et al. (1998) supported this statement, which Christopher and Ryals (1999) brought into context of SCM, by qualitative arguments, but axiomatic and quantitative arguments to substantiate this conjecture have been missing so far. The AS model introduced in Chap. 9 integrates the DES method and the DCF concept to value-based simulation. As outlined in this chapter, this approach facilitates a significantly improved planning of SC configurations as requested by Labitzke et al. (2009). In contrast to simulation-based cost acccounting or cost simulation (see e.g. Labitzke et al. 2009, 2011), the model suggested in Chap. 9 extends the view from a pure cost focus to a value-based approach that simultaneously considers cost- and capital-related value drivers and non-financial factors of SC configuration. Furthermore, this approach helps to cover the need addressed by Chopra and Meindl (2007) to consider all phases of the PLC in decision making for SC configuration as well as the requirement of an early integration of SCM and NPI formulated by Pero and Sianesi (2009) or Pero et al. (2010). Besides, this modeling approach is adequate to consider the interplay of different SC members or to reflect inter-organizational SC aspects of value creation.

Empirical research of the thesis at hand comprises a benchmarking study from the FMCG industry as well as an industrial case example of a cosmetics manufacturer. Especially the relevance of benchmarking for value-based SCM is explained by Losbichler and Rothböck (2006). In the benchmarking study presented in Chap. 6, value impacts are evaluated by analyzing secondary data derived from financial statements of publicly traded firms. This approach is similar to empirical assessments of value impacts resulting from SCM by Reiner and Hofmann (2006), Randall and Farris II (2009b) or Johnson and Templar (2011). Opposed to analyzes conducted by Hendricks and Singhal (2003, 2005b, 2008, 2009), who ex post evaluate value deteriorations resulting from SC deficiencies, the benchmarking study in this thesis is based on a quantitative model which additionally is adequate to ex ante determine future influences of SCM on company value. Furthermore, this underlying model is suitable for assessing value increases of obtained by SCM improvements as well as value losses resulting from poor SCM. The influence of timing and continuity of value impacts outlined and supported by qualitative arguments (see Srivastava et al. 1998) is empirically substantiated by this benchmarking study. Complementary to other studies (see e.g. Capkun et al. 2009; Losbichler and Rothböck 2006; Obermaier and Donhauser 2009; Padachi 2006), the detailed assessment and sensitivity analysis presented in Chap. 6 indicate the relevance of cost of capital and the importance of working capital components for value creation. The case examples of Chaps. 8 and 9 help illustrate the influence of SC dynamics and uncertainties on SC performance and thus support the findings of Fisher et al. (1997), Petrovic (2001), Blackhurst et al. (2004) or Datta and Christopher (2011). Complementary to these manuscripts, a direct link between these non-financial factors and company value is explained, substantiated and quantified in these chapters.

The comprehension of SCM, on which research in this thesis is based, fully covers both dimensions of the product-relationship-matrix introduced by Seuring (2009). The assessment of TSCD options for NPI (see Chaps. 8 and 9) considers all phases of the PLC and hence fully covers the product dimension. The relationship dimension comprises SC configuration, reflected in the tactical SC design scenarios, and SC operation, which according to Wong and Wong (2008) or Gilmour (1999) is taken into account in benchmarking (see Chap. 6). Strategic, tactical and operational aspects of SCM as characterized by Hübner (2007) are reflected in this thesis. The quantitative SC planning model outlined in Chap. 7 aims at strategic aspects, while the case examples in Chaps. 8 and 9 focus SC design on tactical level. The outlined integration of SCM-related value drivers with value driver hierarchies exemplifies how company value is linked to operational SCM activities. This comprehensive perception of SCM exceeds most of other research approaches discussed in the Chaps. 2–4. From the functional perspective, only one third of all manuscripts reviewed in Chap. 4 are based on the broad concept of SCM while the majority of papers limits their focus to specific functions (see Sect. 4.4.2). Models for SC configuration most often are limited to optimizing performance criteria of cost or profitability (see e.g. Meixell and Gargeya 2005; Melo et al. 2009), as outlined in greater detail in Sect. 2.2.5. Process optimization in SC operation is done under consideration of multiple criteria to improve product availability and the utilization of PPE and inventory at reduced cost (see Sect. 2.2.5, Berning et al. 2002; Brandenburg and Tölle 2009) but in most cases a direct link to company value is not considered or given.

Shareholder value and DCF valuation characterize the terminological foundation of the research in this thesis, which reflects insights of Lambert and Burduroglu (2000) and the value comprehension of most reviewed papers on value-based SCM (see findings of Sect. 2.3.2 and Chap. 4). The financial aspects considered in this thesis include the four SCM-related value drivers sales, SC cost, working capital and fixed assets identified by Christopher and Ryals (1999) and thus exceed purely cost-related or profitability-related perspectives on SC performance that are taken by a considerable number of scientific papers on quantitative models for SCM (see e.g. Meixell and Gargeya 2005; Melo et al. 2009). The illustrated relevance of both profitability- and capital-related factors for value-based SCM is in line with approaches of numerous manuscripts (Beamon 1998; Christopher and Ryals 1999; Hofmann and Locker 2009; Lasch et al. 2006; Losbichler and Rothböck 2006; Otto and Obermaier 2009; Walters 1999). In this thesis, an emphasis is put on capital aspects and working capital in particular. This focus reflects the significance of working capital for academic research on SCM, which is outlined by Farris II and Hutchison (2002, 2003) or Randall and Farris II (2009a,b). Unlike Hofmann and Kotzab (2006, 2010), aspects of collaborative working capital management on inter-organizational level are excluded from observation in this thesis. However, the argument that working capital positively influences the financial performance of a firm, as concluded by Padachi (2006) or Capkun et al. (2009), is supported by the findings of this thesis. The empirical assessment of the correlation between developments of working capital including its monetary components and company value presented in this thesis can be seen as an extension of the analysis provided by Obermaier and Donhauser (2009) who empirically assess influences of inventory levels on firm performance. In most sections of this thesis, value impacts of fixed assets are considered ulterior. Although this circumstance might be considered a shortfall of this thesis, other quantitative models for value-based SCM, e.g. the ones proposed by Hahn and Kuhn (2010, 2011), purposely disregard value impacts of fixed assets. Following the insights of Vickery et al. (2003) or Corsten and Gruen (2003), the quantitative model proposed in Chap. 10 is based on the assumption that the extent to which SCM affects sales development is known or at least can be estimated, although the determination of this magnitude is a difficult task (Christopher 2005). As proposed by Walters (1999) and taken up by Hofmann and Locker (2009), the link between these four financial drivers of company value and operational SCM activities is outlined in this thesis. In contrast to other research approaches (see e.g. Lambert and Pohlen 2001; Möller 2003; Neher 2003; Walters 1999), the conceptual frameworks illustrated in Chaps. 8 and 10 are supported systematically by quantitative models and empirically by case examples.

Besides financial value drivers, influences of the non-financial factors uncertainties and dynamics on company value are elaborated in this thesis. This approach reflects requests of Neher (2003), Möller (2003) or Lambert and Pohlen (2001) to consider intangible value aspects. Lee et al. (1997a) addressed the phenomenon of dynamic demand profiles by qualitative arguments, which are supported by quantitative analyses presented in Chaps. 8 and 9. The suitability of NPI situations for analysis of SC dynamics has been stated by Lee (2002) and illustrated at the example of a cosmetics manufacturer by Schilling et al. (2010). Impacts of short- and long-term demand uncertainties are focused in Chaps. 8 and 9, and compared to assessments of the effects on cost and delivery performance provided by Petrovic (2001), influences on inventory levels and replenishment lead times are additionally taken into account in this thesis. Focusing on the FMCG industry for such an empirical research is in line with approaches described by Datta and Christopher (2011). Besides, value impacts arising from the interplay between a cosmetics manufacturer and its supplier are considered in this thesis. However, network aspects of value creation are not investigated as detailed as demanded by Neher (2003), Möller (2003) or Otto and Obermaier (2009). Referring to Srivastava et al. (1998), Christopher and Ryals (1999) explained the relevance of timing and volatility of cash flow effects stemming from SCM by qualitative arguments, which in this thesis is supported by empirical observations presented in Chap. 6 and mathematical evidence given in Chap. 10. The results of the case example evaluated in Chaps. 8 and 9 furthermore empirically support the statement of Christopher and Ryals (1999) that value contributions can be achieved by reducing the RLT.

11.3 Limitations and Further Research Prospects

Limitations and future research directions arise from the circumstance that this thesis does not elaborate on value-based SCM in depth or in length. Hence, some of the research perspectives addressed in related literature (see findings of Chap. 4) are not fully covered by this dissertation. First and foremost, the consideration of inter-organizational aspects and network influences on value creation has to be mentioned in this context. Besides the consideration of the interplay between manufacturer and supplier in the case examples of Chaps. 8 and 9, these aspects were not considered in this dissertation. Additionally, the quantitative models presented in the thesis at hand can be detailed further by adequate metrics to measure value impacts of operational SCM activities. Beyond this, the assessment of value impacts stemming from fixed assets, especially in decision-making for strategic SC design, could be elaborated further. Similarly, value creation in reduction networks requires investigation in greater detail. In this context, closed-loop SCM might bear potential to extend the value comprehension to ecological aspects. Additionally, research on value contribution of social factors in SCM could contribute to bridge the gap between shareholder value and stakeholder value or intangible value. Besides, empirical analyses in other industries or different scenarios and case examples would further validate and strengthen the findings on value-based SCM presented in this dissertation.

Hence, future research directions can be differentiated by three categories – the overall research design, the theory-related research and empirical research. Regarding the overall research design, qualitative research would complement the quantitative approaches of this dissertation and, according to Golicic et al. (2005), contribute to a balanced approach to research on value-based SCM. As stated by

Möller (2003) or Neher (2003), the consideration of inter-organizational aspects in value-based SCM leaves room for further theory-related research. This includes a terminological clarification and definition what should be comprehended as value on network level as well as conceptual frameworks to link this value on network level to SCM processes and activities or to company value. In this context, quantitative models and metrics are needed, e.g. to determine value added on SC or network level and to ensure an appropriate value transfer between different SC members. Other possibilities comprise the theory-related extension of the value comprehension, e.g. to aspects of stakeholder value creation or intangible value. Possible directions for empirical research include the application of different methodologies, e.g. survey research or in-depth case study research, to the field of value-based SCM (Gimenez 2005; Kotzab 2005; Seuring 2005, 2008; Wallenburg and Weber 2005). Furthermore, the field of observation should be extended to different industries for additional empirical validation of the axiomatic models presented in this thesis. The specific characteristics of the FMCG sector explained thoroughly in Sect. 2.3.1 furthermore lead to the question what other factors influence value creation in different industries. Concluding, it can be stated that this dissertation contributes to value-based SCM to a considerable extent, but not exhaustively or terminatory.

Chapter 12
Appendices

12.1 Paper Sample and Categorization for the Content Analysis Given in Chap. 4

The following list comprises the complete sample of papers which were reviewed in the content analysis of Chap. 4. For each paper, this list contains the categorization in the following sequence: journal ("IJLM", "IJPDLM", "SCMIJ"), research design ("case study", "theoretical", "literature review", "modeling", "n.a.", "survey"), purpose of the paper ("describe", "diagnose", "explain", "explore", "intervene", "normative"), level of analysis ("function", "firm", "dyad", "chain", "network", "n.a."), actor of analysis ("carrier", "manufacturer", "n.a.", "retailer"), function of analysis ("e-business/IT", "inventory management", "logistics", "n.a.", "operations management", "others", "purchasing", "quality management", "SCM"), applied value terminology ("company value", "efficiency", "n.a.", "stakeholder value") , proposed research perspective ("extend/validate", "n.a.", "specific")

Anderson and Katz (1998): IJLM, n.a., explain, function, n.a., purchasing, company value, n.a.

Bititci et al. (2004): IJPDLM, theoretical, explain, network, n.a., SCM, stakeholder value, specific

Blankley (2008): IJLM, literature review, describe, firm, n.a., e-business/IT, company value, specific

Cantor and Terle (2010): IJPDLM, theoretical, intervene, firm, carrier, sustainable SCM, company value, specific

Carr et al. (2004): IJPDLM, modeling, normative, firm, n.a., n.a., company value, n.a.

Carter and Rogers (2008): IJPDLM, literature review, intervene, firm, n.a., sustainable SCM, company value, specific

Christopher and Ryals (1999): IJLM, theoretical, explain, network, n.a., SCM, company value, n.a.

M. Brandenburg, *Quantitative Models for Value-Based Supply Chain Management*,
Lecture Notes in Economics and Mathematical Systems 660,
DOI 10.1007/978-3-642-31304-2__12, © Springer-Verlag Berlin Heidelberg 2013

Deane et al. (2009): IJPDLM, modeling, normative, network, n.a., purchasing, company value, extend/validate
Defee and Stank (2005): IJLM, literature review, explore, chain, n.a., SCM, company value, extend/validate
Deitz et al. (2009): IJPDLM, case study, explore, dyad, retailer, inventory management, company value, extend/validate
Emiliani (2003): SCMIJ, theoretical, diagnose, network, n.a., purchasing, company value, specific
Emiliani and Stec (2002a): SCMIJ, theoretical, explain, dyad, n.a., purchasing, company value, n. a.
Emiliani and Stec (2002b): SCMIJ, theoretical, intervene, dyad, n.a., purchasing, stakeholder value, specific
Emiliani and Stec (2005): SCMIJ, survey, diagnose, dyad, manufacturer, purchasing, efficiency, extend/validate
Emiliani et al. (2005): SCMIJ, theoretical, intervene, dyad, n.a., purchasing, stakeholder value, n.a.
Fawcett et al. (2008): SCMIJ, n.a., normative, firm, n.a., SCM, company value, n.a.
Fawcett et al. (2006): IJPDLM, survey, explore, chain, n.a., sustainable SCM, company value, n.a.
Foggin et al. (2004): IJPDLM, survey, diagnose, function, n.a., logistics, stakeholder value, extend/validate
Gaudenzi and Borghesi (2006): IJLM, theoretical, normative, firm, n.a., SC risk management, stakeholder value, extend/validate
Godsell et al. (2010): SCMIJ, case study, describe, firm, manufacturer, SCM, company value, n.a.
Godsell and van Hoek (2009): SCMIJ, case study, explain, firm, n.a., SCM, company value, n.a.
Gupta et al. (2003): IJPDLM, modeling, normative, firm, n.a., inventory management, efficiency, extend/validate
Hammant et al. (1999): IJPDLM, case study, explain, firm, retailer, SCM, company value, n.a.
Hertz et al. (2001): SCMIJ, case study, explain, firm, manufacturer, SCM, efficiency, n.a.
Hofmann (2009): IJPDLM, theoretical, explore, network, carrier, inventory management, company value, extend/validate
Hofmann (2010): IJPDLM, theoretical, explain, network, n.a., SCM, stakeholder value, extend/validate
Holmström et al. (1999): IJLM, theoretical, explain, chain, manufacturer, SCM, stakeholder value, n.a.
Jones et al. (1997): IJPDLM, case study, explain, chain, n.a., logistics, efficiency, specific
Jüttner et al. (2010): IJLM, literature review, explain, firm, n.a., SCM, stakeholder value, specific
Kennett et al. (1998): SCMIJ, case study, describe, firm, manufacturer, quality management, stakeholder value, n.a.

Lambert and Burduroglu (2000): IJLM, theoretical, explain, function, n.a., logistics, company value, specific

Lambert and Pohlen (2001): IJLM, theoretical, normative, chain, n.a., SCM, company value, extend/validate

Love et al. (2004): SCMIJ, theoretical, normative, network, n.a., SCM, company value, n.a.

Lowson (2003): IJPDLM, case study, explore, firm, retailer, SCM, stakeholder value, specific

Mady (1991): IJPDLM, survey, diagnose, firm, manufacturer, inventory management, efficiency, n.a.

McCarthy and Golicic (2002): IJPDLM, case study, explore, firm, manufacturer, SC planning, efficiency, extend/validate

Mena et al. (2009): IJPDLM, case study, explore, dyad, manufacturer, SCM, company value, extend/validate

Moore and Cunningham III (1999): IJPDLM, survey, explore, firm, carrier, sustainable SCM, company value, specific

Norrman and Jansson (2004): IJPDLM, case study, describe, firm, manufacturer, SCM, company value, specific

Parry et al. (2010): SCMIJ, case study, explore, firm, manufacturer, operations management, company value, extend/validate

Peck (2005): IJPDLM, case study, normative, firm, manufacturer, SCM, company value, specific

Pegels (1991): IJPDLM, modeling, explain, firm, n.a., logistics, company value, n.a.

Pohlen and Goldsby (2003): IJPDLM, theoretical, explain, chain, manufacturer, inventory management, company value, extend/validate

Randall and Farris II (2009a): IJPDLM, modeling, normative, chain, n.a., SC finance, company value, specific

Richey Jr. (2009): IJPDLM, theoretical, describe, n.a., n.a., SC risk management, stakeholder value, specific

Sahay and Mohan (2003): IJPDLM, survey, explore, firm, manufacturer, SCM, company value, specific

Spekman and Davis (2004): IJPDLM, theoretical, describe, chain, n.a., SC risk management, stakeholder value, n.a.

Srivastava (2008): IJPDLM, case study, explain, chain, n.a., logistics, stakeholder value, n.a.

Stock and Boyer (2009): IJPDLM, literature review, intervene, n.a., n.a., SCM, stakeholder value, specific

Tibben-Lembke and Rogers (2002): SCMIJ, theoretical, explain, n.a., retailer, logistics, company value, specific

Töyli et al. (2008): IJPDLM, survey, explore, function, n.a., logistics, company value, specific

Trent and Monczka (2003): IJPDLM, survey, explore, firm, n.a., purchasing, company value, specific

Tummala et al. (2006): SCMIJ, case study, explore, firm, manufacturer, SCM, company value, n.a.

Table 12.1 $WACC$ for each company of the benchmarking group

Company	AVO	BDF	CPA	ELA	HEN	KAO	KMB	PRG	RCU	UNI
WACC (%)	7.58	6.64	7.79	7.57	7.56	4.23	7.70	7.72	7.66	6.26

Turner et al. (2004): IJPDLM, case study, explore, firm, manufacturer, n.a., stakeholder value, n.a.

van der Vorst and Beulens (2002): IJPDLM, case study, explore, chain, n.a., SCM, stakeholder value, n.a.

van Hoek (1999): SCMIJ, theoretical, describe, chain, n.a., sustainable SCM, stakeholder value, specific

Vlachopoulou and Manthou (2003): IJPDLM, theoretical, explain, n.a., n.a., e-business/IT, n.a., n.a.

Wagner et al. (2003): SCMIJ, survey, explore, firm, n.a., e-business/IT, company value, extend/validate

Walters (1999): IJPDLM, modeling, explain, function, n.a., logistics, company value, specific

Walters (2004a): IJPDLM, theoretical, explain, firm, n.a., n.a., company value, n.a.

Walters (2004b): IJPDLM, theoretical, describe, network, n.a., n.a., n.a., n.a.

Walters (2006): IJLM, theoretical, explain, firm, n.a., SCM, company value, n.a.

Wu and Chou (2007): IJLM, theoretical, explore, firm, carrier, logistics, n.a., extend/validate

Zeng and Rossetti (2003): IJPDLM, case study, normative, dyad, manufacturer, logistics, efficiency, specific

Zokaei and Simons (2006): IJLM, modeling, explain, chain, n.a., logistics, stakeholder value, specific

12.2 $WACC$ Figures for the Benchmarking Study of Chap. 6

Table 12.1 comprises $WACC$ figures that are calculated for each company of the benchmarking study of Chap. 6.

12.3 Mathematical Proofs for the Lemmata of Chap. 10

12.3.1 Linearity of Value Functions

For time series $C := (C_p)_{p=0}^{P}$ of SC cost, $W := (W_p)_{p=0}^{P}$ of working capital and $S := (S_p)_{p=0}^{P}$ of sales in a horizon of periods $p = 0, \dots, P$, the value functions for SC cost

$$VA^C : \mathbb{R}^P \to \mathbb{R}, (C) \to VA^C(C)$$

and working capital

$$VA^{WC} : \mathbb{R}^P \to \mathbb{R}, (W) \to VA^{WC}(W)$$

are defined as follows:

$$VA^{C}(C) := \sum_{i=1}^{P} \frac{(\frac{S_i}{S_0} \cdot C_0 - C_i) \cdot (1 - T_i)}{(1 + WACC_p)^i} \, .$$

$$VA^{W}(W) := \sum_{i=1}^{P} \frac{(\frac{S_i}{S_{i-1}} \cdot W_{i-1} - W_i)}{(1 + WACC_i)^i} \, .$$

Lemma. *The value functions VA^C and VA^W are linear.*

Proof. The proof is split into first giving evidence for the statement regarding the value function for SC cost and second validating the statement regarding the value function for working capital.

(i) SC cost: For $r \in \mathbb{R}$ and a second time series $K := (K_p)_{p=0}^{P}$ of SC cost in the horizon of periods $p = 0, \dots, P$, the linearity can be calculated straightforward by arithmetical transformations.

Vector addition:

$$VA^{C}(C) + VA^{C}(K) = \sum_{i=1}^{P} \frac{(\frac{S_i}{S_0} \cdot C_0 - C_i) \cdot (1 - T_i)}{(1 + WACC_i)^i} + \sum_{i=1}^{P} \frac{(\frac{S_i}{S_0} \cdot K_0 - K_i) \cdot (1 - T_i)}{(1 + WACC_i)^i}$$

$$= \sum_{i=1}^{P} \frac{(\frac{S_i}{S_0} \cdot (C_0 + K_0) - (C_i + K_i)) \cdot (1 - T_i)}{(1 + WACC_i)^i} = VA^{C}(C + K).$$

Scalar multiplication:

$$VA^{C}(r \cdot C) = \sum_{i=1}^{P} \frac{(\frac{S_i}{S_0} \cdot r \cdot C_0 - r \cdot C_i) \cdot (1 - T_i)}{(1 + WACC_i)^i}$$

$$= r \cdot \sum_{i=1}^{P} \frac{(\frac{S_i}{S_0} \cdot C_0 - C_i) \cdot (1 - T_i)}{(1 + WACC_i)^i} = r \cdot VA^{C}(C) \, .$$

(ii) Working capital: Similarly the linearity property can be shown for the value function of working capital by $r \in \mathbb{R}$ and a second time series $V := (V_p)_{p=0}^{P}$ for working capital in a horizon of periods $p = 0, \dots, P$.

Vector addition:

$$VA^W(V) + VA^W(W) = \sum_{i=1}^{P} \frac{\frac{S_i}{S_{i-1}} \cdot V_{i-1} - V_i}{(1 + WACC_i)^i} + \sum_{i=1}^{P} \frac{\frac{S_i}{S_{i-1}} \cdot W_{i-1} - W_i}{(1 + WACC_i)^i}$$

$$= \sum_{i=1}^{P} \frac{\frac{S_i}{S_{i-1}} \cdot (V_{i-1} + W_{i-1}) - (V_i + W_i)}{(1 + WACC_i)^i} = VA^W(V + W) .$$

Scalar multiplication:

$$VA^W(r \cdot V) = \sum_{i=1}^{P} \frac{\frac{S_i}{S_{i-1}} \cdot r \cdot V_{i-1} - r \cdot V_i}{(1 + WACC_i)^i} = r \cdot \sum_{i=1}^{P} \frac{\frac{S_i}{S_{i-1}} \cdot V_{i-1} - V_i}{(1 + WACC_i)^i} = r \cdot VA^W(V) .$$

$\square$

12.3.2   Proof of Lemma 10.1

Lemma 10.1. *In the case that all value impacts of a company are caused by SCM, the proposed quantitative model calculates the same value added to a company as the standard DCF model.*

Proof. The basic idea of this proof is to show that ceteris paribus (i.e. value impacts which do not stem from SCM are neglected) the sum $VA_p^S + VA_p^C + VA_p^W + VA_p^A$ of the value impacts VA_p^W, VA_p^C, VA_p^S and VA_p^A of the four SC value drivers working capital, SC cost, sales and fixed assets is equal to the change ΔFCF_p of free cash flow of a company in period p.

$$VA_p^{SCM} = VA_p^S + VA_p^C + VA_p^W + VA_p^A$$

$$= (S_p - S_0 - (\frac{S_p}{S_0} - 1) \cdot C_0)) \cdot (1 - T_p) - (\frac{S_p}{S_{p-1}} - 1) \cdot W_{p-1}$$

$$+ (\frac{S_p}{S_0} \cdot C_0 - C_p) \cdot (1 - T_p) + \frac{S_p}{S_{p-1}} \cdot W_{p-1} - W_p + D_p \cdot (1 - T_p) - E_p$$

$$= (S_p - S_0) \cdot (1 - T_p) - (\frac{S_p}{S_0} \cdot C_0 - \frac{S_p}{S_0} \cdot C_0) \cdot (1 - T_p) + (C_0 - C_p) \cdot (1 - T_p)$$

$$+ (\frac{S_p}{S_{p-1}} \cdot W_{p-1} - \frac{S_p}{S_{p-1}} \cdot W_{p-1}) + W_{p-1} - W_p + D_p \cdot (1 - T_p) - E_p$$

$$= (S_p - S_0) \cdot (1 - T_p) - (C_p - C_0) \cdot (1 - T_p) - (W_p - W_{p-1})$$

$$+ D_p \cdot (1 - T_p) - E_p$$

$$= ((S_p - C_p) - (S_0 - C_0)) \cdot (1 - T_p) - (W_p - W_{p-1}) + D_p \cdot (1 - T_p) - E_p .$$

With this, the following equations are obtained to end the proof:

$$VA_p^{SCM} = \Delta\, EBIT - \Delta\, Tax\ expenses_p - \Delta\, Working\ capital_p$$
$$+ \Delta\, Depreciation\ expenses_p - \Delta\, Net\ capital\ expenditures_p$$
$$= \Delta\, Free\ cash\ flow_p .\qquad\qquad\qquad\square$$

12.3.3 Proof of Lemma 10.2

Lemma 10.2. *Amplifying a monotonically increasing and value creating sales development generates additional value.*

Proof. Let $S := (S_p)_{p=0}^P$ be a monotonous growing time series of sales which in a horizon of periods $p = 0, \ldots, P$ results in positive value contribution, i.e. $VA^S(S) > 0$ at given time series of working capital $W := (W_p)_{p=0}^P$ and SC cost $C := (C_p)_{p=0}^P$. Let an additional growth of this sales development be given by a monotonous growing time series $R := (R_p)_{p=0}^P$ of sales which has the same initial level and exceeds S in all subsequent periods, i.e. $R_0 = S_0$ and $R_i > S_i$ for all $p \in \{1, \ldots, P\}$.

To proof the statement it is sufficient to show $VA^S(R) - VA^S(S) > 0$:

$$VA^S(R) - VA^S(S)$$

$$= \sum_{i=1}^P \frac{(R_i - R_0 - (\frac{R_i}{R_0} - 1) \cdot C_0) \cdot (1 - T_i) - (\frac{R_i}{R_{i-1}} - 1) \cdot W_{i-1}}{(1 + WACC_i)^i}$$

$$- \sum_{i=1}^P \frac{(S_i - S_0 - (\frac{S_i}{S_0} - 1) \cdot C_0) \cdot (1 - T_i) - (\frac{S_i}{S_{i-1}} - 1) \cdot W_{i-1}}{(1 + WACC_i)^i}$$

$$= \sum_{i=1}^P \frac{(R_i - S_i - \frac{R_i - S_i}{S_0} \cdot C_0) \cdot (1 - T_i) - (\frac{R_i}{R_{i-1}} - \frac{S_i}{S_{i-1}}) \cdot W_{i-1}}{(1 + WACC_i)^i}$$

$$\geq \sum_{i=1}^P \frac{((1 - \frac{C_0}{S_0}) \cdot (1 - T_i) - \frac{W_{i-1}}{S_{i-1}}) \cdot (R_i - S_i)}{(1 + WACC_i)^i} .$$

By showing $(1 - \frac{C_0}{S_0}) \cdot (1 - T_i) - \frac{W_{i-1}}{S_{i-1}} > 0$, the proof ends. For simplicity reasons, tax rate T and performance ratios $\frac{C}{S}$ and $\frac{W}{S}$ of cost C and working capital W are assumed constant, i.e. the right hand side of the last equality given above can be rearranged to:

$$((1 - \frac{C}{S}) \cdot (1 - T) - \frac{W}{S}) \cdot \sum_{i=1}^P \frac{R_i - S_i}{(1 + WACC_i)^i} .$$

The developments of sales S, cost C and working capital W are assumed to be value creating from cost and working capital. Therefore one obtains:

$$0 < FCF = (S - C) \cdot (1 - T) - W \text{ and hence } 0 < (1 - \frac{C}{S}) \cdot (1 - T) - \frac{W}{S}. \quad \square$$

12.3.4 Proof of Lemma 10.3

Lemma 10.3. *Accelerating or enhancing improvements of SC cost performance in a deterioration-free SC cost development increases the resulting value contribution.*

Proof. The proof is split into first giving evidence for the statement regarding acceleration and second validating the statement regarding enhancement of SC cost impacts.

(i) Acceleration: Let $C := (C_p)_{p=0}^{P}$ and $S := (S_p)_{p=0}^{P}$ be time series of SC cost and sales in a horizon of periods $p = 0, \ldots, P$. Assume C is deterioration-free and shows an improvement of SC cost performance in period $q + 1$, i.e. $\frac{C_{q+1}}{S_{q+1}} <$ $\frac{C_q}{S_q}$ for a $q \in \{0, \ldots, P - 1\}$ and $\frac{C_{i+1}}{S_{i+1}} \leq \frac{C_i}{S_i}$ for all $i \in \{0, \ldots, P\}$.

Defining K by $K_{i-1} := \frac{S_{i-1}}{S_i} \cdot C_i$ for $i \in \{q, q + 1\}$ and $K_i := C_i$ for all $i \in \{0, \ldots, P\}\backslash\{q - 1, q\}$ results in a deterioration-free time series K of SC cost with an improvement of SC cost performance in period q, i.e. K simply accelerates the improvement of SC cost performance of C to an earlier period. This follows directly from the definition of K.

For $i = q - 2$:

$$\frac{K_{q-2}}{S_{q-2}} = \frac{C_{q-2}}{S_{q-2}} \geq \frac{C_{q-1}}{S_{q-1}} \geq \frac{C_q}{S_q} = \frac{K_{q-1}}{S_{q-1}}.$$

For $i = q - 1$:

$$\frac{K_{q-1}}{S_{q-1}} = \frac{1}{S_{q-1}} \cdot (\frac{S_{q-1}}{S_q} \cdot C_q) = \frac{C_q}{S_q} > \frac{C_{q+1}}{S_{q+1}} = \frac{1}{S_q} \cdot (\frac{S_q}{S_{q+1}} \cdot C_{q+1}) = \frac{K_q}{S_q}.$$

For $i = q$:

$$\frac{K_q}{S_q} = \frac{C_{q+1}}{S_{q+1}} = \frac{K_{q+1}}{S_{q+1}}.$$

For all other $i \in \{0, \ldots, q - 3, q + 1, \ldots, P\}$:

$$\frac{K_{i-1}}{S_{i-1}} = \frac{C_{i-1}}{S_{i-1}} \geq \frac{C_i}{S_i} = \frac{K_i}{S_i}.$$

To proof the statement for acceleration it is sufficient to show $VA^C(K) > VA^C(C)$:

$$VA^C(K) - VA^C(C) = VA^C(K - C)$$

$$= \sum_{i=1}^{P} \frac{(\frac{S_i}{S_0} \cdot (K_0 - C_0) - (K_i - C_i)) \cdot (1 - T_i)}{(1 + WACC_i)^i}$$

$$= \frac{(\frac{S_{q-1}}{S_0} \cdot (K_0 - C_0) - (K_{q-1} - C_{q-1})) \cdot (1 - T_{q-1})}{(1 + WACC_{q-1})^{q-1}}$$

$$+ \frac{(\frac{S_q}{S_0} \cdot (K_0 - C_0) - (K_q - C_q)) \cdot (1 - T_q)}{(1 + WACC_q)^q}$$

$$= \frac{(C_{q-1} - K_{q-1}) \cdot (1 - T_{q-1})}{(1 + WACC_{q-1})^{q-1}} + \frac{(C_q - K_q) \cdot (1 - T_q)}{(1 + WACC_q)^q}$$

$$= \frac{(C_{q-1} - \frac{S_{q-1}}{S_q} \cdot C_q) \cdot (1 - T_{q-1})}{(1 + WACC_{q-1})^{q-1}} + \frac{(C_q - \frac{S_q}{S_{q+1}} \cdot C_{q+1}) \cdot (1 - T_q)}{(1 + WACC_q)^q}$$

$$> 0.$$

The last inequality can be seen easily by considering that C is deterioration-free and has an improvement in period $q + 1$. C is deterioration-free, i.e. $\frac{C_{q-1}}{S_{q-1}} \geq \frac{C_q}{S_q}$, which results in the inequality $C_{q-1} - \frac{S_{q-1}}{S_q} \cdot C_q \geq 0$. C shows an improvement in period $q+1$, i.e. $\frac{C_q}{S_q} > \frac{C_{q+1}}{S_{q+1}}$, which results in the inequality $C_q - \frac{S_q}{S_{q+1}} \cdot C_{q+1} > 0$.

(ii) Enhancement: Let $C := (C_p)_{p=0}^{P}$ and $K := (K_p)_{p=0}^{P}$ be time series of SC cost for a time series $S := (S_p)_{p=0}^{P}$ of sales in a horizon of periods $p = 0, \ldots, P$. Assume $K_q < C_q$ for one $q \in \{1, \ldots, P\}$ and $K_i := C_i$ for all $i \in \{1, \ldots, P\}\backslash\{q\}$, i.e. K shows an enhanced SC cost performance in period q compared to C, because $\frac{K_q}{S_q} < \frac{C_q}{S_q}$. Due to the linearity of the value function for SC cost, the proof for this statement is straightforward by showing $VA^C(K) > VA^C(C)$:

$$VA^C(K) - VA^C(C) = VA^C(K - C) = \sum_{i=1}^{P} \frac{(\frac{S_i}{S_0} \cdot (K_0 - C_0) - (K_i - C_i)) \cdot (1 - T_i)}{(1 + WACC_i)^i}$$

$$= \frac{(C_q - K_q) \cdot (1 - T_q)}{(1 + WACC_q)^q} > 0. \qquad \square$$

12.3.5 Proof of Lemma 10.4

Lemma 10.4. *In cases of constant WACC which is not exceeded by the sales growth rate and a deterioration-free improvement of working capital performance, an accelerated or enhanced improvement of the working capital performance results in higher value contributions.*

Proof. Let $WACC$ be constant, i.e. $WACC_i := \alpha \in \mathbb{R}$ for all $i \in \{0, \dots, P\}$, and let $S := (S_p)_{p=0}^{P}$ be a time series for sales in a horizon of periods $p \in \{0, \dots, P\}$ with a growth rate limited by $WACC$, i.e. $\alpha > \frac{S_{p+1}-S_p}{S_p}$ for all $p \in \{0, \dots, P-1\}$. The proof is split into first giving evidence for the statement regarding acceleration and second validating the statement regarding enhancement of working capital impacts.

(i) Acceleration: Let $W := (W_p)_{p=0}^{P}$ be a time series of working capital which shows a deterioration-free development of working capital performance and an improvement of working capital performance in period $p \geq 2$, i.e. $\frac{W_i}{S_i} \leq \frac{W_{i-1}}{S_{i-1}}$ for all $i = 0, \dots, P$ and $\frac{W_{p+1}}{S_{p+1}} < \frac{W_p}{S_p}$ for a $p \in \{2, \dots, P\}$. Define $V :=$ $(V_i)_{i=1}^{P}$ by $V_p := \frac{S_p}{S_{p+1}} \cdot W_{p+1}$ and $V_i := W_i$ for all $i \in \{1, \dots, P\}\backslash\{p\}$. Then V is a deterioration-free working capital development which shows an improvement in period $p-1$, because $\frac{V_p}{S_p} = \frac{W_{p+1}}{S_{p+1}} < \frac{W_p}{S_p} \leq \frac{W_{p-1}}{S_{p-1}} = \frac{V_{p-1}}{V_{p-1}}$ and $\frac{V_{i-1}}{S_{i-1}} = \frac{W_{i-1}}{S_{i-1}} \geq \frac{W_i}{S_i} = \frac{V_i}{S_i}$ for all $i \in \{1, \dots, P\}$.

The acceleration part of the proof is completed by showing $VA^W(V) > VA^W(W)$:

$$VA^W(V) - VA^W(W) = VA^W(V-W) = \sum_{i=1}^{P} \frac{\frac{S_i}{S_{i-1}} \cdot (V_{i-1} - W_{i-1}) - (V_i - W_i)}{(1 + WACC_i)^i}$$

$$= \frac{\frac{S_p}{S_{p-1}} \cdot (V_{p-1} - W_{p-1}) - (V_p - W_p)}{(1 + WACC_p)^p} + \frac{\frac{S_{p+1}}{S_p} \cdot (V_p - W_p) - (V_{p+1} - W_{p+1})}{(1 + WACC_{p+1})^{p+1}}$$

$$= \frac{\frac{S_{p+1}}{S_p} \cdot (V_p - W_p)}{(1 + WACC_{p+1})^{p+1}} - \frac{V_p - W_p}{(1 + WACC_p)^p}$$

$$= \frac{\frac{S_{p+1}}{S_p} \cdot (\frac{S_p}{S_{p+1}} \cdot W_{p+1} - W_p)}{(1 + WACC_{p+1})^{p+1}} - \frac{\frac{S_p}{S_{p+1}} \cdot W_{p+1} - W_p}{(1 + WACC_p)^p}$$

$$= \frac{\frac{S_{p+1}}{S_p} \cdot (\frac{S_p}{S_{p+1}} \cdot W_{p+1} - W_p)}{(1 + \alpha)^{p+1}} - \frac{(\frac{S_p}{S_{p+1}} \cdot W_{p+1} - W_p) \cdot (1 + \alpha)}{(1 + \alpha)^{p+1}}$$

$$= \frac{(\frac{S_{p+1}}{S_p} - (1 + \alpha)) \cdot (\frac{S_p}{S_{p+1}} \cdot W_{p+1} - W_p)}{(1 + \alpha)^{p+1}}.$$

W shows an improvement of working capital performance in period p, i.e. $\frac{W_{p+1}}{S_{p+1}} < \frac{W_p}{S_p}$ and hence $\frac{S_p}{S_{p+1}} \cdot W_{p+1} - W_p < 0$. From the prerequisite that the sales growth rate does not exceed the constant cost of capital $WACC = \alpha$ it can be obtained that $\frac{S_{p+1}}{S_p} - (1+\alpha) \leq 0$ by the following transformations:

$$\alpha \geq \frac{S_{p+1} - S_p}{S_p} \tag{12.1}$$

$$\Longleftrightarrow\ 0 \geq \frac{S_{p+1} - S_p}{S_p} - \alpha \tag{12.2}$$

$$\Longleftrightarrow\ 0 \geq \frac{S_{p+1}}{S_p} - (1+\alpha) . \tag{12.3}$$

A combination of both inequalities shows that the numerator of the last fraction is greater than 0 which completes the acceleration part of the proof.

(ii) Enhancement: Let $V := (V_p)_{p=0}^{P}$ and $W := (W_p)_{p=0}^{P}$ be time series of working capital with $V_0 = W_0$ and $V_i \leq W_i$ for all $i \in \{1, \dots, P\}$ and $V_p < W_p$ for a $p \in \{1, \dots, P\}$. It is sufficient to show $VA^W(V) > VA^W(W)$:

$$VA^W(V) - VA^W(W) = VA^W(V - W) = \frac{\sum_{i=1}^{P} (\frac{S_i}{S_{i-1}} \cdot (V_{i-1} - W_{i-1}) - (V_i - W_i))}{(1 + WACC_i)^i}$$

$$= \frac{\sum_{i=1}^{P} (\frac{S_i}{S_{i-1}} \cdot (V_{i-1} - W_{i-1}) - (V_i - W_i))}{(1+\alpha)^i}$$

$$= \frac{\frac{S_1}{S_0} \cdot (V_0 - W_0)}{1 + \alpha} + \sum_{i=1}^{P-1} (-\frac{V_i - W_i}{(1+\alpha)^i} + \frac{\frac{S_{i+1}}{S_i} \cdot (V_i - W_i)}{(1+\alpha)^{i+1}}) - \frac{V_P - W_P}{(1+\alpha)^P}$$

$$\geq \sum_{i=1}^{P-1} (-\frac{V_i - W_i}{(1+\alpha)^i} + \frac{\frac{S_{i+1}}{S_i} \cdot (V_i - W_i)}{(1+\alpha)^{i+1}}) = \sum_{i=1}^{P-1} \frac{\frac{S_{i+1}}{S_i} \cdot (V_i - W_i) - (V_i - W_i) \cdot (1+\alpha)}{(1+\alpha)^{i+1}}$$

$$= \sum_{i=1}^{P-1} \frac{(\frac{S_{i+1}}{S_i} - (1+\alpha)) \cdot (V_i - W_i)}{(1+\alpha)^{i+1}} > 0 .$$

The last inequality follows from the definition of V and W and the prerequisite of the correlation between sales growth and cost of capital:

$$V_p - W_p < 0 \text{ and } V_i - W_i \leq 0 \text{ for all } i \in \{0, \dots, P\} .$$

$$\frac{S_{i+1}}{S_i} - (1+\alpha) \leq 0 \text{ for all } i \in \{0, \dots, P-1\} . \qquad \square$$

12.3.6   Proof of Lemma 10.5

Lemma 10.5. *Increasing the volatility of sales, SC cost or working capital developments can result in higher value contributions compared to more smooth developments.*

Proof. The proof is done by giving appropriate numerical examples.

Assume a time horizon of three periods $p = 0, 1, 2$ and constant sales $S = 100\,\text{m}\,€$, constant tax rate $T = 25\,\%$ and constant $WACC = 10\,\%$.

Constant developments of working capital $W_i = 20\,\text{m}\,€$ and SC cost $C_i = 30\,\text{m}\,€$ for $i \in \{0, 1, 2\}$ have no volatility but, as can be seen by Lemma 10.6 do not generate value ($VA^W = 0\,\text{m}\,€$ and $VA^C = 0\,\text{m}\,€$).

Achieving intermediate improvements of working capital ($W_1 = 20\,\text{m}\,€$) or SC cost ($C_1 = 20\,\text{m}\,€$) increases the volatility of the respective value driver but results in value contribution ($VA^W = 0.8\,\text{m}\,€$ and $VA^C = 6.8\,\text{m}\,€$).   □

12.3.7   Proof of Lemma 10.6

Lemma 10.6. *Deterioration-free developments of SC cost performance or working capital performance do not result in value losses. Constant developments of SC cost performance or working capital performance do not create value, while continuous improvements of SC cost performance or working capital performance result in value creation.*

Proof. The proof is split into first giving evidence for the statement regarding working capital and second validating the statement regarding SC cost.

(i) Working capital: Let $W := (W_p)_{p=0}^P$ and $S := (S_p)_{p=0}^P$ be time series of working capital and sales which show a deterioration-free development in a horizon of periods $p = 0, \ldots, P$, i.e. $\frac{W_p}{S_p} \leq \frac{W_{p-1}}{S_{p-1}}$ for all $p = 0, \ldots, P$. Considering that $S_p > 0$ for all $p = 0, \ldots, P$, these inequalities can be rearranged to $0 \leq \frac{S_p}{S_{p-1}} \cdot W_{p-1} - W_p$ for all $p = 1, \ldots, P$. As the right hand side of the last inequation is defined as VA_p^W, the proof that deterioration-free developments of the working capital performance do not result in value losses is complete.

Turning these inequations into equations (simply write "=" instead of "≤") shows that constant developments of the working capital performance do not affect company value.

Assuming that $W := (W_p)_{p=0}^P$ and $S := (S_p)_{p=0}^P$ show a continuous improvement in a period $q \in \{1, \ldots, P\}$, i.e. $\frac{W_{q-1}}{S_{q-1}} > \frac{W_q}{S_q}$ and $\frac{W_{i-1}}{S_{i-1}} \geq \frac{W_i}{S_i}$ for all $i \in \{1, \ldots, P\}\backslash\{q\}$, implies $VA_q^W > 0$. This proves that continuous improvements of the working capital performance result in value creation.

Table 12.2 Status of publication and presentation

Chapter	Publication	Conference
4	Brandenburg (2011)	Hamburg international conference on logistics HICL 2011 (Hamburg, Germany, September 8–9, 2011)
5	Brandenburg and Seuring (2010b)	8th international Heinz Nixdorf symposium IHNS 2010 (Paderborn, Germany, April 21–22, 2010)
6	Brandenburg and Seuring (2010a)	22nd NOFOMA conference (Kolding, Denmark, June 10–11, 2010)
7	Brandenburg and Seuring (2010c)	Hamburg International Conference on Logistics HICL 2010 (Hamburg, Germany, September 2–3, 2010)
9	Brandenburg and Schilling (2012)	Workshop of the "Gesellschaft für Operations Research e. IV. ", working groups "Wirtschaftsinformatik" and "Entscheidungstheorie und -praxis" (Hamburg, Germany, March 30–April 1, 2011)
10	Brandenburg and Seuring (2011)[a]	"Logistikmanagement LM11" (Bamberg, Germany, September 28–30, 2011)[a]
	Brandenburg (2012)[a]	"17th international Working Seminar on Production Economics" (Innsbruck, Austria, February 20–24, 2012)[a]

[a]Partially published and presented

(ii) SC cost: Let $C := (C_p)_{p=0}^P$ and $S := (S_p)_{p=0}^P$ be time series of SC cost and sales which show a deterioration-free development in a horizon of periods $p = 0, \ldots, P$, i.e. $\frac{C_p}{S_p} \leq \frac{C_{p-1}}{S_{p-1}}$ for all $p = 1, \ldots, P$. This implies $\frac{C_p}{S_p} \leq \frac{C_0}{S_0}$ for all $p \in \{1, \ldots, P\}$. Considering that $S_p > 0$, this inequality can be rearranged to $0 \leq \frac{S_p}{S_0} \cdot C_0 - C_p$ for all $p \in \{1, \ldots, P\}$ and finally $0 \leq (\frac{S_p}{S_0} \cdot C_0 - C_i) \cdot (1 - T_p)$ for all $p \in \{1, \ldots, P\}$. As the right hand side of the last inequation is defined as VA_p^C, the proof for the first statement regarding value impacts of deterioration-free developments of SC cost is complete.

By turning these inequations into equations (simply write "=" instead of "≤") the proof of the second statement regarding value impacts of constant developments of SC cost is obtained.

Assuming that $C := (C_p)_{p=0}^P$ and $S := (S_p)_{p=0}^P$ show a continuous improvement in a period $q \in \{1, \ldots, P\}$, i.e. $\frac{C_{q-1}}{S_{q-1}} > \frac{C_q}{S_q}$ and $\frac{C_{i-1}}{S_{i-1}} \geq \frac{C_i}{S_i}$ for all $i \in \{1, \ldots, P\} \setminus \{q\}$, implies $VA_q^C > 0$. and thus proves the third statement regarding value impacts resulting from continuous improvements of the SC cost performance.   □

12.4   Status of Publication and Presentation of the Chaps. 4–10

The Chaps. 4–10 contain manuscripts that have been previously published in peer-reviewed journals or edited books or were presented at scientific conferences (as summarized in Table 12.2). These manuscripts are reprinted in this thesis by courtesy of Erich Schmidt Verlag, Berlin, EUL Verlag, Lohmar – Köln, Shaker Verlag, Aachen, and Springer Verlag, Heidelberg.

The manuscripts were carefully revised. Especially, parameters, acronyms and nomenclature used in these papers were harmonized to ensure a homogeneous terminology in this dissertation. The article structure of these manuscripts is inherited unchanged to the respective chapters in order to facilitate reading selected chapters of this thesis.

References

Adebanjo, D., and R. Mann. 2000. Identifying problems in forecasting consumer demand in the fast moving consumer goods sector. *Benchmarking: An International Journal* 7(3): 223–230.

Akkermans, H.A., P. Bogerd, E. Yücesan, and L.N. van Wassenhove. 2003. The impact of ERP on supply chain management: Exploratory findings from a european delphi study. *European Journal of Operational Research* 146(2): 284–301.

Alvarado, U.Y., and H. Kotzab. 2001. Supply chain management – The integration of logistics in marketing. *Industrial Marketing Management* 30: 183–198.

Anderson, M.G., and P.B. Katz. 1998. Strategic sourcing. *International Journal of Logistics Management* 9(1): 1–13.

Anderson, E.W., C. Fornell, and S.K. Mazvancheryl. 2004. Customer satisfaction and shareholder value. *Journal of Marketing* 68: 172–185.

Atasu, A., V.D.R. Guide Jr., and L.N. van Wassenhove. 2008. Product reuse economics in closed-loop supply chain research. *Production and Operations Management* 17(5): 483–496.

Attaran, M., and S. Attaran. 2007. Collaborative supply chain management – The most promising practice for building efficient and sustainable supply chains. *Business Process Management Journal* 13(3): 390–404.

Ayag, Z. 2005. An integrated approach to evaluating conceptual design alternatives in a new product development environment. *International Journal of Production Research* 43(4): 687–713.

Bahrami, K. 2002. Improving supply chain productivity through horizontal cooperation – The case of consumer goods manufacturers. In *Cost management in supply chains*, ed. S. Seuring and M. Goldbach, 213–250. Heidelberg: Physica.

Barney, J. 1991. Firm resources and sustained competitive advantage. *Journal of Management* 17(1): 99–120.

Basnet, C., J. Corner, J. Wisner, and K.C. Tan. 2003. Benchmarking supply chain management practice in New Zealand. *Supply Chain Management: An International Journal* 8(1): 57–64.

Bauer, T. 2011. *Empirische Ausgestaltung von Supply Chain Controlling Systemen für das wertorientierte Supply Chain Controlling und das Supply Chain Performance Management (Empirical embodiment of supply chain management accounting systems for value-based supply chain management accounting and supply chain performance management)*. Kassel: Kassel University Press.

Beamon, B.M. 1998. Supply chain design and analysis: Models and methods. *International Journal of Production Economics* 55(3): 281–294.

Beamon, B.M. 1999. Measuring supply chain performance. *International Journal of Operations and Production Management* 19(3): 275–292.

Berlien, O., A.S. Kirsten, J. Oelert, and R. Schutt. 2006. Wertsteigerung durch das Konzernprogramm *best* bei ThyssenKrupp (Value creation by the corporate program *best* at ThyssenKrupp). In *Wertorientiertes management (Value-based management)*, ed. N. Schweickart and A. Töpfer, 597–608. Berlin: Springer.

Bernandes, E., and M. Hanna. 2009. A theoretical review of flexibility, agility and responsiveness in the operations management literature. *International Journal of Operations and Production Management* 29(1): 30–63.

Berning, G., M. Brandenburg, K. Gürsoy, V. Mehta, and F.-J. Tölle. 2002. An integrated system solution for supply chain optimization in the chemical process industry. *OR Spectrum* 24(4): 371–401.

Bertrand, J.W.M., and J.C. Fransoo. 2002. Operations management research methodologies using quantitative modeling. *International Journal of Operations and Production Management* 22(2): 241–264.

Bhutta, K.S., and F. Huq. 1999. Benchmarking – Best practices: An integrated approach. *Benchmarking: An International Journal* 6(3): 254–268.

Bhutta, K.S., F. Huq, and F. Maubourguet. 2002. Efficient consumer response – Increasing efficiency through cooperation. In *Cost management in supply chains*, ed. S. Seuring and M. Goldbach, 195–212. Heidelberg: Physica.

Bilgen, B., and H.-O. Günther. 2008. A MILP model for production and distribution planning in the consumer goods supply chains. In *Operations research proceedings 2008*, ed. B. Fleischmann, K.-H. Borgwardt, R. Klein, and A. Tuma, 179–184. Heidelberg: Springer.

Bilgen, B., and H.-O. Günther. 2010. Integrated production and distribution planning in the fast moving consumer goods industry: A block planning approach. *OR Spectrum* 32(4): 927–955.

Billington, C.A., and T.C. Davis. 1992. Manufacturing strategy analysis: Models and practice. *Omega* 20(5–6): 587–595.

Biswas, S., and Y. Narahari. 2004. Object oriented modeling and decision support for supply chains. *European Journal of Operational Research* 153(3): 704–726.

Bititci, U.S., V. Martinez, P. Albores, and J. Parung. 2004. Creating and managing value in collaborative networks. *International Journal of Physical Distribution and Logistics Management* 34(3/4): 251–268.

Black, F., and M. Scholes. 1973. The pricing of options and corporate liabilities. *Journal of Political Economy* 81: 637–654.

Blackhurst, J., T. Wu, and P. O'Grady. 2004. Network-based approach to modelling uncertainty in a supply chain. *International Journal of Production Research* 42(8): 1639–1658.

Blanchard, C., C.L. Comm, and D.F.X. Mathaisel. 2008. Adding value to service providers: Benchmarking Wal-Mart. *Benchmarking: An International Journal* 15(2): 166–177.

Blankley, A. 2008. A conceptual model for evaluating the financial impact of supply chain management technology investments. *International Journal of Logistics Management* 19(2): 156–182.

Bloemhof-Ruwaard, Jaqueline M., Jo van Nunen, Jurriaan Vroom, Ad van der Linden, and Annemarie Kraal. 2002. One and two way packaging in the dairy sector. In *Quantitative approaches to distribution logistics and supply chain management*, ed. Andreas Klose, M. Grazia Speranza, and Luk N. van Wassenhove, 115–127. Berlin: Springer.

Bottani, E., and R. Montanari. 2010. Supply chain design and cost analysis through simulation. *International Journal of Production Research* 48(10): 2859–2886.

Brandenburg, M. 2011. A systematic review of literature on value-based supply chain management. In *International supply chain management and collaboration practices*, ed. W. Kersten, T. Blecker, and C. Jahn, 283–296. Lohmar: EUL Verlag.

Brandenburg, M. 2012. Impacts of supply chain management on company value. In *17th International Working Seminar on Production Economics*, eds. R.W. Grubbström and H. Hinterhuber. Pre-prints Vol. 2, Congress Innsbruck, Innsbruck/Austria, 101–114.

Brandenburg, M., and T. Menke. 2008. Quantifizierung von Wertbeiträgen aus Änderungen von Supply Chain Kosten und Working Capital. (Quantification of value contributions resulting from changes of supply chain cost and working capital). *Zeitschrift für Controlling and Management* 52(3): 168–174.

Brandenburg, M., and R. Schilling. 2010. Value impacts of dynamics and uncertainty in tactical supply chain design for new product introduction. In *Proceedings of the German-Italian conference on the interdependencies between new product development and supply chain management*, 26–39. Hamburg: TuTech.

Brandenburg, M., and R. Schilling. 2012. Value impacts of dynamics and uncertainty in tactical supply chain design for new product introduction. In *Wirtschaftsinformatik, Entscheidungstheorie und -praxis (Business informatics, decision theory and practice)*, ed. M. Geiger, J. Geldermann, and S. Voß, 23–46. Aachen: Shaker.

Brandenburg, M., and S. Seuring. 2010a. The influence of supply chain cost and working capital on company value: Benchmarking companies from the fast moving consumer goods industry. *Logistics Research* 3(4): 233–248.

Brandenburg, M., and S. Seuring. 2010b. A model for quantifying impacts of supply chain cost and working capital on the company value. *Lecture Notes in Business Information Processing* 46: 107–117.

Brandenburg, M., and S. Seuring. 2010c. Value-based strategic supply chain planning. In *Pioneering solutions in supply chain management – A comprehensive insight into current management approaches*, Operations and technology management, vol. 14, W. Kersten, T. Blecker, and C. Lüthje, 185–196. Berlin: Erich Schmidt Verlag.

Brandenburg, M., and S. Seuring. 2011. Quantifying impacts of supply chain management on company value. In *Logistikmanagement – Herausforderungen, Chancen und Lösungen Bd. II (Logistics management – Challenges, chances and solutions Vol. II)*, ed. E. Sucky, B. Asdecker, A. Dobhan, S. Haas, and J. Wiese, 117–142. Bamberg: University of Bamberg Press.

Brandenburg, M., and F.-J. Tölle. 2009. MILP-based campaign scheduling in a specialty chemicals plant: A case study. *OR Spectrum* 31(1): 141–166.

Brandt, W., and P. Zencke. 2006. Wertorientierte Unternehmensführung bei der SAP AG. (Value-based management at SAP AG). In *Wertorientiertes Management (Value-based management)*, ed. N. Schweickart and A. Töpfer, 609–636. Berlin: Springer.

Brealey, R.A., S.C. Myers, and F.Allen. 2008. *Principles of corporate finance*, 9th ed. Boston/Irwin: McGraw-Hill.

Brewer, P.C., and T.W. Speh. 2000. Using the balanced scorecard to measure supply chain performance. *Journal of Business Logistics* 21(1): 75–93.

Burgess, K., J.S. Prakash, and R. Koroglu. 2006. Supply chain management: A structured literature review and implications for future research. *International Journal of Operations and Production Management* 26 (7): 703–729.

Butler, R.J. 2003. *Supply chain design for new products*. Atlanta/GA, USA: Georgia Institute of Technology.

Butler, R., J. Ammons, and J. Sokol. 2006. Planning the supply chain network for new products: A case study. *Engineering Management Journal* 18(2): 35–43.

Cachon, G.P., and M. Fisher. 1997. Campbell Soup's continuous replenishment program: Evaluation and enhanced inventory decision rules. *Production and Operations Management* 6(3): 266–276.

Cachon, G.P., and M. Fisher. 2000. Supply chain inventory management and the value of shared information. *Management Science* 46(8): 1032–1048.

Camm, J.D., T.E. Chorman, F.A. Dill, J.R. Evans, D.J. Sweeney, and G.W. Wegryn. 1997. Blending OR/MS, judgement, and GIS: Restructuring P&G's supply chain. *Interfaces* 27(1): 128–142.

Caniato, F., R. Golini, and M. Kalchschmidt. 2010. Global supply chain configurations and drivers. In *Proceedings of the 17th international annual EurOMA conference*, ed. R. Sousa. Porto: Catholic University of Portugal.

Cantor D.E., and M. Terle. 2010. Applying a voluntary compliance model to a proposed transportation safety regulation. *International Journal of Physical Distribution and Logistics Management* 40(10): 822–846.

Capkun, V., A.P. Hameri, and L.A. Weiss. 2009. On the relationship between inventory and financial performance in manufacturing companies. *International Journal of Operations and Production Management* 29(8): 789–806.

Cappello, A., M. Lösch, and C. Schmitz. 2006. Achieving top performance in supply chain management. In *Value creation – Strategies for the chemical industry*, 2nd ed, ed. F. Budde, U.-H. Felcht, and H. Frankemöller, 281–296. Weinheim: Wiley.

Caridi, M., M. Pero, and A. Sianesi. 2009. The impact of NPD projects on supply chain complexity: An empirical research. *International Journal of Design Engineering* 2(4): 380–397.

Carr, P., M. Rainbird, and D. Walters. 2004. Measuring the implications of virtual integration in the new economy: A process-led approach. *International Journal of Physical Distribution and Logistics Management* 34(3/4): 358–372.

Carter, C.R., and D.S. Rogers. 2008. A framework of sustainable supply chain management: Moving toward new theory. *International Journal of Physical Distribution and Logistics Management* 38(5): 360–387.

Chang, Y., and H. Makatsoris. 2001. Supply chain modeling using simulation. *International Journal of Simulation* 2(1): 24–30.

Chauhan, S., R. Nagi, and J.-M. Proth. 2004. Strategic capacity planning in supply chain design for a new market opportunity. *International Journal of Production Research* 42(11): 2197–2206.

Chenhall, R. H. 2005. Integrative strategic performance measurement systems, strategic alignment of manufacturing, learning and strategic outcomes: An exploratory study. *Accounting, Organizations and Society* 30(5): 395–422.

Chopra, S., and P. Meindl. 2007. *Supply chain management – Strategy, planning and operations*, 3rd ed. Upper Saddle River: Prentice Hall.

Christensen, W., R. Germain, and L. Birou. 2007. Variance vs. average: Supply chain lead-time as a predictor for financial performance. *Supply Chain Management: An International Journal* 12(5): 349–357.

Christopher, M. 2000. The agile supply chain – Competing in volatile markets. *Industrial Marketing Management* 29: 37–44.

Christopher, M. 2005. *Logistics and supply chain management – Creating value-adding networks*, 3rd ed. Harlow: Prentice Hall.

Christopher, M., and J. Gattorna. 2005. Supply chain cost management and value-based pricing. *Industrial Marketing Management* 34: 115–121.

Christopher, M., and H. Lee. 2004. Mitigating supply chain risk through improved confidence. *International Journal of Physical Distribution and Logistics Management* 34(5): 388–396.

Christopher, M., and L. Ryals. 1999. Supply chain strategy: Its impact on shareholder value. *International Journal of Logistics Management* 10(1): 1–10.

Christopher, M., and D.R. Towill. 2002. Developing market specific supply chain strategies. *International Journal of Logistics Management* 13(1): 1–14.

Christopher, M., H. Peck, and D. Towill. 2006. A taxonomy for selecting global supply chain strategies. *International Journal of Logistics Management* 17(2): 277–287.

Chwif, L., M. Pereira Barretto, and E. Saliby. 2002. Supply chain analysis: Spreadsheet or simulation? In *Proceedings of the winter simulation conference*, ed. E. Yücesan, C.-H. Chen, J. Showdon, and J. Charnes, 59–66. New York: ACM; Piscataway: IEEE.

Claes, P.C.M. 2006. Management control and value-based management: Compatible or not? In *Performance measurement and management control: Improving organizations and society*, ed. M.J. Epstein and J.-F. Manzoni, 269–301. Oxford/San Diego/Amsterdam/Boston: Elsevier.

Coenenberg, A.G., and R. Salfeld. 2003. *Wertorientierte Unternehmensführung (Value-based management)*. Stuttgart: Schäffer-Poeschel.

Cohen, S., and J. Roussel. 2005. *Strategic supply chain management – The five disciplines for top performance*. New York: McGraw-Hill.

Comelli, M., P. Fenies, and N. Tchernev. 2008. A combined financial and physical flows evaluation for logistic process and tactical production planning: Application in a company supply chain. *International Journal of Production Economics* 112: 77–95.

Conway, D.G., and C.T. Ragsdale. 1997. Modeling optimization problems in the unstructured world of spreadsheets. *Omega* 25(3): 313–322.

Cooper, M.C., D.M. Lambert, and J.D. Pagh. 1997. Supply chain management – More than a new name for logistics. *International Journal of Logistics Management* 8(1): 1–14.

Copeland, T., T. Koller, and J. Murrin. 2005. *Valuation: Measuring and managing the value of companies*, 4th ed. New York: Wiley.

Corsten, D., and T. Gruen. 2003. Desperately seeking shelf availability: An examination of the extent, the causes, and the efforts to address retail out-of-stocks. *International Journal of Retail and Distribution Management* 31(12): 605–617.

Croom, S., P. Romano, and M. Giannakis. 2000. Supply chain management: An analytical framework for critical literature review. *European Journal of Purchasing and Supply Management* 6: 67–83.

Croxton, K.L., S.J. Garcia-Dastugue, D.M. Lambert, and D.S. Rogers. 2001. The supply chain management processes. *International Journal of Logistics Management* 12(2): 13–36.

Daganzo, C.F. 2003. *A theory of supply chains*. Berlin: Springer.

Damodaran, A. 2005. Valuation approaches and metrics: A survey of the theory and evidence. *Foundations and Trends in Finance* 1(8): 693–784.

Damodaran, A. 2009. Damodaran online. http://pages.stern.nyu.edu/~adamodar/ accessed. Accessed 7 July 2009.

Damodaran, A. 2011a. *Applied corporate finance*, 3rd ed. Hoboken: Wiley.

Damodaran, A. 2011b. *The little book of valuation – How to value a company, pick a stock, and profit*. Hoboken: Wiley.

Danne, C., and P. Häusler. 2010. Assessing the effects of assortment complexity in consumer goods supply chains. *Lecture Notes in Business Information Processing* 46: 118–129.

Datta, P.P., and M.G. Christopher. 2011. Information sharing and coordination mechanisms for managing uncertainty in supply chains: A simulation study. *International Journal of Production Research* 49(3): 765–803.

Dattakumar, R., and R. Jagadeesh. 2003. A review of literature in benchmarking. *Benchmarking: An International Journal* 10(3): 176–209.

Deane, J.K., C.W. Craighead, and C.T. Ragsdale. 2009. Mitigating environmental and density risk in global sourcing. *International Journal of Physical Distribution and Logistics Management* 39(10): 861–883.

de Brito, M.P., S.D.P. Flapper, and R. Dekker. 2002. Reverse logistics: A review of case studies, Tech. rep., Erasmus University Rotterdam, the Netherlands. Econometric Institute Report EI 2002-21.

Defee, C.C., and T.P. Stank. 2005. Applying the strategy-structure-performance paradigm to the supply chain environment. *International Journal of Logistics Management* 16(1): 28–50.

Deitz, G., H. Hansen, and R.G. Richey. 2009. Coerced integration: The effects of retailer supply chain technology mandates on supplier stock returns. *International Journal of Physical Distribution and Logistics Management* 39(10): 814–825.

Dekker, R., E. van Asperen, G. Ochtman, and W. Kusters. 2009. Floating stocks in FMCG supply chains: Using intermodal transport to facilitate advance deployment. *International Journal of Physical Distribution and Logistics Management* 39(8): 632–648.

de Wet, J.H. 2005. EVA versus traditional accounting measures of performance as drivers of shareholder value – A comparative analysis. *Meditari Accountancy Research* 13(2): 1–16.

Donaldson, T., and L.E. Preston. 1995. The stakeholder theory of the corporation: Concepts, evidence, and implications. *The Academy of Management Review* 20(1): 65–91.

Dowlatshahi, S. 2005. A strategic framework for the design and implementation of remanufacturing operations in reverse logistics. *International Journal of Production Research* 43(16): 3455–3480.

Duffy, M. 2004. How Gillette cleaned up its supply chain. *Supply Chain Management Review* 8: 20–27.

ELA. 2004. Differentiation for performance – Results of the fifth quinquennial European logistics study "Excellence in logistics 2003/2004", Tech. rep., ELA European Logistics Association and A. T. Kearney Management Consultants.

Emiliani, M.L. 2003. The inevitability of conflict between buyers and sellers. *Supply Chain Management: An International Journal* 8(2): 107–115.

Emiliani, M.L., and D.J. Stec. 2002a. Realizing savings from online reverse auctions. *Supply Chain Management: An International Journal* 7(1): 12–23.

Emiliani, M.L., and D.J. Stec. 2002b. Squaring online reverse auctions with the caux round table principles for business. *Supply Chain Management: An International Journal* 7(2): 92–100.

Emiliani, M.L., and D.J. Stec. 2005. Wood pallet suppliers' reaction to online reverse auctions. *Supply Chain Management: An International Journal* 10(4): 278–288.

Emiliani, M.L., D.J. Stec, and L.P. Grasso. 2005. Unintended responses to a traditional purchasing performance metric. *Supply Chain Management: An International Journal* 10(3): 150–156.

Farris II, M.T., and P.D. Hutchison. 2002. Cash-to-cash: The new supply chain management metric. *International Journal of Physical Distribution and Logistics Management* 32(4): 288–298.

Farris II, M.T., and P.D. Hutchison. 2003. Measuring cash-to-cash performance. *International Journal of Logistics Management* 14(2): 83–91.

Fawcett, S.E., J.A. Ogden, G.M. Magnan, and M.B. Cooper. 2006. Organizational commitment and governance for supply chain success. *International Journal of Physical Distribution and Logistics Management* 36(1): 22–35.

Fawcett, S.E., G.M. Magnan, and M.W. McCarter. 2008. Benefits, barriers, and bridges to effective supply chain management. *Supply Chain Management: An International Journal* 13(1): 35–48.

Fischer, M.L. 1997. What is the right supply chain for your product? *Harvard Business Review* 75: 105–116.

Fisher, M.L., J.H. Hammond, W.R. Obermeyer, and A. Raman. 1994. Making supply meet demand in an uncertain world. *Harvard Business Review*, 72: 83–93.

Fisher, M., J. Hammond, W. Obermeyer, and A. Raman. 1997. Configuring a supply chain to reduce the cost of demand uncertainty. *Production and Operations Management* 6(3): 211–225.

Fleischmann, M., J.M. Bloemhoff-Ruwaard, R. Dekker, E. van der Laan, J.A.E.E. van Nunen, and L.N. van Wassenhove. 1997. Quantitative models for reverse logistics: A review. *European Journal of Operational Research* 103: 1–17.

Fleischmann, B., H. Meyr, and M. Wagner. 2008. Advanced planning. In *Supply Chain Management and Advanced Planning*, eds. H. Stadtler and C. Kilger, 81–106. Heidelberg: Springer.

Foggin, J.H., J.T. Mentzer, and C.L. Monroe. 2004. A supply chain diagnostic tool. *International Journal of Physical Distribution and Logistics Management* 34(10): 827–855.

Fong, S.W., E.W.L. Cheng, and D.C.K. Ho. 1998. Benchmarking: A general reading for management practitioners. *Management Decision* 36(6): 407–418.

Forrester, J.W. 1961. *Industrial dynamics*. Cambridge: MIT.

Förster, Andrea, Knut Haase, and Michael Tönnies. 2006. Ein modellgestützter Ansatz zur mittelfristigen Produktions- und Ablaufplanung für eine Brauerei (A model-based approach for mid-term production and operations planning for a brewery). *Zeitschrift für Betriebswirtschaft* 76(12): 1255–1274.

Franke, J., D. Pfaff, R. Elbert, M. Gomm, and E. Hofmann. 2005. Die Financial Chain im Supply Chain Management: Konzeptionelle Einordnung und Identifikation von Werttreibern (The financial chain in supply chain management: Conceptual positioning and identification of value drivers). In *Wirtschaftsinformatik 2005: eEconomy, eGovernment, eSociety (Business informatics 2005: eEconomy, eGovernment, eSociety)*, ed. O.K. Ferstel, E.J. Sinz, S. Eckert, and T. Isselhorst, 567–584. Heidelberg: Physica.

Frankel, R., T.J. Goldsby, and J.M. Whipple. 2002. Grocery industry collaboration in the wake of ECR. *International Journal of Logistics Management* 13(1): 57–72.

Freeman, R.E. 1984. *Strategic management: A stakeholder approach*. Boston: Pitman.

Freiwald, S. 2005. *Supply Chain Design – Robuste Planung mit differenzierter Auswahl der Zulieferer (Supply chain design – Robust planning with differentiated supplier selection)*. Frankfurt/M: Peter Lang.

Fullerton, R.R., and W.F. Wempe. 2009. Lean manufacturing, non-financial performance measures, and financial performance. *International Journal of Operations and Production Management* 29(3): 214–240.

Gabriel, C. 2003. *Strategisches supply chain design (Strategic supply chain design)*. Bamberg: Difo-Druck.

Gaudenzi, B., and A. Borghesi. 2006. Managing risks in the supply chain using the AHP method. *International Journal of Logistics Management* 17(1): 114–136.

Geginat, J., B. Morath, R. Wittmann, and P. Knüsel. 2006. Kapitalkosten als strategisches Entscheidungskriterium. (Cost of capital as a strategic decision criterion.), Tech. rep., Roland Berger Strategy Consultants, München.

Gilmour, Peter. 1999. Benchmarking supply chain operations. *International Journal of Physical Distribution and Logistics Management* 5(4): 259–266.

Gimenez, C. 2005. Case studies and surveys in supply chain management research – Two complementary methodologies. In *Research methodologies in supply chain management*, ed. H. Kotzab, S. Seuring, M. Müller, and G. Reiner, 315–330. Heidelberg: Physica.

Godsell, J., and R. van Hoek. 2009. Fudging the supply chain to hit the number: Five common practices that sacrifice the supply chain and what financial analysts should ask about them. *Supply Chain Management: An International Journal* 14(3): 171–176.

Godsell, J., A. Birtwistle, and R. van Hoek. 2010. Building the supply chain to enable business alignment: Lessons from British American Tobacco (BAT). *Supply Chain Management: An International Journal* 15(1): 10–15.

Goetschalckx, M., and B. Fleischmann. 2008. Strategic network design. In *Supply chain management and advanced planning*, 4th ed, ed. H. Stadtler and C. Kilger, 117–132. Berlin: Springer.

Goldbach, M. 2002. Organizational settings in supply chain costing. In *Cost management in supply chains*, ed. S. Seuring and M. Goldbach, 89–108. Heidelberg: Physica.

Golicic, S.L., D.F. Davis, and T.M. McCarthy. 2005. A balanced approach to research in supply chain management. In *Research methodologies in supply chain management*, ed. H. Kotzab, S. Seuring, M. Müller, and G. Reiner, 15–30. Heidelberg: Physica.

Gomm, M.L. 2010. Supply chain finance: Applying finance theory to supply chain management to enhance finance in supply chains. *International Journal of Logistics, Research and Applications* 13(2): 133–142.

Graves, S., and S. Willems. 2005. Optimizing the supply chain configuration for new products. *Management Science* 51(8): 1165–1180.

Grinyer, J. 1985. Earned economic income: A theory of matching. *Abacus* 23: 43–54.

Gruca, T.S., and L.L. Rego. 2005. Customer satisfaction, cash flow and shareholder value. *Journal of Marketing* 69: 115–130

Gudehus, T., and H. Kotzab. 2009. *Comprehensive logistics*. Heidelberg: Springer.

Guide Jr., V.D.R., and L.N. van Wassenhove. 2009. The evolution of closed-loop supply chain research. *Operations Research* 57(1): 10–18.

Guide Jr., V.D.R., T.P. Harrison, and L.N. van Wassenhove. 2003. The challenge of closed-loop supply chains. *Interfaces* 33(6): 3–6.

Guillen, G., F.D. Mele, A. Espuna, and L. Puigjaner. 2005. Multiobjective supply chain design under uncertainty. *Chemical Engineering Science* 60: 1535–1553.

Gunasekaran, A., and B. Kobu. 2007. Performance measures and metrics in logistics and supply chain management: A review of recent literature (1995–2004) for research and applications. *International Journal of Production Research* 45(12): 2819–2840.

Gunasekaran, A., C. Patel, and R. McGaughey. 2004. A framework for supply chain performance measurement. *International Journal of Production Economics* 87: 333–347.

Günther, H.O. 2005. Supply chain management and advanced planning systems: A tutorial. In *Supply chain management und logistik – optimierung, simulation, decision support (Supply chain management and logistics – optimisation, simulation, decision support)*, ed. H.O. Günther, D.C. Mattfeld, and L. Suhl, 3–40. Heidelberg: Physica.

Günther, H.O. 2008. The block planning approach: A case study application from the beverage industry. *Proceedings of the 2008 IEEE*, 359–363. DOI: 10.1109/IEEM.2008.4737891.

Günther, H.O., and H. Meyr. 2009. *Supply chain planning – Quantitative decision support and advanced planning solutions*. Berlin/Heidelberg/New York: Springer.

Günther, H.O., and P. van Beek, ed. 2003. *Advanced planning and scheduling solutions in process industry*. Berlin/Heidelberg/New York: Springer.

Günther, H.O., D.C. Mattfeld, and L. Suhl. 2005. *Supply chain management und logistik – optimierung, simulation, decision support (Supply chain management and logistics – optimisation, simulation, decision support)*. Heidelberg: Physica.

Günther, H.O., M. Grunow, and M. Neuhaus. 2006. Realizing block planning concepts in make-and-pack production using MILP modeling and SAP APO©. *International Journal of Production Research* 44(18–19): 3711–3726.

Gupta, Y., P.S. Sundararaghavan, and M.U. Ahmed. 2003. Ordering policies for items with seasonal demand. *International Journal of Physical Distribution and Logistics Management* 33(6): 500–518.

Hahn, G.J., and H. Kuhn. 2010. Optimising a value-based performance indicator in mid-term sales and operations planning. *Journal of the Operational Research Society* 62: 515–525.

Hahn, G.J., and H. Kuhn. 2011. Value-based performance and risk management in supply chains: A robust optimization approach. *International Journal of Production Economics*. doi:10.1016/j.ijpe.2011.04.002.

Halldorsson, A., and J. Arlbjørn. 2005. Research methodologies in supply chain management – What do we know? In *Research methodologies in supply chain management*, ed. H. Kotzab, S. Seuring, M. Müller, and G. Reiner. Heidelberg: Physica.

Hammant, J., S.M. Disney, P. Childerhouse, and M.M. Naim. 1999. Modelling the consequences of a strategic supply chain initiative of an automotive aftermarket operation. *The International Journal of Physical Distribution and Logistics Management* 29(9): 535–550.

Handfield, R.B., and E. L. Nichols. 1999. *Introduction to supply chain management*. Upper Saddle River: Prentice-Hall.

Handfield, R.B., and E.L. Nichols. 2002. *Supply chain redesign – Transforming supply chains into integrated value systems*. Upper Saddle River: Financial Times Prentice Hall.

Hanman, S. 1997. Benchmarking your firm's performance with best practice. *International Journal of Logistics Management* 8(2): 1–18.

Harland, C.M. 1996. Supply chain management: Relationships, chains and networks. *British Academy of Management* 7: 650–673.

Hartman, J.C. 2000. On the equivalence of net present value and economic value added as measures of a project's economic worth. *Engineering Economist* 45: 158–165.

Haug, A., A. Pedersen, and J.S. Arlbjørn. 2010. ERP system strategies in parent-subsidiary supply chains. *International Journal of Physical Distribution and Logistics Management* 40(4): 298–314.

Hawawini, G., and C. Viallet. 2002. *Finance for executives – Managing for value creation*, 2nd ed. Mason: Thomson/South-Western.

Heikkilä, J. 2002. From supply to demand chain management: Efficiency and customer satisfaction. *Journal of Operations Management* 20: 747–767.

Hendricks, K., and V. Singhal. 1997. Delays in new product introductions and the market value of the firm: The consequences of being late in the market. *Management Science* 43(4): 422–436.

Hendricks, K., and V. Singhal. 2003. The effect of supply chain glitches on shareholder wealth. *Journal of Operations Management* 21: 501–522.

Hendricks, K., and V. Singhal. 2005a. Association between supply chain glitches and operating performance. *Management Science* 51(5): 695–711.

Hendricks, K., and V. Singhal. 2005b. An empirical analysis of the effect of supply chain disruptions on long-run stock price performance and equity risk of the firm. *Production and Operations Management* 14(1): 35–52.

Hendricks, K., and V. Singhal. 2008. The effect of supply chain disruptions on shareholder value. *Total Quality Management* 19(7–8): 777–791.

Hendricks, K., and V. Singhal. 2009. Demand-supply mismatches and stock market reaction: Evidence from excess inventory announcements. *Manufacturing and Service Operations Management* 11(3): 509–524.

Hendricks, Kevin B., Vinod R. Singhal, and Christine I. Wiedman. 1995. The impact of capacity expansion on the market value of the firm. *Journal of Operations Management* 12: 259–272.

Henkel. 2000–2010. Annual reports. http://www.henkel.de/investor-relations/downloads-archiv-10481.htm. Accessed 25 Feb 2011.

Henkel. 2004–2009. Annual reports. http://www.henkel.de/investor-relations/downloads-archiv-10481.htm. Accessed 6 July 2009.

Hertz, S., J.K. Johansson, and F. de Jager. 2001. Customer-oriented cost cutting: Process management at Volvo. *Supply Chain Management: An International Journal* 6(3): 128–141.

Higuchi, T., and M. Troutt. 2004. Dynamic simulation of the supply chain for a short life cycle product-lessons from the Tamagotchi case. *Computers and Operations Research* 31(7): 1097–1114.

Hillman, A.J., and G.D. Keim. 2001. Shareholder value, stakeholder management, and social issues: What's the bottom line? *Strategic Management Journal* 22: 125–139.

Hofmann, E. 2006. Quantifying and setting off network performance. *International Journal for Networking and Virtual Organisations* 3(3): 317–339.

Hofmann, E. 2009. Inventory financing in supply chains: A logistics service provider-approach. *International Journal of Physical Distribution and Logistics Management* 39(9): 716–740.

Hofmann, E. 2010. Linking corporate strategy and supply chain management. *International Journal of Physical Distribution and Logistics Management* 40(4): 256–276.

Hofmann, E., and R. Elbert. 2004. Collaborative Cash Flow Management – Financial Supply Chain Management als Herausforderung der Netzkompetenz (Collaborative cash flow management – Financial supply chain management as challenge of the network competency). In *Netzkompetenz in Supply Chains – Grundlagen und Umsetzung (Network competency in supply chains – Basics and implementation)*, ed. H.-C. Pfohl, 93–117. Wiesbaden: Gabler.

Hofmann, Erik, and Herbert Kotzab. 2006. Developing and discussing a supply chain-oriented model of collaborative working capital management. In *Track 11 "Globalization in the Value Chain": IFSAM, 2006*, 1–30. Berlin: IFSAM.

Hofmann, Erik, and Herbert Kotzab. 2010. A supply chain-oriented approach of working capital management. *Journal of Business Logistics* 31(2): 305–330.

Hofmann, E., and A. Locker. 2009. Value-based performance measurement in supply chain: A case study from the packaging industry. *Production Planning and Control* 20(1): 68–81.

Holmström, J., W.E. Hoover Jr., E. Eloranta, and A. Vasara. 1999. Using value reengineering to implement breakthrough solutions for customers. *International Journal of Logistics Management* 10(2): 1–12.

Honkomp, S., S. Lombardo, O. Rosen, and J. Pekny. 2000. The curse of reality – Why process scheduling optimization problems are difficult in practice. *Computers and Chemical Engineering* 24(2–7): 323–328.

Horstmann, Michael. 2003. Henkel: Erfolgreiche Neustrukturierung der Kosmetikproduktion in Europa (Henkel: Successful restructuring of the cosmetics production in Europe). In *Supply Chain Champions – Was sie tun und wie Sie einer werden (Supply chain champions – what they do and how you become one)*, ed. Ulrich Thonemann, Klaus Behrenbeck, Raimund Diederichs, Jochen Gropietsch, Jörn Küpper, and Markus Leopoldseder, 168–176. Wiesbaden: Gabler.

Huan, S.H., S.K. Sheoran, and G. Wang. 2004. A review and analysis of supply chain operations reference (scor) model. *Supply Chain Management: An International Journal* 9(1): 23–29.

Huan, S.H., S.K. Sheoran, and H. Keskar. 2005. Computer-assisted supply chain configuration based on supply chain operations (SCOR) model. *Computers and Industrial Engineering* 48: 377–394.

Hübner, R. 2007. *Strategic supply chain management in process industries: An application to specialty chemicals production network design.* Heidelberg: Springer.

Humphrey, J. 2003. Globalization and supply chain networks: The auto industry in Brazil and India. *Global Networks* 3(2): 121–141.

Ivanov, D., B. Sokolov, and J. Kaeschel. 2010. Integrated adaptive design and planning of supply networks. *Lecture Notes in Business Information Processing* 46: 152–163.

Jayaram, J. 2008. Supplier involvement in new product development projects: Dimensionality and contingency effects. *International Journal of Production Research* 46(13): 3717–3735.

Jehle, M. 2005. *Wertorientiertes supply chain management und supply chain controlling (Value-based supply chain management and supply chain management accounting)*. Frankfurt/M: Peter Lang.

Jensen, M.C. 2001. Value maximization, stakeholder theory and the corporate objective function. *European Financial Management* 7(3): 297–317.

Johnson, M., and S. Templar. 2011. The relationships between supply chain and firm performance: The development and testing of a unified proxy. *The International Journal of Physical Distribution and Logistics Management* 41(2): 88–103.

Jones, D.T., P. Hines, and N. Rich. 1997. Lean logistics. *The International Journal of Physical Distribution and Logistics Management* 27(3/4): 153–173.

Jung, J.Y., G. Blau, J.F. Pekny, G.V. Reklaitis, and D. Eversdyk. 2004. A simulation based optimization approach to supply chain management under demand uncertainty. *Computers and Chemical Engineering* 28: 2087–2106.

Jüttner, U., M. Christopher, and J. Godsell. 2010. A strategic framework for integrating marketing and supply chain strategies. *International Journal of Logistics Management* 21(1): 104–126.

Kannegiesser, M., H.-O. Günther, P. van Beek, M. Grunow, and C. Habla. 2009. Value chain management for commodities: A case study from the chemical industry. In *Supply chain planning – Quantitative decision support and advanced planning solutions*, ed. H.O. Günter and H. Meyr, 283–313. Berlin/Heidelberg/New York: Springer.

Kaplan, S.N., and R.S. Ruback. 1995. The valuation of cash flow forecasts. *Journal of Financial Economics* 25: 191–212.

Keebler, J.S., and R.E. Plank. 2009. Logistics performance measurement in the supply chain: A benchmark. *Benchmarking: An International Journal* 16(6): 785–798.

Keebler, J.S., D.A. Durtsche, K.B. Manrodt, and D.M. Ledyard. 1999. *Keeping score – Measuring the business value of logistics in the supply chain*. Oak Brook: Council of Logistics Management.

Kelm, K.M., V.K. Narayanan, and G.E. Pinches. 1995. Shareholder value creation during R&D innovation and commercialization stages. *The Academy of Management Journal* 38(3): 770–786.

Kelton, W., R. Sadowski, and D. Sadowski. 2002. *Simulation with arena*, 2nd ed. New York: McGraw-Hill.

Kennett, J., M. Fulton, P. Molder, and H. Brooks. 1998. Supply chain management: The case of a UK baker preserving the identity of Canadian milling wheat. *Supply Chain Management: An International Journal* 3(3): 157–166.

Kersten, W., and T. Blecker. 2006. *Managing risks in supply chains – How to build reliable collaboration in logistics*. Berlin: Erich Schmidt Verlag.

Kersten, W., M. Böger, P. Hohrath, and H. Späth. 2006. Supply chain risk management: Development of a theoretical and empirical framework. In *Managing risks in supply chains – How to build reliable collaboration in logistics*, ed. W. Kersten and T. Blecker, 3–17. Berlin: Erich Schmidt Verlag.

Kleijnen, P. 2005. Supply chain simulation tools and techniques: A survey. *International Journal of Simulation and Process Modelling* 1(1/2): 82–89.

Kleijnen, J.P.C., and M. T. Smits. 2003. Performance metrics in supply chain management. *Journal of the Operational Research Society* 54: 507–514.

Knorren, N., and J. Weber. 1997. *Shareholder value (in German)*, Advanced controlling, vol. 2. Vallendar. WHU Otto-Reischim-Hochschule.

Kotzab, H. 2005. The role and importance of survey research in the field of supply chain management. In *Research methodologies in supply chain management*, ed. H. Kotzab, S.Seuring, M. Müller, and G. Reiner, 125–138. Heidelberg: Physica.

Kotzab, H., and C. Teller. 2002. Cost efficiency in supply chains – A conceptual discrepancy? Logistics cost management between desire and reality. In *Cost management in supply chains*, ed. S. Seuring and M. Goldbach, 233–250. Heidelberg: Physica.

Krikke, Harold, Costas P. Pappis, Giannis T. Tsoulfas, and Jaqueline M. Bloemhof-Ruwaard. 2002. Extended design principles for closed loop supply chains: Optimising economic, logistic and environmental performance. In *Quantitative approaches to distribution logistics and supply chain management*, ed. Andreas Klose, M. Grazia Speranza, and Luk N. van Wassenhove, 61–74. Berlin: Springer.

Krikke, H., I. le Blanc, and S. van de Velde. 2004. Product modularity and the design of closed-loop supply chains. *California Management Review* 46(2): 23–39.

Kumar, D., O.P. Singh, and J. Singh. 2010. An analytical framework for critical literature review of supply chain design. *International Journal of Information and Systems Science* 6(3): 293–317.

Labitzke, N., T.S. Spengler, and T. Volling. 2009. Applying decision-oriented accounting principles for the simulation-based design of logistics systems in production. In *Proceedings of the 2009 winter simulation conference*, ed. M. Rossetti, R. Hill, B. Johansson, A. Dunkin, and R.G. Ingalls, 2496–2508. Austin: Omnipress.

Labitzke, N., T. Volling, and T.S. Spengler. 2011. Wertorientierte simulation zur unterstützung der logistischen prozessgestaltung bei der stahlherstellung (Value-based simulation to support logistics process design in steel production). *Zeitschrift für Betriebswirtschaft (Journal of Business Economics)* 81(7–8): 771–803.

Lambert, D., and R. Burduroglu. 2000. Measuring and selling the value of logistics. *International Journal of Logistics Management* 11(1): 1–17.

Lambert, D.M., and M.C. Cooper. 2000. Issues in supply chain management. *Industrial Marketing Management* 29: 65–83.

Lambert, D., and T. Pohlen. 2001. Supply chain metrics. *International Journal of Logistics Management* 12(1): 1–19.

Lambert, D.M., M.C. Cooper, and J.D. Pagh. 1998. Supply chain management: Implementation issues and research opportunities. *International Journal of Logistics Management* 9(2): 1–19.

Lasch, R., A. Lemke, and T. Schindler. 2006. Der Beitrag der Logistik zur wertorientierten Unternehmensführung (The contribution of logistics to value-based management). In *Wertorientiertes Management (Value-based management)*, ed. N. Schweickart and A. Töpfer, 271–300. Berlin: Springer.

Lee, H.L. 2002. Aligning supply chain strategies with product uncertainties. *California Management Review* 44(3): 105–119.

Lee, T.Y.S. 2008. Supply chain risk management. *International Journal of Information and Decision Science* 1(1): 98–114.

Lee, H., V. Padmanabhan, and S. Whang. 1997a. The bullwhip effect in supply chains. *Sloan Management Revlew* 38(3): 93–102.

Lee, H., V. Padmanabhan, and S. Whang. 1997b. Information distortion in a supply chain: The bullwhip effect. *Management Science* 43(4): 546–558.

Lee, H.L., K.S. So, and C.S. Tang. 2000. The value of information sharing in a two-level supply chain. *Management Science* 46(5): 626–643.

Lockamy, A., and K. McCormack. 2004. Linking SCOR planning practices to supply chain performance – An exploratory study. *International Journal of Operations and Production Management* 24(12): 1192–1218.

Losbichler, H., and M. Rothböck. 2006. Creating shareholder value through value-driven supply chain management. In *Managing risks in supply chains – How to build reliable collaboration in logistics*, ed. W. Kersten and T. Blecker, 281–296. Berlin: Erich Schmidt Verlag.

Love, P.E.D., Z. Irani, and D.J. Edwards. 2004. A seamless supply chain management model for construction. *Supply Chain Management: An International Journal* 9(1): 43–56.

Lowson, R.H. 2003. How supply network operations strategies evolve. *International Journal of Physical Distribution and Logistics Management* 33(1): 75–91.

Lueg, R., and U. Schäffer. 2010. Assessing empirical research on value-based management: Guidelines for improved hypothesis testing. *Journal für Betriebswirtschaft* 60: 1–47.

Luehrmann, T.A. 1997. Using APV: A better tool for valuing operatons. *Harvard Business Review* 75: 145–154.

Lummus, R.R., and R.J. Vokurka. 1999. Defining supply chain management: A historical perspective and practical guidelines. *Industrial Management and Data Systems* 99(1): 11–17.

Madden, B.J. 1998. The CFROI valuation model. *The Journal of Investing* 7(1): 31–44.

Mady, M.T. 1991. Effect of industry type on inventory investments and structure: The Egyptian case. *International Journal of Physical Distribution and Logistics Management* 21(9): 30–36.

Maire, J.L., V. Bronet, and M. Pillet. 2005. A typology of 'best practices' for a benchmarking process. *Benchmarking: An International Journal* 12(1): 45–60.

Malmi, T., and S. Ikäheimo. 2003. Value based management practices-some evidence from the field. *Management Accounting Research* 14(3): 235–254.

Manuj, I., J. Mentzer, and M. Bowers. 2009. Improving the rigor of discrete-event simulation in logistics and supply chain management. *International Journal of Physical Distribution and Logistics Management* 39(3): 172–201.

Marquai, A., R. Alcantara, and M. Christopher. 2010. Using the systematic literature review procedure to identify the root causes of out-of-stock in retail supply chains. In *Proceedings of the 17th international annual EurOMA conference*, ed. R. Sousa. Porto: Catholic University of Portugal.

Mayring, P. 2008. *Qualitative inhaltsanalyse (Qualitative content analysis)*, 10th ed. Weinheim: Beltz.

McCarthy, T.M., and S.L. Golicic. 2002. Implementing collaborative forecasting to improve supply chain performance. *International Journal of Physical Distribution and Logistics Management* 32(6): 431–454.

McKinnon, A., and M. Forster. 2000. European logistical and supply chain trends: 1999–2005, Tech. rep., Heriot-Watt University Edinburgh.

Meixell, M.J., and V.B. Gargeya. 2005. Global supply chain design: A literature review and critique. *Transportation Research Part E* 41: 531–550.

Melnyk, S., R. Lummus, R. Vokurka, L. Burns, and J. Sandor. 2009. Mapping the future of supply chain management: A delphi study. *International Journal of Production Research* 47(16): 4629–4653.

Melo, M.T., S. Nickel, and F. Saldanha-da Gama. 2009. Facility location and supply chain management – A review. *European Journal of Operational Research* 196: 401–412.

Mena, C., A. Humphries, and R. Wilding. 2009. A comparison of inter- and intra-organizational relationships: Two case studies from UK food and drink industry. *International Journal of Physical Distribution and Logistics Management* 39(9): 762–784.

Mentzer, J., W. DeWitt, J. Keebler, S. Min, N. Nix, C. Smith, and Z. Zacharia. 2001. Defining supply chain management. *Journal of Business Logistics* 22(2): 1–25.

Meredith, J. 1993. Theory building through conceptual methods. *International Journal of Operations and Production Management* 13(3): 3–11.

Meredith, J., K.A. Raturi, K. Amoako-Gyampah, and B. Kaplan. 1989. Alternative research paradigms in operations. *Journal of Operations Management* 8: 297–326.

Metze, T. 2010. *Supply Chain Finance – Die wertorientierte Analyse und Optimierung des Working Capital in Supply Chains (Supply chain finance – The value-based analysis and optimization of working capital in supply chains)*. Lohmar: EUL Verlag.

Meyer, H. 2006. Wertsteigerung durch Neuausrichtung der Heidelberger Druckmaschinen AG (Value increase by realignment of Heidelberger Druckmaschinen AG). In *Wertorientiertes Management (Value-based management)*, ed. N. Schweickart and A. Töpfer, 649–658. Berlin: Springer.

Meyr, H., and H. Stadtler. 2008. Types of supply chains. In *Supply chain management and advanced planning*, 4th ed, ed. H. Stadtler and C. Kilger, 65–80. Berlin: Springer.

Miebach Consulting. 2004. SCM in der Konsumgüterbranche 2004. (SCM in consumer goods industry 2004), Tech. rep., Miebach Consulting and Lebensmittel Zeitung.

Mikkola, J.H. 2005. Modeling the effect of product architecture modularity in supply chains. In *Research methodologies in supply chain management*, ed. H. Kotzab, S. Seuring, M. Müller, and G. Reiner, 493–508. Heidelberg: Physica.

Min, H., and G. Zhou. 2002. Supply chain modeling: Past, present, future. *Computers and Industrial Engineering* 43: 231–249.

Min, S., J.T. Mentzer, and R.T. Ladd. 2007. A market orientation in supply chain management. *Journal of the Academy of Marketing Science* 35: 507–522.

Modigliani, F., and M. Miller. 1958. The cost of capital, corporation finance and the theory of investment. *American Economic Review* 48: 261–197.

Mollenkopf, D., and G.P. Dapiran. 2005. World-class logistics: Australia and New Zealand, *International Journal of Physical Distribution and Logistics Management* 35(1): 63–74.

Möller, K. 2003. Supply Chain Valuation – Wertschöpfung in und durch Supply Chain Networks (Supply chain value – value creation in an by supply chain networks). In *Supply chain controlling in theorie und praxis (Supply chain management accounting in theory and practice)*, ed. W. Stölzle and A. Otto, 49–82. Wiesbaden: Gabler.

Moore, K.R., and W.A. Cunningham III. 1999. Social exchange behavior in logistics relationships: A shipper perspective. *International Journal of Physical Distribution and Logistics Management* 29(2): 103–121.

Morana, R., and S. Seuring. 2007. End-of-life returns of long-lived products from end customer-insights from an ideally set up closed-loop supply chain. *International Journal of Production Research* 45(18–19): 4423–4437.

Morana, R., and S. Seuring. 2011. A three level framework for closed-loop supply chain management – Linking society, chain and actor level. *Sustainability* 3: 678–691.

Mukhopadhyay, S.K., and A.K. Barua. 2003. Supply chain cell activities for a consumer goods company. *International Journal of Production Research* 41(2): 297–314.

Myers, S. 1974. Interactions in corporate finance and interaction decisions – Implications for capital budgeting. *Journal of Finance* 29: 1–25.

Neher, A. 2003. Wertorientierung im Supply Chain Controlling (Value orientation in supply chain management accounting). In *Supply chain controlling in theorie und praxis (Supply chain management accounting in theory and practice)*, ed. W. Stölzle and A. Otto, 27–47. Wiesbaden: Gabler.

Neuner, C. 2009. *Konfiguration internationaler Produktionsnetzwerke unter Berücksichtigung von Unsicherheit (Configuration of international production networks under consideration of uncertainty)*. Wiesbaden: Gabler.

New, S.J. 1996. A framework for analysing supply chain improvement. *International Journal of Operations and Production Management* 16(4): 19–34.

Nienhaus, J., A. Ziegenbein, and C. Duijts. 2006. How human behaviour amplifies the bullwhip effect – A study based on the beer distribution game online. *Production Planning and Control* 17(6): 547–557.

Norrman, A., and U. Jansson. 2004. Ericsson's proactive supply chain risk management approach after a serious sub-supplier accident. *International Journal of Physical Distribution and Logistics Management* 34(5): 434–456.

Obermaier, R., and A. Donhauser. 2009. Disaggregate and aggregate inventory to sales ratios over time: The case of german corporations 1993–2005. *Logistics Research* 1: 95–111.

O'Leary, D.E. 2000. Supply chain processes and relationships for electronic commerce. In *Handbook on electronic commerce*, ed. M. Shaw, R. Blanning, T. Strader, and A. Whinston, 431–444. Heidelberg: Springer.

Otto, A. 2002. *Management und Controlling von Supply Chains (Management and management accounting of supply chains)*. Wiesbaden: Gabler.

Otto, A., and R. Obermaier. 2009. How can supply networks increase firm value? A causal framework to structure the answer. *Logistics Research* 1: 131–148.

Ottosson, E., and F. Weissenrieder. 1996. Cash value added – A new method for measuring financial performance, Tech. rep., Department of Economics, Gothenburg University.

Padachi, Kesseven. 2006. Trend in working capital management and its impact on firms' performance: An analysis of mauritian small manufacturing companies. *International Review of Business Research Papers* 2(2): 45–58.

Palsson, H., and O. Johansson. 2009. Supply chain integration obtained through uniquely labelled goods – A survey of Swedish manufacturing industries. *International Journal of Physical Distribution and Logistics Management* 39(1): 28–46.

Parry, G., J. Mills, and C. Turner. 2010. Lean competence: Integration of theories in operations management practice. *Supply Chain Management: An International Journal* 15(3): 216–226.

Pauwels, K., J. Silva-Risso, S. Srinivasan, and D. M. Hanssens. 2004. New products, sales promotions, and firm value: The case of the automobile industry. *Journal of Marketing* 68: 142–156.

Peck, H. 2005. Drivers of supply chain vulnerability: An integrated framework. *International Journal of Physical Distribution and Logistics Management* 35(4): 210–232.

Pegels, C.C. 1991. Alternative methods of evaluating capital investments in logistics. *International Journal of Physical Distribution and Logistics Management* 21(2): 19–25.

Pero, M., and A. Sianesi. 2009. Aligning supply chain management and new product development: A theoretical framework. *International Journal of Electronic Customer Relationship Management* 3(3): 301–317.

Pero, M., N. Abdelkafi, A. Sianesi, and T. Blecker. 2010. A framework for the alignment of new product development and supply chains. *Supply Chain Management: An International Journal* 15(2): 115–128.

Perona, M. 2002. A new customer-oriented methodology to evaluate supply chain lost sales costs due to stockout in consumer goods sector. In *Cost management in supply chains*, ed. S. Seuring and M. Goldbach, 289–307. Heidelberg: Physica.

Petrovic, D. 2001. Simulation of supply chain behaviour and performance in an uncertain environment. *International Journal of Production Economics* 71: 429–438.

Pfohl, H.C., and M. Gomm. 2009. Supply chain finance: Optimizing financial flows in supply chains. *Logistics Research* 1: 149–161.

Pohlen, T.L., and T.J. Goldsby. 2003. VMI and SMI programs: How economic value added can help sell the change. *International Journal of Physical Distribution and Logistics Management* 33(7): 565–581.

Porter, Michael E. 1998. *Competitive strategy: Techniques for analyzing industries and competitors*. New York: Free Press.

Poston, R., and S. Grabinski. 2001. Financial impacts of enterprise resource planning implementations. *International Journal of Accounting Information Systems* 2(23): 271–294.

Pourakbar, M., A. Sleptchenko, and R. Dekker. 2009. The floating stock policy in fast moving consumer goods supply chains, *Transportation Research Part E* 45(1): 39–49.

Ramezani, C.A., L. Soenen, and A. Jung. 2002. Growth, corporate profitability, and value creation. *Financial Analysts Journal* 62(6): 56–67.

Randall, W., and M. Farris II. 2009a. Supply chain financing: Using cash-to-cash variables to strengthen the supply chain. *International Journal of Physical Distribution and Logistics Management* 39(8): 669–689.

Randall, W., and M. Farris II. 2009b. Utilizing cash-to-cash to benchmark company performance. *Benchmarking: An International Journal* 16(4): 449–461.

Rappaport, A. 1998. *Creating shareholder value*. New York: The Free Press.

Reiner, G. 2005. Supply chain management research methodologies using quantitative models based on empirical data. In *Research methodologies in supply chain management*, ed. H. Kotzab, S. Seuring, M. Müller, and G. Reiner, 431–444. Heidelberg: Physica.

Reiner, G., and P. Hofmann. 2006. Efficiency analysis of supply chain processes. *International Journal of Production Research* 44(23): 5065–5087.

Reiner, G., and R. Schodl. 2003. A model for the support and evaluation fo strategic supply chain design. In *Strategy and organization in supply chains*, ed. S. Seuring, M. Müller, M. Goldbach, and U. Schneidewind, 305–320. Heidelberg: Physica.

Reiner, G., and M. Trcka. 2004. Customized supply chain design: Problems and alternatives for a production company in the food industry. A simulation based analysis. *International Journal of Production Economics* 89: 217–229.

Richey Jr., R.G. 2009. The supply chain crisis and disaster pyramid: A theoretical framework for understanding preparedness and recovery. *International Journal of Physical Distribution and Logistics Management* 39(7): 619–628.

Ritchie, B., and C. Brindley. 2007. Supply chain risk management and performance – A guiding framework for future development. *International Journal of Operations and Production Management* 27(3): 303–322.

Rockwell Automation, ed. 2007. Arena^{TM} user's guide, http://literature.rockwellautomation.com/idc/groups/literature/documents/um/arena-um001_-en-p.pdf. Accessed 7 Sep 2010.

Ross, S.A., R.W. Westerfield, and J.F. Jaffe. 2002. *Corporate finance*, 6th ed. New York: McGraw-Hill.

Ryan, H.E., and E.A. Trahan. 1999. The utilization of value-based management: An empirical analysis. *Financial Practice and Education* 9(1): 46–58.

Ryan, H.E., and E.A. Trahan. 2007. Corporate financial control mechanisms and firm performance: The case of value-based management systems. *Journal of Business Finance and Accounting* 34(1–2): 111–138.

Saad, S., and N. Gindy. 1998. Handling internal and external disturbances in responsive manufacturing environment. *Production Planning and Control* 9(8): 760–770.

Sachan, A., and S. Datta. 2008. Review of supply chain management and logistics research. *International Journal of Physical Distribution and Logistics Management* 35(9): 664–705.

Sahay, B.S., and R. Mohan. 2003. Supply chain management practices in Indian industry. *International Journal of Physical Distribution and Logistics Management* 33(7): 582–606.

Sanchez, A.M., and M.P. Perez. 2005. Supply chain flexibility and firm performance – A conceptual model and empirical study in the automotive industry. *International Journal of Operations and Production Management* 25(7): 681–700.

Sandholm, T., D. Levine, M. Concordia, P. Martyn, R. Hughes, J. Jacobs, and D. Begg. 2006. Changing the game in strategic sourcing at Procter and Gamble: Expressive competition enabled by optimization. *Interfaces* 36(1): 55–68.

Schilling, G. 1996. Working capital's role in maintaining corporate liquidity. *TMA Journal* 16: 4–7.

Schilling, R., H. Kuhn, and M. Brandenburg. 2010. Simulation-based evaluation of tactical supply chain design scenarios for new product introduction. In *Proceedings of the 17th international annual EurOMA conference*, ed. R. Sousa. Porto: Catholic University of Portugal.

Schmenner, R.W., and M.L. Swink. 1998. On theory in operations management. *Journal of Operations Management* 17(1): 97–113.

Schnetzler, M.J., and P. Schönsleben. 2007. The contribution and role of information management in supply chains: A decomposition-based approach. *Production Planning and Control* 18(6): 497–513.

Schnetzler, M., A. Sennheiser, and M. Weidemann. 2004. Supply chain strategies for business success. In *Proceedings of the international IMS forum 2004: "Global challenges in manufacturing"* Politecnico di Milano, Milan/Italy.

Schweickart, N., and A. Töpfer. 2006. *Wertorientiertes Management (Value-based management)*. Berlin/Heidelberg: Springer.

Seifert, D. 2002. *Collaborative planning, forecasting and replenishment*. Bonn: Galileo Press.

Seuring, S. 2001. Supply chain costing – A conceptual framework. In *Cost management in supply chains*, ed. S. Seuring and M. Goldbach, 15–30. Heidelberg/New York: Physica.

Seuring, S. 2005. Case study research in supply chains – An outline and three examples. In *Research methodologies in supply chain management*, ed. H. Kotzab, S. Seuring, M. Müller, and G. Reiner, 235–250. Heidelberg: Physica.

Seuring, S. 2006. Supply chain controlling: Summarizing recent developments in german literature. *Supply Chain Management: An International Journal* 11(1): 10–14.

Seuring, S. 2008. Assessing the rigor of case study research in supply chain management. *Supply Chain Management: An International Journal* 13(2): 128–137.

Seuring, S. 2009. The product-relationship-matrix as framework for strategic supply chain design based on operations theory. *International Journal of Production Economics* 120(1): 221–232.

Seuring, S., and S. Gold. 2012. Conducting content-analysis based literature reviews in supply chain management. *Supply Chain Management: An International Journal* 17(5): 544–555.

Seuring, S., and M. Goldbach. 2001. *Cost management in supply chains*. Heidelberg/New York: Physica.

Seuring, S., and M. Müller. 2008. From a literature review to a conceptual framework for sustainable supply chain management. *Journal of Cleaner Production* 16: 1699–1710.

Seuring, S., M. Müller, M. Westhaus, and R. Morana. 2005. Conducting a literature review – The example of sustainability in supply chains. In *Research methodologies in supply chain management*, ed. H. Kotzab, S. Seuring, M. Müller, and G. Reiner, 91–106. Heidelberg: Physica.

Shapiro, J. 2007. *Modeling the supply chain*, 2nd ed. Duxbury. Brooks/Cole: Thompson.

Shepherd, C., and H. Günter. 2006. Measuring supply chain performance: Current research and future directions. *International Journal of Productivity and Performance Management* 55(3/4): 242–258.

Siemieniuch, C., F. Waddell, and M. Sinclair. 1999. The role of 'partnership' in supply chain management for fast-moving consumer goods: A case study. *International Journal of Logistics Research and Applications* 2(1): 87–101.

Silver, E., D. Pyke, and R. Peterson. 1998. *Inventory management and production planning and scheduling*, 3rd ed. New York: Wiley.

Simatupang, T.M., and R. Sridharan. 2005. An integrative framework for supply chain collaboration. *International Journal of Logistics Management* 16(2): 257–274.

Simchi-Levi, D., X. Chen, and J. Bramel, eds. 2005. *The logic of logistics: Theory, algorithms and applications for logistics and supply chain management*, 2nd ed. Heidelberg: Springer.

Slagmulder, R. 2002. Managing costs across the supply chain. In *Cost management in supply chains*, ed. S. Seuring and M. Goldbach, 75–88. Heidelberg: Physica.

Smith, H.J. 2003. The shareholders vs. stakeholders debate. *MIT Sloan Management Review* 44(4): 85–90.

Smith, A. 2004. Emerging markets – Can they offset the european slowdown? Tech. rep., Citigroup Global Markets Inc. Smith Barney, London.

Spekman, R.E., and E.W. Davis. 2004. Risky business: Expanding the discussion on risk and the extended enterprise. *International Journal of Physical Distribution and Logistics Management* 34(5): 414–433.

Sridharan, U.V., W.R. Caines, and C.C. Patterson. 2005. Implementation of supply chain management and its impact on the value of firms. *Supply Chain Management: An International Journal* 10(4): 313–318.

Srivastava, S.K. 2008. Value recovery network design for product returns. *International Journal of Physical Distribution and Logistics Management* 38(4): 141–162.

Srivastava, R.K., A.S. Tasadduq, and L. Fahey. 1998. Market-based assets and shareholder value: A framework for analysis. *Journal of Marketing* 62: 2–18.

Stadtler, H. 2005. Supply chain management and advanced planning – Basis, overview and challenges. *European Journal of Operational Research* 163: 575–588.

Stadtler, H., and C. Kilger, eds. 2008. *Supply chain management and advanced planning*. Berlin/Heidelberg/New York: Springer.

Stemmler, L. 2002. The role of finance in supply chain management. In *Cost management in supply chains*, ed. S. Seuring and M. Goldbach, 165–176. Heidelberg: Physica.

Stemmler, L., and S. Seuring. 2003. Finanzwirtschaftliche Elemente in der Lieferkettensteuerung: Erste überlegungen zu einem Konzept des Supply Chain Finance (Financial elements in the control of supply chains: First considerations for a supply chain finance concept). *Logistik Management* 5(4): 27–37.

Sterman, J.D. 1989. Modeling managerial behavior: Misperceptions of feedback in a dynamic decision making experiment. *Management Science* 35(3): 321–339.

Stewart, G.B. 1991. *The quest for value: The EVA management guide*. New York: Harper Business.

Stock, J.R., and S.L. Boyer. 2009. Developing a consensus definition of supply chain management: A qualitative study. *International Journal of Physical Distribution and Logistics Management* 39(8): 690–711.

Stölzle, W. 2002. Supply chain controlling und performance management – Konzeptionelle Herausforderungen für das supply chain management (Supply chain management accounting and performance management – conceptual challenges for the supply chain management). *Logistik Management* 4(3): 10–21.

Suang, H., and L. Wang. 2009. The status and development of logistics cost management: Evidence from Mainland China. *Benchmarking: An International Journal* 16(5): 657–670.

Supply-Chain Council, ed. 2006. *Supply chain operations reference model SCOR version 8.0.* Pittsburgh: Supply-Chain Council.

Tahmassebi, T. 1998. An approach to management of multilevel distribution systems for consumer goods and chemicals industry under information uncertainty. *Computers and Chemical Engineering* 22: S263–S270.

Tan, K.C. 2001. A framework of supply chain management literature. *European Journal of Purchasing and Supply Management* 7: 39–48.

Tan, G.W., M.J. Shaw, and B. Fulkerson. 2000. Web-based global supply chain management. In *Handbook on electronic commerce*, ed. M. Shaw, R. Blanning, T. Strader, and A. Whinston, 457–478. Heidelberg: Springer.

Tan, K.C., V.R. Kannan, C.-C. Hsu, and G.K. Leong. 2010. Supply chain information and relational alignments: Mediators of EDI on firm performance. *International Journal of Physical Distribution and Logistics Management* 40(5): 377–394.

Teller, C., and H. Kotzab. 2003. Increasing competitiveness in the grocery industry – Success factors in supply chain partnering. In *Strategy and organization in supply chains*, ed. S. Seuring, M. Müller, M. Goldbach, and U. Schneidewind, 149–164. Heidelberg: Physica.

Terzi, S., and S. Cavalieri. 2004. Simulation in the supply chain context: A survey. *Computers in Industry* 53: 3–16.

Tibben-Lembke, R.S., and D.S. Rogers. 2002. Differences between forward and reverse logistics in a retail environment. *Supply Chain Management: An International Journal* 7(5): 271–282.

Töyli, J., L. Häkkinen, L. Ojala, and T. Naula. 2008. Logistics and financial performance: An analysis of 424 Finnish small and medium-sized enterprises. *International Journal of Physical Distribution and Logistics Management* 38(1): 57–80.

Trent, R.J., and R.M. Monczka. 2003. Understanding integrated global sourcing. *International Journal of Physical Distribution and Logistics Management* 7(33): 607–629.

Truong, T.H., and F. Azadivar. 2005. Optimal design methodologies for configuration of supply chains. *International Journal of Production Research* 43(11): 2217–2236.

Tsiakis, P., N. Shah, and C.C. Pantelides. 2001. Design of multi-echelon supply chain networks under demand uncertainty. *Industrial and Engineering Chemistry Research* 40(16): 3585–3604.

Tummala, V.M.R., C.L.M. Phillips, and M. Johnson. 2006. Assessing supply chain management success factors: A case study. *Supply Chain Management: An International Journal* 11(2): 179–192.

Tuominen, T., N. Kitaygorodskaya, and P. Helo. 2009. Benchmarking Russian and Finnish food industry supply chains. *Benchmarking: An International Journal* 16(3): 415–431.

Turner, T., V. Martinez, and U. Bititci. 2004. Managing the value delivery process. *International Journal of Physical Distribution and Logistics Management* 34(3/4): 302–318.

Vahrenkamp, R. 2005. *Logistik – Management und Strategien (Logistics – Management and strategies)*, 5th ed. München/Wien: Oldenbourg.

Vahrenkamp, R., and C. Siepermann. 2007. *Risikomanagement in Supply Chains – Gefahren abwehren, Chancen nutzen, Erfolg generieren (Risk management in supply chains – mitigating threats, exploiting opportunities, creating success)*. Berlin: Erich Schmidt Verlag.

van der Vorst, J.G.A.J., and A.J.M. Beulens. 2002. Identifying sources of uncertainty to generate supply chain redesign strategies. *International Journal of Physical Distribution and Logistics Management* 32(6): 409–430.

van Hoek, R.I. 1999. From reversed logistics to green supply chains. *Supply Chain Management: An International Journal* 4(3): 129–134.

van Hoek, R.I., and P. Chapman. 2006. From tinkering around the edge to enhancing revenue growth: Supply chain-new product development. *Supply Chain management: An International Journal* 11(5): 385–389.

van Nyen, P.L.M.V., J.W.M. Bertrand, H.P.G. van Ooijen, and N.J. Vandaele. 2009. Supplier managed inventory in the OEM supply chain: The impact of relationship types on total costs and cost distribution. In *Supply chain planning – Quantitative decision support and advanced planning solutions*, ed. H.O. Günther and H. Meyr, 219–246. Heidelberg: Springer.

Vanpoucke, E., K.K. Boyer, and A. Vereecke. 2009. Supply chain information flow strategies: An empirical taxonomy. *International Journal of Operations and Production Management* 29(12): 1213–1241.

Vaziri, H.K. 1992. Using competitive benchmarking to set goals. *Quality Progress* 25: 81–85.

Vickery, S.K., J. Jayaram, C. Droge, and R. Calatone. 2003. The effects of an integrative supply chain strategy on customer service and financial performance: An analysis of direct versus indirect relationships. *Journal of Operations Management* 21(5): 523–539.

Villegas, F., and N. Smith. 2006. Supply chain dynamics: Analysis of inventory vs. order oscillations trade-off. *International Journal of Production Research* 44(6): 1037–1054.

Vlachopoulou, M., and V. Manthou. 2003. Partnership alliances in virtual markets. *International Journal of Physical Distribution and Logistics Management* 33(3): 254–267.

Wagner, S.M. 2008. Cost management practices for supply chain management: An exploratory analysis. *International Journal of Services and Operations Management* 4(3): 296–320.

Wagner, B.A., J. Fillis, and U. Johansson. 2003. E-business and e-supply strategy in small and medium sized businesses (SMEs). *Supply Chain Management: An International Journal* 8(4): 343–354.

Wall, F., and R. Schröder. 2009. *Controlling zwischen Shareholder Value und Stakeholder Value (Management accounting between shareholder value and stakeholder value)*. München: Oldenbourg.

Wallace, J.S. 1997. Adopting residual income-based compensation plans: Do you get what you pay for? *Journal of Accounting and Economics* 24: 275–300.

Wallenburg, C.M., and J. Weber. 2005. Structural equation modeling as a basis for theory development within logistics and supply chain management research. In *Research methodologies in supply chain management*, ed. H. Kotzab, S. Seuring, M. Müller, and G. Reiner, 171–186. Heidelberg: Physica.

Walters, D. 1999. The implications of shareholder value planning and management for logistics decision making. *International Journal of Physical Distribution and Logistics Management* 29(4): 240–258.

Walters, D. 2004a. A business model for the new economy. *International Journal of Physical Distribution and Logistics Management* 34(3/4): 346–357.

Walters, D. 2004b. New economy – New business models – New approaches. *International Journal of Physical Distribution and Logistics Management* 34(3/4): 219–229.

Walters, D. 2006. Effectiveness and efficiency: The role of demand chain management. *International Journal of Logistics Management* 17(1): 75–94.

Walters, D. 2008. Demand chain management + response management = increased customer satisfaction. *International Journal of Physical Distribution and Logistics Management* 38(9): 699–725.

Wang, J., and Y.-F. Shu. 2007. A possibilistic decision model for new product supply chain design. *European Journal of Operational Research* 177(2): 1044–1061.

Weber, J., U. Bramsemann, C. Heineke, and B. Hirsch. 2002a. *Erfahrungen mit Value Based Management (Experiences with value-based management)*, Advanced controlling, vol. 27/28. Vallendar: WHU, Lehrstuhl für Betriebswirtschaftslehre insbesondere Controlling und Telekommunikation.

Weber, J., U. Bramsemann, C. Heineke, and B. Hirsch. 2002b. *Value Based Management erfolgreich umsetzen (Implementing value-based management successfully)*, Advanced controlling, vol. 25. Vallendar: WHU-Otto-Beisheim-Hochschule, Lehrstuhl für Betriebswirtschaftslehre.

Weber, J., U. Bramsemann, C. Heineke, and B. Hirsch. 2004. *Wertorientierte Unternehmenssteuerung: Konzepte – Implementierung – Praxisstatements (Value-based management: Concepts – implementation – statements from practice)*. Wiesbaden: Gabler.

Weimer, G., and S. Seuring. 2009. Performance measurement in business process outsourcing decisions – Insights from four cases. *Strategic Outsourcing: An International Journal* 2(3): 275–292.

White, G.P. 1996. A survey and taxonomy of strategy-related performance measures for manufacturing. *International Journal of Operations and Production Management* 16(3): 42–61.

Wilding, R. 1998. The supply chain complexity triangle: Uncertainty generation in the supply chain. *International Journal of Physical Distribution and Logistics Management* 28(8): 599–616.

Williams, B.D., and T. Tokar. 2008. A review of inventory management research in major logistics journals. *International Journal of Logistics Management* 19(2): 212–232.

Winkler, H., and B. Kaluza. 2006. Integrated performance- and risk management in supply chains – Basics and methods. In *Managing risks in supply chains – How to build reliable collaboration in logistics*, ed. W. Kersten and T. Blecker, 19–36. Berlin: Erich Schmidt Verlag.

Wojanowski, R., V. Verter, and T. Boyaci. 2007. Retail-collection network design under deposit-refund. *Computers and Operations Research* 34(2): 324–345.

Wong, W.P., and K.Y. Wong. 2008. A review on benchmarking of supply chain performance measures. *Benchmarking: An International Journal* 15(1): 25–51.

Wong, C., J. Arlbjørn, and J. Johansen. 2005. Supply chain management practices in toy supply chains. *Supply Chain management: An International Journal* 10(5): 367–378.

Wouda, F.H.E., Paul van Beek, J.G.A.J. van der Vorst, and Heiko Tacke. 2003. An application of mixed-integer linear programming models on the redesign of the supply network of Nutricia Dairy and Drinks Group in Hungary. In *Advanced planning and scheduling solutions in process industry*, ed. H.-O. Günther and Paul van Beek, 183–199. Heidelberg: Springer.

Wu, Y.C.W., and Y.H. Chou. 2007. A new look at logistics business performance: Intellectual capital perspective. *International Journal of Logistics Management* 18(3): 41–63.

Wynstra, F., and E. ten Pierick. 2000. Managing supplier involvement in new product development: A portfolio approach. *European Journal of Purchasing and Supply Management* 6: 49–57.

Yang, B.R. 2000. Supply chain management: Developing visible design rules across organizations. In *Handbook on electronic commerce*, ed. M. Shaw, R. Blanning, T. Strader, and A. Whinston, 445–456. Heidelberg: Springer.

Yang, D., T. Xiao, and H. Shen. 2009. Pricing, service level and lot size decisions of a supply chain with risk-averse retailers: Implications to practitioners. *Production Planing and Control* 20(4): 320–331.

Young, D.S., and S.F. O'Byrne. 2001. *EVA and value based management: A practical guide to implementation*, 1st ed. New York: McGraw-Hill.

Zeng, A.Z., and C. Rossetti. 2003. Developing a framework for evaluating the logistics costs in global sourcing processes: An implementation and insights. *International Journal of Physical Distribution and Logistics Management* 33(9): 785–803.

Zimmermann, K., and S. Seuring. 2009. Two case studies on developing, implementing and evaluating a balanced scorecard in distribution channel dyads. *International Journal of Logistics, Research and Applications* 12(1): 63–81.

Zokaei, A.K., and D.W. Simons. 2006. Value chain analysis in consumer focus improvement: A case study of the UK red meat industry. *International Journal of Logistics Management* 17(2): 311–331.